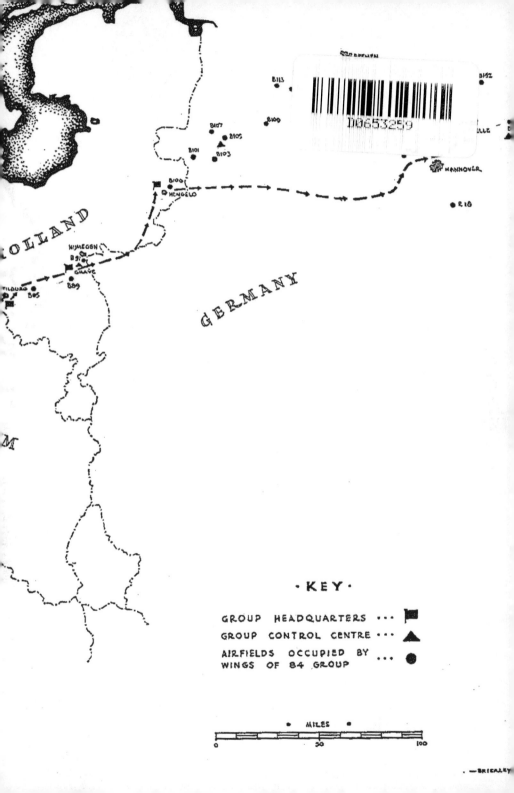

HOLLAND

GERMANY

B113

B152

B107

2105

B103

B101

B100

HENGELO

HANNOVER

R18

NIJMEGEN

B91

GRAVE

TILBURG

B85

B89

· K E Y ·

GROUP HEADQUARTERS · · ·

GROUP CONTROL CENTRE · · ·

AIRFIELDS OCCUPIED BY · · ·
WINGS OF 84 GROUP

· MILES ·

0   50   100

—BRICKLEY

BE BOLD

BE BOLD

AIR CHIEF MARSHAL
SIR FREDERICK ROSIER
GCB, CBE, DSO

WITH DAVID ROSIER

GRUB STREET   LONDON

Published by
Grub Street
4 Rainham Close
London
SW11 6SS

Copyright © Grub Street 2011
Copyright text © Air Chief Marshal Sir Frederick Rosier and David Rosier 2011
Copyright foreword © Air Chief Marshal Sir Michael Graydon 2011
Copyright appreciation © Christopher Shores 2011

British Library Cataloguing in Publication Data
Rosier, Frederick.
  Be bold.
  1. Rosier, Frederick. 2. Fighter pilots--Great Britain--
  Biography. 3. Great Britain. Royal Air Force--Officers--
  Biography. 4. World War, 1939-1945--Aerial operations,
  British. 5. World War, 1939-1945--Personal narratives,
  British.
  I. Title II. Rosier, David.
  940.5'44'941'092-dc22

  ISBN-13: 9781906502973

Cover design by Sarah Driver
Edited by Sophie Campbell
Formatted by Sarah Driver

Printed and bound by MPG Ltd, Bodmin, Cornwall

Grub Street Publishing only uses
FSC (Forest Stewardship Council) paper for its books.

CONTENTS

FOREWORD

Keeping a diary is something that few people do today unless they are politicians looking to make a buck. And whilst we have seen recently instances of some generals recording their life story, to the best of my knowledge, no senior airman or sailor has done so for quite some time. More's the pity I suppose because there is much to say as our armed forces are steadily eroded to impotence. Nevertheless, one should be careful, for such accounts are too often tarnished by selective memory and self-justification.

My own efforts in the mid 1990s are certainly not for publication even if I could now find them!

Sir Fred Rosier's story is different. Firstly, and unusually, it covers two seminal periods of the twentieth century which have defined our lives today. The Second World War, extensively analysed still, devastated the lives of millions in so many countries; and the Cold War which extended for some forty-five years, most of my service life, touched virtually every corner of the planet in one way or another.

These memoirs, the main sources of which were his personal papers and the letters he wrote to Het as his girlfriend and later his wife of fifty-nine years, were written for no other purpose than to keep a record. People did then, and how much we have all gained from such memories often scribbled on old notebooks or scraps of paper. I doubt that emails will carry the same interest or natural elegance should they be unearthed in the future.

Fred's recollections, now collated into chapters by his eldest son David, are a delight. They are, as one would expect from a man who took pleasure in the simple expression of ideas, refreshingly uncomplicated. He wrote as he spoke, without pretence, as he saw things at the time, and with no eye on the judgement of history.

His love of the Royal Air Force and of life shines through, as does his integrity. The reader will not learn much of why Fred Rosier was thought of so highly as an operational commander; nor perhaps will he or she appreciate just how influential were his views with allies because of the respect in which he was held. Sir Fred was too modest to tell us this. But those who had the privilege of working for him will know. They will recall

The author as one of Sir Graydon's suprise guests on This is your Life, 1993.

the man who looked the part, who played the violin, who could drink a glass of water placed on the ground without using his hands, and a man who could hold a roomful of tough nuts in the palm of his hands with the power of his words and his matchless sense of timing. And for the younger generation, it will, I hope, be of interest for its intriguing look into another world, and another time.

Mostly however, it is a rattling good story.

Air Chief Marshal Sir Michael Graydon

APPRECIATION

Fighter pilots are something of a 'breed apart', and Fred Rosier was certainly no exception to this. At the conclusion of hostilities in 1945, amongst those born within the British Isles many who had survived the war intact stayed in the Royal Air Force. Generally speaking, and perhaps not surprisingly, the majority and particularly those who had distinguished themselves during the war, would follow successful careers, either in the service, or in other chosen professions or industries.

Of those remaining in the service, at least twenty reached 'Air' rank, more than half of these receiving promotions beyond the rank of air vice-marshal. Indeed, two achieved the ultimate appointment as marshals of the Royal Air Force. Of this 'elite' group, four became air officers commanding (AOC) Fighter Command, and one of a similar position with Bomber Command. One of the former quartet was Sir Frederick Rosier.

Of this select group of twenty, twelve had joined the regular RAF in the years prior to the outbreak of war. Of the seven who had entered the service following the commencement of hostilities, no less than three had been serving with the Cambridge University Air Squadron, one was a member of the exclusive Auxiliary Air Force, and two had joined the Volunteer Reserve before September 1939. Only one was too young to have commenced any form of service before this date, but he had 'history', being the son of an air vice-marshal who had been a First World War fighter 'ace'. Of this latter group, two commenced their service as sergeants, one of them, Neil Cameron, ultimately becoming one of the marshals of the RAF, and chief of the defence staff.

Against this background, it is particularly interesting to note Fred Rosier's entry to the service in 1935. It needs to be remembered that at that time the United Kingdom – and England in particular – was considerably more 'class conscious' than it is today. All the rest of the dozen future leaders were the product of the public school system, or similar establishments in the Commonwealth; indeed, three were also products of the RAF College, Cranwell. Fred records how on commencing his training, he was the only state school pupil in his group. That he was accepted for training for a short service commission, and by his fellow officers, says much for his personality, probably considerably reinforced by his sporting prowess, not least on the rugby field.

Serving initially with one of Fighter Command's most notable squadrons, he rapidly became a flight commander and an accomplished fighter pilot. Moving in these circles, he came increasingly to build a wide range of friends amongst the close-knit community of the command. One of the fascinating aspects of his account, to this reader at least, is the liberal 'seasoning' thereof with the well-known names of many of the pilots with whom he served.

His posting to form and command a new unit at the outbreak of war meant that he did not enter action as part of an established and well-practised 'team', as would have no doubt been the case had he still been with 43 Squadron in June 1940. Being shot down and quite badly burned so early in the war meant that he was effectively out of action during the months which followed, preventing his chance to become one of the 'aces' of the Battle of Britain.

The move to the active, but difficult, Western Desert theatre the following year rapidly provided opportunities for his leadership skills to be demonstrated to the full, resulting in he and his close friend, 'Bing' Cross becoming the operational leaders of the first two fighter wings of the Western Desert Air Force in time for Operation Crusader, the biggest British offensive of the war up to that time – November 1941.

The extent of the successful tactics and operations he and Cross developed and led despite their squadrons being equipped with aircraft of generally inferior performance to the opposition, resulted in the awards both received of the Distinguished Service Order in February 1942 at the end of the Crusader operation. At this time only four such awards had previously been made to fighter pilots of RAF, Middle East, since the outbreak of war there in June 1940. The experiences gained during that period rendered Fred an enthusiast for inter-service co-operation which he was able to develop to excellent effect during the rest of the war, accompanied by concurrent rapid promotion.

Whilst the section devoted to the war years may require some further background reading, it nonetheless has fascinating detail. Moreover, the latter part of the book dealing with his subsequent career I found to be most enjoyable and illuminating, and of great interest. It rapidly becomes clear that he was one of the 'chosen few', earmarked at higher levels for future high command. Consequently the usually enjoyable and varied postings he received prepared him admirably for what was to come on his way to the top.

I only had the pleasure of meeting Sir Frederick once, at Grub Street's publication party for 'Bing' Cross' autobiography; I wish I had been able to see him again and get to know him better. However, the book very clearly brings out the humanity, generosity, sense of fun and attractive personality, as well as the great professional gifts of this outstanding officer. Being asked to write this appreciation of him came as a rare privilege and a great pleasure.

Christopher Shores, March 2011

INTRODUCTION

I should first apologise that this book has taken so long to come to fruition. In the years before he died in 1998, I persuaded my father to write down as much as he could remember about his early life and RAF career. He had never been particularly forthcoming about this but from the various tales I had heard over the years, I felt that the story of his rather remarkable life might be of interest to his grandchildren and to future generations in years to come.

Sadly my father died before the book was completed – he got as far as the end of the Second World War and so I enlisted my mother's help to finish the project. You will therefore be able to detect a slight change in style and perhaps emphasis as my mother, who also sadly died before the book was published, had an elephantine memory for detail.

My task has been to edit both my father's and my mother's writings. I have added detail from the many letters my father wrote to my mother from when they started 'going out' in the early thirties to the end of the Second World War. I have also added detail from my father's first log book starting in August 1935 through to when he took over command of 229 Squadron in October 1940, from 229 Squadron Operational Records and from my father's subsequent log books. In addition, I have drawn on articles my father wrote and from various books written about the war. In order to complete the story I wrote the final few chapters. They are therefore based on my memory of events and probably do not cover adequately the 'political' aspects entailed in my father's last few jobs.

My siblings Elisabeth, Nicholas and John have helped me with additional stories and have encouraged me to 'get on and finish it', for which I thank them enormously.

I would also like to thank Julia Johnstone and Sally Price who have spent hours deciphering my longhand manuscript scrawl and typing draft after draft.

Finally, I would like to thank Air Chief Marshal Sir Michael 'Mike' Graydon for reading through the draft and for his comments and suggestions.

David Rosier

Rosier family crest

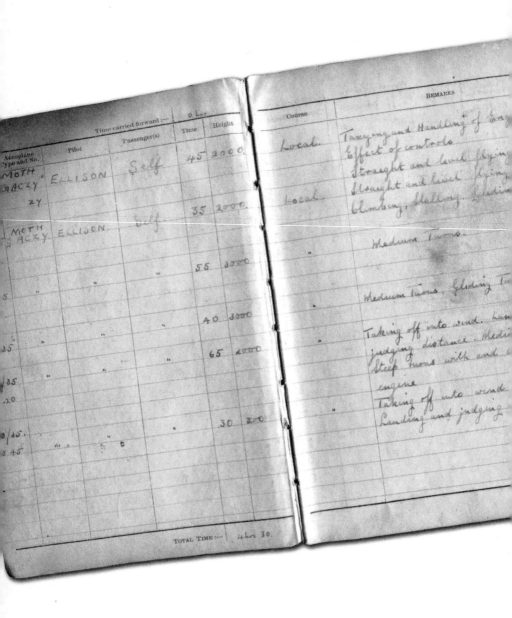

Aeroplane Type and No.	Pilot	Passenger(s)	Time	Height	Course	REMARKS
		Time carried forward :—	0 h.			
MOTH GACZY ZY	ELLISON	Self	45	2000	Local.	Taxeying and Handling of eng. Effect of controls. Straight and level flying.
MOTH A-ZY	ELLISON.	Self	35	2000	Local.	Straight and level flying. Climbing. Stalling. Gliding
		"	55	3000	"	Medium Turns.
5	"	"	40	3000	"	Medium Turns. Gliding T
35	"	"	65	2000	"	Taking off into wind. Lan judging distance. Medi Steep Turns with and engine
35 .20	"	"			"	
2/45. 5 45	"	"	6	30	300	"	Taking off into wind Landing and judging
		TOTAL TIME :—	4 hrs 30.			

Extract from the author's log book

Chapter 1
GROWING UP AND LEARNING TO FLY

MY EARLY LIFE

I was born in Wrexham, North Wales in my grandma's house, 48 Bradley Road, on 13th October, 1915. I was the first son of Ernest George Rosier and his second wife Frances Elisabeth, née Morris. My father's first wife Ruth, by whom he had two sons, had died in 1912 and he married Frances in December 1913. The elder of my two half-brothers, Hugh, was pleasant and good-natured, he worked on a farm; the younger, Phillip, seemed to me to be a strange lad. I remember that each one came to visit us two or three times a year. Hugh died when I was aged sixteen; but by then Phillip had already disappeared out of our lives.

I was six months old when my father's job as an engineer on the Great Western Railway took us to Corwen, a small town twelve miles west of Wrexham on the River Dee. My father, who had briefly been a teacher, had many interests: gardening, playing the flute and keeping up to date with the development of wireless and the improvements in sound reproduction. He made the original 'cats whiskers' wireless with headphones, later graduating to the new sets using valves and loudspeakers.

But his main interest was in wood carving and cabinet-making which he taught at night school in Corwen. In the parish church there is a carved oak font cover made from an old oak pew presented by him as a memorial to those of the parish who died in the First World War. Other examples of his work, which include a carved oak sideboard, are in our cottage in Wales.

As for my mother, she was kind and good-natured, always putting our interests first. The relationship between her and my father was close and mostly harmonious; but I can recall occasions when she lost her temper with him. She was careful about spending money; he was a spendthrift, running up debts, mostly on buying technical magazines, carving tools and radio parts, which we could ill afford. Then came the fireworks!

During the eleven years we spent in Corwen we lived in a terrace house just above the town itself. At the back was Pen-y-Pigyn Mountain, with moorlands stretching out far beyond. There in summer we picked wineberries for jam making. From the front of the house we had an expansive view of the mountains beyond the valley of the River Dee, in which I learned to swim and fish.

At the age of five I went to the National School (C of E) and although I remember very little of my time there, the teaching must have been good. Age nine I passed the scholarship to the County School at Bala. The ruling by the Merioneth Education Committee that entrants to its county schools should be ten on 1st September worked against me and consequently, I had to wait for a further year until September 1926 when I was nearly eleven to start there.

I travelled daily by a Great Western Railway train on the twelve-mile journey to Bala. My friends and I would often spend our lunchtime at the side of Bala Lake, back then it was just a huge, empty expanse of water. Now it has been developed by the Welsh Tourist Board as a water sports centre.

Like my father, I enjoyed music. For a few months I took piano lessons but these were stopped because I did not practice enough. Next I tried the violin, which I found much more to my liking. I had a good teacher and practiced regularly, alongside joining the church choir.

During our time in Corwen my twin sisters, Marian and Rose, and my brother Bill were born.

In 1927, after only two terms at Bala, I had to leave and move to

Wrexham County School, Grove Park, because my father's job had taken us to Gwersyllt, a small village three miles from Wrexham. We lived in two houses in Gwersyllt, both railway tied, then in 1933 we moved into a newly built semi-detached house in Rhosddu, Wrexham which my father called Ramsbury Cottage after the village in Wiltshire where he was born.[1]

I was very happy in my new school, which had a fine reputation for academic and sporting achievements. Unfortunately, I did little work. The sciences, mathematics and geography were the only subjects in which I was interested. Not surprisingly in 1930, I failed to matriculate in the Central Welsh Board (CWB) School Certificate examination. As I could not pass English which was necessary for matriculation, I had to take it a second time in 1931 and then for a third time in 1932 before passing. In those days, without passing you could not advance to the sixth form. Having finally got there, and only concentrating on the subjects that interested me, two years later in 1934 I gained the Higher School Certificate of the CWB in mathematics, physics and chemistry.

Sports were my top priority during my time at school. I was in the rugger team for four years and was captain in my last year. I was in the tennis team for four years and captain for two. I was also captain of the swimming team and, for the record, a school prefect for three years and house captain for my final two years.

In 1934 I was selected as hooker for the North Wales schoolboys' team against South Wales. The match, played at Ruabon School, was, not surprisingly, an overwhelming victory for the South Wales boys. At least two of their side became household names – Davies and Tanner were first choice as three-quarters for Wales for many years. Wilf Wooler from the North, after winning his Blue at Cambridge, was for many years captain of the Welsh team.

Whenever possible I played for Wrexham Rugby Club – a pleasant but inebriated bunch. Indeed, the first time I ever drank too much was after an away match for Wrexham 1st XV against Birkenhead Park.

Twice a week I cycled the three miles to St. Mark's church in Wrexham for choir practice, and twice every Sunday for Matins and Evensong. For a year or two I was the treble soloist, and still remember the words of my favourite solo 'Oh, for the Wings of a Dove ...' My

The author playing Malvolio in a performance of Twelfth Night
whilst at Wrexham County School, Grove Park, 1933.

violin playing had progressed so well that I played in the school's small
orchestra and later in the Denbighshire Youth Orchestra.

I also enjoyed acting, taking a leading part in a number of school
plays. On one occasion, when playing Malvolio in Twelfth Night with
my usual fervour, I flung my chain of office across the stage with such
vigour that it landed with a crash on the stage lights, fusing the lot.
The resulting total darkness raised laughter and raucous cheers from
the audience, composed mainly of fellow school mates. They ap-
proved, but the reaction of the master in charge was quite different.
I was invited to join an amateur dramatic club. I well remember tour-
ing the local parish halls and miners' institutes playing 'The Tolpuddle
Martyrs' – this was thought to be very worthwhile by most of my fellow actors who were to a man socialists and trade union activists.

In my last years at school I became interested in a very active and
attractive girl called Hettie Blackwell. She captained Grove Park Girls'
school hockey and tennis teams and later played hockey for Denbighshire. She came first in many field sports, winning the Senior
Athletics Cup. At first I think I was impressed by the sight of her
well shaped legs but clearly there was more to it than that. She must
also have been good academically for she romped through to her

Higher School Certificate in 1933. That September whilst I, poor chap, was still at school, she went to St Mary's College, Bangor where she studied to become a school teacher. During that time I wrote to her every Friday.

In the winter of 1934, my mother was not well and in February, the terrible pain in the base of her spine she had been suffering with was diagnosed as cancer. She was admitted to the War Memorial Hospital in Wrexham, where she died a few months later. She was buried in Gwersyllt Parish churchyard where my father, who died in 1942 whilst I was in the Western Desert, was also laid to rest. This was one of the saddest moments of my life and it was only after my mother's death that I realised what a dominant influence she had been.

> *16th February 1934*
> *My Dearest Hettie,*
> *I'm not going to write much tonight because I'm utterly fagged out – after being up till two o'clock every morning. Mother's very ill – had to take her to hospital last Sunday. She's practically paralysed from the waist downwards.*
>
> *I'm taking the part of a German colonel in the house play for Eisteddfod. Thanks very much for that valentine card, and I'm awfully sorry I forgot your birthday.*

Having gained my Higher School Certificate in 1934 I had to think of the future. As we had little money, in order to go to university it was necessary that I gained a scholarship. My failure to be awarded one by both Manchester and Bangor caused me to look around for something else to do. As unemployment was extremely high in Wrexham and there were no jobs to be had other than in the mines, I decided to stay at school and play rugger while applying for jobs. That November I wrote to Het about a weekend trip to London I made with my father when I visited the Science Museum and saw a football match between Sheffield and the 'Spurs' ending the day at Her Majesty's Theatre seeing a performance of C.B. Cochran's review Streamline. It is worth noting that a cheap day return from Wrexham to London cost ten shillings

(50p) at that time.

> *15th March 1935*
> *I applied for the police force last Monday. I have also*
> *applied for a post as police inspector in the Colonies.*
> *It would be absolutely great if I could obtain one be-*
> *cause commencing salary is about £350 per year.*

I also applied for the new police college which the Metropolitan Commissioner of Police Lord Trenchard (the founder of the RAF), was establishing at Hendon in 1935. I seem to remember that a successful graduate would do six months 'on the beat' before becoming a sub-inspector.

When I went up to London for the interview at Scotland Yard I was told that I was too young, but could be interviewed again the following year. With the object of looking older I decided to grow a moustache. It was pretty awful – gingerish – but I persevered with it for some time.

I should mention here that in the RAF during the war I met many graduates of Hendon Police College. They could always be spotted by their smartness and bearing. Amongst those who reached air rank were Air Chief Marshal Sir William Coles, Air Commodore Paddy Kearon and Air Commodore Bill Stewart, who were all friends of mine. Like them, I feel sure that I would have left the Metropolitan Police in 1939 to join the RAF.

On arriving back in Wrexham, I realised that I was going to have to earn some money and with skills learned both from my father and from books, I decided to be an electrician. Undercutting the opposition, I charged only £1 for installing a lighting point, on which I made about 2/6d profit (12½p from 100p). It was almost always a dirty and time-consuming job. I also repaired shoes and mended bicycles. One day after I had mended a puncture for Het, her mother told her that she should not allow me to help her again. She warned her that: "she must not be beholden to strange boys!"

My early interest in aeroplanes had been whetted by seeing Britain win the 1928 Schneider Trophy race at Calshot, when I was on holiday with my relations in Wiltshire. I was astonished and amazed to witness seaplanes going so fast. I had also attended two of the annual RAF displays at Hendon where I had marvelled at the skill of the pilots. During those years I had taken every opportunity to cycle the fourteen miles from my home to RAF Sealand, a flying training school. There I had a close view over the hedge of aircraft being made ready to fly by their instructors and pupils and of take-off and landing practice. Thus in the spring of 1935 I was overjoyed to read that suitable applicants would be considered for short service commissions in the RAF. 'short service' meant four years followed by a gratuity of £300. I filled in and forwarded the necessary forms. Het's father signed a form as guarantee of my good character. As a result I was summoned for interview at the Air Ministry in London. At Adastral House, Kingsway, then the home of the Air Ministry, I went before a panel of five or six officers before being subjected to a rigorous medical examination.

To my delight, quite soon after I received a letter informing me that I had been granted a short service commission but that, 'it was doubtful whether I would be called upon for duty before August'. In a letter to Het I wrote: 'I have been walking on air all day long, isn't it a good job that I failed to get into the Metropolitan Police.'

A short time later I received my marching orders requiring me to report to the Bristol Flying School at Filton, before noon on 26th August next. While at Bristol I would undergo my ab initio training, a course of elementary flying where I would have civilian status. If my flying proved satisfactory I would, after six weeks, be posted to the RAF depot at Uxbridge where I would be commissioned as an acting pilot officer on probation. I wrote to Het:

I have to fill in numerous forms. The first of these my father saw had on it 'name of relative we are to correspond with in case of casualty'. They have given me detailed instructions as to what I have to wear while at Bristol: lounge suits, sports jacket and slacks, dinner jacket suit, full evening dress (tails) etc. They have also told me what I have to wear when I go to Uxbridge and have my uniform. I am not to wear service slacks there – but have to wear breeches.

That August I camped at Rhyl for ten days returning to Wrexham for a few days before leaving by train for Bristol on Sunday 25th August, arriving at Filton at six in the evening.

LEARNING TO FLY
AUGUST 1935-MAY 1936

Filton, just outside Bristol, as well as being the location of the Bristol Flying School, was the home of The Bristol Aeroplane Company, makers of aero engines and of the Bulldog and Gauntlet fighters. The City of Bristol RAF Auxiliary Squadron, flying Sidestrands, was also based on the airfield.

Civil flying schools had been set up for the basic training of pilots due to the inability of the RAF to cope with the number of pilots needed to satisfy the recent decision to expand – proof the government at last was seeing sense. Director of Flying Cyril Unwins, was also the chief test pilot of Bristols, and was famous for his high altitude flying; he was the first man to fly over Everest. The flying and ground instructors were mostly ex-RAF. My instructor, a most likeable chap, was Flying Officer Ellison, then a twenty-six-year-old reserve officer.

We aspiring pilots were fifteen strong; five were ex-RAF boy apprentices from Halton and Cranwell who were due to become sergeant pilots. These had already served in squadrons for about six years as fitters, armourers, wireless operators etc. The rest of us, who were due to become officers, were a varied lot; some straight from school, others older, who had been dissatisfied with their jobs in civilian life and two ex-Mercantile Marine officers who were unable to get jobs in the merchant navy which was then in decline because of the state of the economy.

We prospective officers lodged in a house called Brooklands, situated next to the aerodrome, while the 'would be' sergeant pilots had to find other digs because NCOs were not allowed to associate with officers. I wrote in a letter to Het, 'the fellows here are all jolly good sports'. Other than me, all of those destined to be officers had been at public schools, but there was no noticeable class divide. Two of them had their own cars while another two had had their licences suspended, for 'driving in a manner dangerous to the public'. In general we operated as a group and together visited the better pubs in Bristol.

I wrote to Het on my first evening:

I have become a club member of the flying school which cost me two and sixpence and consequently I have a wonderful lunch of five courses with coffee in the lounge afterwards for one and sixpence and afternoon tea costing six pence.

I remember being somewhat apprehensive before my first flight in a Tiger Moth on Tuesday 27th August 1935. Although this was my first ever flight – and, despite my instructor subjecting me to stalls, rolls and loops, I revelled in it and showed no signs of air sickness. I wrote to Het that evening, 'I had a wonderful time of it today'.

7th September 1935 was a great day in my life. After twelve hours and fifteen minutes dual flying, I went solo for twenty minutes flying at 300 feet. In my log book I wrote: 'Taking off and landing – what a fortunate Tiger'.

We flew everyday and also attended endless lectures on the principles of flight. For me flying was the main excitement and challenge. In retrospect however, I *was* rather foolish to 'chance my arm' by flying under the Clifton Suspension Bridge!

On 24th September I received my Certificate of Competency and 'A' licence (No. 8389) after thirty hours flying, twenty dual and ten solo. I also noted in a letter to Het, 'I am slightly out of funds as I bought a sports jacket yesterday for thirty-five shillings' (or £1.75).

On 11th October I completed my first solo, cross country flight from Filton to Andover and return in ninety minutes. Three days later I had a flying test with T W Campbell, the chief flying instructor. This I passed, thereby completing my ab initio training course. I left Filton on 17th October after seven weeks, and fifty-two hours flying.

After a few days' leave those of us who had passed the course moved on to Uxbridge, the RAF depot, where on 21st October we were gazetted as acting pilot officers on probation. There we were joined by other groups who had completed their initial training at other civil flying schools. Many hours over the next two weeks were spent drilling on the parade ground where we were turned from a rabble into a reasonable bunch of men. It was here that we had our first introduction to service life. We were made to study, and to laboriously amend the

King's Regulations. We were briefed on service etiquette and were given practical guidance on how to behave in the mess.

On Thursday we have a guest night to which the RAF band attends. Drinks are first served in the anteroom. Then we go in to dinner during the course of which we are not allowed to mention ladies' names, politics or religion.

On the first day (Monday) we had orders to proceed into London after lunch and go to the tailors to be measured up for our uniforms. I went to Moss Bros in Covent Garden with six others. We went into London again on Wednesday for the first fitting and again on Friday for the second. The uniform altogether will cost £65.

My complete kit, which arrived before I left Uxbridge, comprised flying boots, shoes, socks, shirts (including stiff shirts), service uniform, breeches and puttees, greatcoat, mess kit including two waistcoats – one for formal wear – mess wellington boots and a tin trunk. My uniform allowance covered the lot.

On passing out from Uxbridge on 3rd November I became 37425 Pilot Officer F. E. Rosier. From Uxbridge the whole course of about thirty short service commission officers was posted to No.1 Course at the newly-established 11 Flying Training School at Wittering, three miles south of Stamford in Lincolnshire. I was posted to B Flight where my instructor was Sergeant Johnson. The Central Flying School (CFS) had vacated Wittering and returned to Upavon where it had been founded in 1915.

Our curriculum was divided between classroom, workshops, the barrack square and flying. The aircraft we used was the trainer version of the Hawker Hart light bomber, a bi-plane with an open cockpit, powered by a Rolls-Royce engine. The pupil sat in the front cockpit, with the instructor behind him. In comparison with the Tiger Moth it was powerful and fast, cruising at about 150 mph. 13th November was another red letter day: I went solo on the Hart.

At Wittering, as well as work, there was plenty of time to play sport and I played rugger for the 1st XV regularly. One of the members of the course, Tom Dalton-Morgan, a very good scrum half, used to drive me to Leicester to spend an occasional evening with Het who was by then teaching at a school near Coalville. Tom, a close friend of mine, had a distinguished war record. He commanded 43 Squadron in the Battle of Britain and later as a group captain on the operations staff of 2nd Tactical Air Force was an exceptionally gifted staff officer. Unfortunately he was a 'Jekyll and Hyde' figure who in 1952 ultimately had to leave the service.

On 20th January 1936 I lost three months' seniority (and some leave) for disobeying orders forbidding us to do aerobatics. On a passenger test with my fitter, LAC Williams, I rightly thought that no one could see what I was doing above the clouds. I was not to know that my fitter would be so violently sick that when we landed he would have to be lifted from the aircraft. Whilst he was led away I was ordered to clean up the back cockpit. However, this incident was luckily soon forgotten and on 25th January I was authorised to wear my 'flying badge' or 'wings'.

My great ambition was to become a fighter pilot and it was therefore a very proud moment when I was transferred from the Hart trainer to C Flight to fly the Hawker Fury.

My first flight in a Fury – K1937 – was on 20th February, and a month later I recorded in my log book on 24th March that I 'led a formation on a battle climb – time to 16,000 feet – eight and a half minutes'.

The last month of our flying training was spent at an armament training camp at Catfoss, north of Hull, where we fired at ground targets and at 'sleeves' towed behind our aircraft. On our return to Wittering on 20th April I was graded 'above average' as a pilot, and what was even better news was told that my next posting was to be to 43 (F) Squadron at Tangmere. I could not have wished for better for 43 – 'The Fighting Cocks' – was one of the most famous fighter squadrons in the RAF.

At the same time, a great friend of mine, Johnny Walker, was posted to 1 (F) Squadron, also famous, and also at Tangmere. So after twenty-

nine hours and thirty minutes solo on Furies, on 6th May I set off for Sussex. Little did I know when saying goodbye to Wittering and the medieval town of Stamford that I would return there in August 1940 during the Battle of Britain.

Chapter 2

THE WORLD'S FINEST FLYING CLUB

43 SQUADRON AT TANGMERE
MAY 1936-AUGUST 1939

Tangmere is situated three miles from Chichester, close to the south coast, and importantly south of the Downs. As a result it has one of the best weather factors in the country. Having been the home of both 1 Squadron and 43 Squadron since 1926 there was great rivalry between the squadrons both at work and at play.

I spent the next three years at what was affectionately known as 'Tangle-bury' with what was without doubt one of the finest squadrons in the RAF. At that time 43 Squadron held both the trophy for gunnery and the Sassoon trophy for the annual pin-pointing competition. The first two of these years were carefree when I felt that I belonged to one of the most exclusive flying clubs in the world. The third was the year we exchanged our Furies for Hurricanes and prepared for a war that seemed inevitable.

43 Squadron had two flights, each with six Furies, powered by a 580 hp Rolls-Royce Kestrel V-12 supercharged, water-cooled engine. I was posted to B Flight, commanded by Flight Lieutenant J W C 'Hank' More who was an exceptional pilot, and also a world-class squash player. A Flight was commanded by Flight Lieutenant R I G MacDougall who was also the acting squadron commander. My first flight in a Fury from Tangmere was on 13th May 1936.

For the first few weeks Johnny Walker and I, whilst treated reasonably in the mess, were seldom invited out to parties, pubs and visits to local towns by the other officers in the squadrons. Had it not been for Johnny's car (I could not afford one), we would have been limited to playing squash together, staying in the mess, or walking the three miles to the Dolphin, situated just opposite Chichester Cathedral. Incidentally, I once damaged Johnny's car when I went into a ditch, having gone too fast around a bend. I did pay for the repairs however. After a few weeks that 'treatment' in the mess came to an end when we were told that we could wear our squadron ties. We had been accepted. In those days it was normal for newly arrived officers to undergo a period of probation.

A little bit about the daily routine: the batman I shared with another officer would awaken me with a cup of tea at 7.00 a.m., the curtains would be drawn, the bath filled, my clothes for the day laid out, and my shoes polished. After breakfast I would go down to the flight office and we would then fly two or three times a day. The summer routine was to rise at 6.00 a.m. and to work until 1:00 p.m., leaving the afternoon free for sports and for sailing at West Wittering and Itchenor.

My log book for June 1936 lists some of the training carried out that month as: 'Camera gun attacks on other aircraft, instrument flying, formation flying, cross country flights, pinpointing, slow flying and spinning, message bag dropping, battle climb to 25,000 feet with full war load and high altitude flying.'

Mess kit – blue waistcoats – was worn for dinners in the mess on Mondays, Tuesdays and three Thursdays in the month; the remaining Thursday being regarded as 'formal' at which full mess kit – white waistcoats – was worn. On Fridays we wore dinner jackets and on Wednesdays, Saturdays and Sundays, it was tweed jackets.

The food in the mess was excellent. My pay as a pilot officer was about £18 a month; out of this my mess dues covering subscriptions, food and drink came to £8 and my tailor's bill to £2, leaving about £8 spending money. This sounds very little but £1 could buy over forty pints of beer or twenty-three packets of cigarettes. For £5 I could have a good night out in London and return with some change.

A couple of months after arriving at Tangmere, on 8th July I was detailed to give a flypast and solo aerobatic display at Andover for General Milch, the inspector general of the German air force, and some of his senior officers, who had been visiting the RAF Staff College. Towards the end of the display my engine cut out whilst I was doing an upward role. I attempted in vain to restart it by putting the Fury into a dive and soon realised that I was left with a long glide to the airfield. In trying to stretch the glide, in full view of the high-powered spectators, I stalled and spun in whilst attempting a forced landing. I thought I had broken my legs in the crash but in the event I sustained nothing more than bad concussion. I was flown in an obsolete Virginia to the Royal Navy Hospital at Haslar, near Lee-on-Solent. I forget how long I stayed but I know that I was back flying by 22nd July, thirteen days later. Incidentally, Het has always maintained that this incident was one of the reasons the Germans considered that the RAF would be a 'push over'.

Whilst on sick leave I went by bus from Liverpool to Windermere to see Het who, with a few old college friends, had organised a hike in the Lake District. They were staying in hostels run by the Youth Hostels Association which had only been founded in 1929 but was already growing rapidly in numbers and popularity, probably because the cost was only one shilling (5p) for a night's lodging. I spent the three nights sleeping under the stars under blankets smuggled out to me by the girls.

On occasions we practiced with the army and I note from my log book that, on 1st September I flew to Old Sarum with Flight Lieutenant More and Pilot Officer Bitmead where we made 'low flying attacks on the Tank Corps'. In the remarks column I wrote 'a brush with the military'.

We practiced formation flying endlessly and had a flight aerobatic team, where we flew in diamond formation, which consisted of Flight Lieutenant More, Pilot Officer Bitmead, Pilot Officer Hollings and myself. We also practiced squadron formations and on 29th October we carried out a flypast in squadron formation for the AOC's annual inspection.

For our long weekends I was sometimes allowed to take my Fury away. Mostly I flew to Sealand, refuelling en-route at Bicester. My destination was Wrexham. I stayed at my home in Rhosddu but spent most of my time with Het.

On 30th October, on one such mission, I flew cross country to Sealand to see Het for the weekend. I was flying in a Hart and was accompanied by Pilot Officer Hollings in a Fury. We hit bad weather nearing Sealand, and Hollings, who was formating on me, lost contact with me in thick cloud. On landing I was told he had crashed near Hawarden in thick mist and had been killed. Three days later I attended his funeral at Stockport.

The Court of Enquiry, at which I was accompanied by Flight Lieutenant More, was held at RAF Northolt and little blame, if any, for the accident must have been apportioned to me for in December I was asked to take over command of B Flight from More. He had been posted to the Fleet Air Arm, and went on to distinguish himself as the squadron commander of 73 Squadron in France in early 1940. He was later posted to the Far East where he became a prisoner of war, and was lost when a Japanese ship full of prisoners, en-route to Japan, was sunk by an American submarine. Much later in 1962, when he was an admiral in Bahrain, I met that submarine commander – Rear Admiral Eugene Fluckey, known as 'Lucky Fluckey'. He was a frequent visitor to Aden where I was stationed.

At the age of twenty-one and a flight commander with 43 Squadron, life for me could not have been better. I was a member of the finest flying club in the world. In my flight I had very good pilots and the ground crew had tremendous spirit. We worked hard and the social life was hectic. Sports, which took up much of our spare time, included rugger, squash, golf, tennis and cricket and in the summer we regularly went to the beach at West Wittering and sailed from Itchenor. Once in 1938 I played at Arundel Castle for the Duke of Norfolk's XI against the 'Sussex Gentlemen'.

In February 1937 Squadron Leader R E 'Dickie' Bain took over command of the squadron and I wrote in a letter to Het that I played golf at Goodwood on Sunday 21st February with Caesar Hull and Johnny Walker. That year I had hoped to win selection to carry out the single aerobatic display at the annual Hendon Air Display, but I was 'off flying' due to illness on the day in late April that the inter-squadron competition was held.

A highlight of the year was the squadron reunion dinner held at the Savoy on 16th April, attended by former squadron members Sholto Douglas and Harold Balfour, later Lord Douglas of Kirtleside and Lord Balfour of Inchrye.

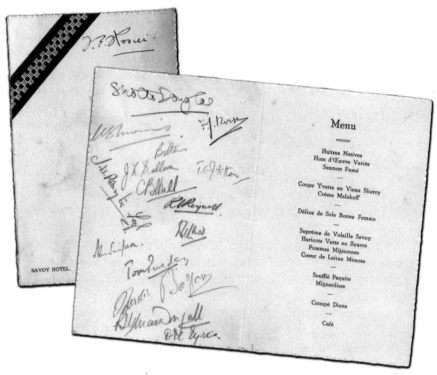

The Savoy menu, signed by the squadron members at the reunion dinner

I noted in a letter to Het that 9th June was 'a full day's holiday for the King's birthday and we spent nearly all the day on the beach'. Further highlights were the squadron formation of fourteen machines at the Empire Air Display and the summer exercise in August when my flight intercepted and attacked a flight of five Hinds at 10,000 feet over Petworth. In October I flew to North Weald with Caesar Hull and Eyres to take the promotion examinations. Later that month on 27th

October we went to Warmwell in Dorset for our annual armament training camp. The live firing took place at Chesil Beach and I averaged 149, the highest score in the squadron. During the camp however, I hit a drogue, damaging the centre section of my Fury and forcing me to land close by at Chickerell near Weymouth.

In 1937 my contemporaries from 43 Squadron in the mess, which we shared with 1 Squadron were Pilot Officer Caesar Hull, a Rhodesian by birth who had been brought up in South Africa and who was killed in September 1940 while commanding the squadron; Pilot Officer Ralph Bentley, who twenty-five years later was chief of the air staff of the Rhodesian Air Force when I was AOC in Aden; the Canadians, Pilot Officers Joe Sullivan who was killed in France in May 1940, and Pat Christie; Malcolm 'Crackers' Carswell, a New Zealander, and the British contingent, John Simpson, Eyres, Bitmead, Folkes and Cox who was killed in the Battle of Britain.

In addition to the officers there were several sergeant pilots in the squadron. Most notable of these were 'Killy' Kilmartin, Frank Carey, a very good rugby player who had an outstanding war record and was later to be commissioned, retiring in 1962 as a group captain, and Jim Hallowes.

In January 1938 I was sent on an air-firing instructor's course at Sutton Bridge with Johnny Walker of 1 Squadron. Later that month I spent a weekend with Caesar Hull and Johnny Walker at John Simpson's house in Essex which he shared with Hector Bolitho. In the grounds they had made their own air strip. During the weekend we visited Cambridge and Saffron Waldron.

In January and February 1938 we did a lot of night-flying in Demons in order to be fully trained when we got our Hurricanes. On 28th March I noted that, with John Simpson and one other, I flew cross country from Tangmere to Grantham for morning tea and refuelling, and then on to Catterick for lunch. After lunch we returned via Hucknall making a detour to Coalville in Leicestershire where Het was still teaching.

Our weekends were always free unless we were duty officer. One Saturday in 1938 I drove up to Coalville on my newly-acquired motor cycle to see Het and to take her up for her first flight. I managed to get a Tiger Moth from Desford, the local flying club, took off and began to show her how good a pilot I was. It was not long before she started to feel sick and in the hope that it would make her feel better, I told her that I was uncertain of our position and that her job was to tell me the names of railway stations we were flying over. It worked. The motor cycle did not. On the way back to Tangmere it broke down. I never rode it again.

In May 1938 we took part in an Empire Day flying display and on 25th June after much practice, we carried out a squadron formation air drill at an air display held at Gatwick organised by the *Daily Express* following the demise of the annual Hendon Air Display. The day was very windy and we had great difficulty maintaining the line abreast flypast. That summer I led six Furies in what was the official RAF Aerobatic Team and little did I know that this was to be the swansong of the aerobatic Fury.

For the first two weeks of August we went on our annual air firing/armament camp at Aldergrove in Northern Ireland where I wrote in my log book that I scored 420 and 390 which caused 'repercussions that night – Squadron Leader Hall's rye whisky'.

Although rumours of war abounded on our return we went on summer leave and four of us – Caesar Hull and 'Crackers' Carswell from my squadron and Mac Boal, from the newly arrived 217 General Reconnaissance Squadron (with Ansons) – chartered a 26 foot cutter. With plenty of food and drink aboard, we set off one evening from Itchenor for Dieppe. Less than an hour later the engine seized, forcing us to anchor for the night. Next morning, having agreed that we would continue using the sail alone, we made fast progress across the Channel. All went well until nightfall when we lost our dinghy as the tow-rope had parted. Nearing the French coast, we were led into the harbour of St. Valéry en Caux by a friendly local yachtsman.

We stayed in St. Valéry for two days and on the third day, having decided that we had drunk far more 'vin blanc cassis' than was good for the liver, we left. Once outside the harbour before setting course, we fired off a distress rocket to acknowledge the kindness of the locals.

Our destination was Ouistreham where we had promised to meet Sergeant Kilmartin, who was participating in a cross-channel race. Unfortunately, the weather deteriorated fast and west of Le Havre in the area of 'Rochers du Calvados' the wind was so strong that we had to reef the sails. However, the fates were looking kindly on us for we were sighted by a French trawler which, with great difficulty, managed to get a line to us. There followed several tense hours of wondering whether our boat would stand the strain of being towed in rough seas; but all went well and we were towed into Ouistreham harbour.

Deciding that we had enough francs for two or three days in Paris we set off there by train the next day. Paris was wonderful. We did the rounds of Montmartre and Montparnasse by night and by day. However, the news in the papers of possible war and the sight of sloppy French soldiers in the streets convinced us that we had better get back to the UK and Tangmere. Arriving back at Ouistreham our boat was a pitiful sight but, with continuous baling, we managed to cross the Channel, reach Itchenor and beach the boat. There was much argument as to how much we owed the owner. Eventually we paid nothing, as his insurance saw to it.

On our return to Tangmere on 29th August preparations had started in earnest to put the station and the squadrons on a war footing. All our machines were made serviceable so that they could leave the ground within three minutes of an alarm. A few weeks later on 26th September, I noted in my log book, 'Recalled from Sealand owing to crisis. Crisis week – efficient flapping'. We bought dark green, dark earth and black paint in Chichester and to our dismay camouflaged our beautiful silver Furies. The sparkling white hangars of Tangmere were painted drab greens and browns and air raid shelters were built. The aerodrome itself was camouflaged to represent hedges, ploughed fields, roads, haystacks etc. In addition, as the Fury was immediately designated night operational, as well as day, torches were bought with which to see our instruments in the dark. They may have been of some help in half-light, but in the dark the flames from the short stub exhaust pipes restricted our night vision. In this regard it should be noted that the Fury had no navigation lights, no signalling lights and no illumination in the cockpit (i.e. the dials were not luminous).

Thank God the war did not start in 1938. On 30th September Chamberlain came back from Munich proclaiming 'Peace in our Time' which gave us another year to prepare for war. As a fighting service to be reckoned with the RAF was unprepared. Admittedly, squadrons were beginning to be equipped with the new eight-gun Hurricanes and a few Spitfires, but they were slow in coming. Had war started that autumn, we would not have stood a chance in our Furies, by then the slowest fighter in the RAF. Even against bombers they were not fast enough.

But at last, towards the end of 1938, the great day came when 43 Squadron was presented with Hurricanes. On 18th November I did my first solo in Hurricane L1690 'wheels down', and on the morning of 29th November, having flown to the Hawker factory at Brooklands in a Demon with Squadron Leader Bain, I collected one of 43 Squadron's first two Hurricanes L1725 and flew it back to Tangmere. I soon felt at home in it and was excited by its performance – with a top speed of 318 mph it was fifty per cent faster than a Fury – and by its armament of eight Browning.303 machine guns.

We then spent the next few days doing 'high drag' flights, i.e. with wheels down and cockpit hood open, until by mid-December the full establishment of sixteen Hurricanes had arrived.

On 7th December in order to show off our new aeroplanes several of us flew to Debden in Essex for a cocktail party, which was unfortunately marred by George Feeny force landing in a nearby field.

On 6th January 1939 we carried out our final squadron formation in our Furies and a few days later I flew to Castle Bromwich in a Hurricane where I had been given the job of assessing the resident airfield of 605 Auxiliary Squadron in its suitability for operating Hurricanes. On arrival there I was met by the squadron assistant adjutant who introduced himself as Pilot Officer Smallwood, to which I am told, I pompously replied that I was Flying Officer Rosier. Without exception the auxiliaries gave me a warm welcome. One in particular, Flying Officer Mitchell, of Mitchell & Butler the Midlands brewers, lent me his expensive car for a few days. 'Splinters' Smallwood and I became close friends until as Air Chief Marshal Sir Denis Smallwood he died in 1997.

My stay at Castle Bromwich was longer than I anticipated because I had to wait for suitable winds to trial take-offs and landings in the required directions. It was during this time that I attended a local funeral of a Tangmere NCO who had been killed in an aircraft crash. Splinters and I went together – he as the 605 Squadron rep and I representing 43 Squadron. After the funeral we were taken along to the parents' house for an Irish 'wake', which was something new to us. In no time we were under the influence with never-ending Guinness, whisky, etc consumed in an atmosphere quite the opposite to that which we had expected.

In February 1939 our Furies finally departed to the maintenance unit at Kemble. My last flight in a Fury was on 21st February when I noted in my log book, 'last flight in Queen of North and South. Perfect'.

Three other events that spring were of particular importance to me. The first was that in January I heard that I had passed the examination for a specialist permanent commission. Out of the 250 who took the exam I came thirteenth. Having to choose between navigation, signals, armament and engineering, I decided on the latter. It would entail a two-year specialist course at the RAF School of Aeronautical Engineering at Henlow in Bedfordshire, followed by a further year at Cambridge University. Caesar Hull and Johnny Walker from Tangmere were unlucky.

The second was that in February 1939 the promotion of Peter Townsend to flight lieutenant resulted in him taking over command of B Flight, which I had commanded for over two years, and I became adjutant while remaining attached to B Flight. Although I must admit to having felt somewhat put out by this change, I accepted that Peter's seniority gave him the right to be a flight commander. I liked Peter although he was difficult to get to know as he was very shy and rather aloof. In his book *Duel of Eagles* Peter writes of a 'wake' which took place in the mess on 22nd April 1939, the night that Flying Officer John Rotherham was killed in an accident while we were night-flying. There we got slowly drunk as I played 'Orpheus in the Underworld' on my violin.

The third, and most important of all, was that on 1st April Het and I were engaged to be married.

My last few months with the squadron that spring and summer were spent training hard for a war which we all felt was by now unavoidable. During this time, for training purposes, I occasionally flew the squadron's dual-controlled Fairey Battle. We endlessly practiced aircraft interceptions, air-firing, instrument flying and battle climbs under operational conditions. On Empire Air Day, the 20th May, a huge crowd came to Tangmere to see the new Hurricanes carry out an aerobatic display.

In early August 1939 43 Squadron was involved in the United Kingdom air exercises held in conjunction with the French air force. They played the enemy, and during the action I carried out a battle climb to 32,000 feet with Pilot Officer Folkes and Sergeant Berry.

The squadron was 'mobilised' on 5th August, by which time I had handed over as adjutant to John Simpson and my last flight with 43 was on 17th August when I recorded in my log book, 'war inevitable'.

I left the Fighting Cocks with great regret. My three years at Tangmere had been marvellous and I hated leaving my many friends there. I also hated the idea of not flying with those friends in the war which was clearly about to start.

I had commanded B Flight for two years as a pilot officer and a flying officer whilst the normal rank for the post was flight lieutenant. I believe I was the first to organise and lead a flight aerobatic team of four; three in V formation and one in the box behind. During my two years in command I had the good fortune to have had very good pilots, Pilot Officers Bentley, Eyres, Simpson, Sullivan, Cox, Folkes and Christie, and Sergeants Hallowes, Shawyer, Berry, Hall and Carey. Sadly, most of them did not survive the war. I also had dedicated maintenance crews from the most junior airmen to the flight sergeants.

However, all the pilots and I were highly critical of the restrictive operational training we had to follow. It was assumed by the 'powers that be' that training in fighter combat was unnecessary because the range of German fighters operating from their home bases would not allow them to escort bombers attacking the UK. The result was that provision was made only for close formation flying and set attacks against bombers. This meant that dog fighting practice – fighter v fighter – was out. But we sometimes used to manage it when the CO, Dicky Bain, an 'ancient' thirty-seven year old, was away. He was not there to see the resultant oil marks on the wings which were 'incompatible with peacetime standards of cleanliness'.

HENLOW AND 229 SQUADRON
SEPTEMBER 1939-MAY 1940

The course at Henlow started on 27th August. One of the first people I met was Flying Officer Cedric Masterman, who had just returned from the North West Frontier. He was to become David's godfather, and a life-long friend. The engineering course was a great change from squadron life, but I soon settled down, made new friends, and set to work with a will.

For the first practical task we were given a piece of metal, measuring devices and some files, with which we had to make a spanner. I was so pleased with mine that I had it plated and took to carrying it as a lucky charm in the top left pocket of my uniform jacket. It must have worked for I survived the war. Sadly, it was stolen just as the war ended.

Within a week of the course starting came Neville Chamberlain's broadcast on 3rd September with the grave but exciting news that we were at war with Germany. It did not take long before my new friend Cedric Masterman and I, determined to get back to active flying, came to the conclusion that slacking at work and bad behaviour were the means to accomplish this. From being near the top of the course we were soon bottom; we drank too much and even failed to stand to attention when the national anthem was played.

It was not long before the commandant, an air commodore, sent for us. He said it was clear enough what we were up to but it was now time for us to return to normality because there was absolutely no chance of getting off the course and returning to squadron flying. Leaving his office we said, "Bloody old fool" and continued with our bad behaviour.

Het and I had been engaged for some months (since April Fools' Day!) and we thought, with the start of the war, that it was time to get married. I made the arrangements with the vicar of Henlow Parish church and on Saturday 30th September, by special licence (at a cost of £25), we were married at the church of St. Mary the Virgin. Cedric Masterman was my best man and Stewart, Het's brother, gave her away. Members of the course provided the Guard of Honour. Sadly, for operational reasons, no-one from 43 Squadron was able to attend the wedding. However I still have the telegram sent by the adjutant, Flying Officer Simpson: 'Good luck and congratulations to you both from all in 43.'

Following the ceremony we drove away in Cedric's Wolseley sports car to the mess at Henlow and drank champagne. Later that evening we were guests at a dinner at the George and Dragon in Baldock. It was a merry party and it still amazes me how we found the way to our first home, a dreary flat in Garrison Court, Hitchin.

The next morning we awoke to the noise of pebbles, thrown by some of my friends, hitting the bedroom window. They took no notice of my shouting "push off" but with much laughter told me that I was posted. I thought they were pulling my leg but later, upon our arrival in the mess, I saw that it was true. The posting notice simply stated that with immediate effect I was to proceed to 52 Operational Training Unit

(OTU) at Aston Down, in Gloucestershire in the rank of flight lieutenant.

So, on the Monday I returned my wife of less than two days to her mother. We parted, on platform one of Paddington Station – she for Wrexham and I for Swindon and then Stroud.

But my posting to Aston Down was short lived. Two days later on Wednesday 4th October, as I was buying a car, I was telephoned and told to report with all my luggage to Air Vice-Marshal Leigh-Mallory at his 12 Group HQ at Hucknall, at 9.30 a.m. the following morning. "Night-fighters will be important in this war," he said, "... and I am sending you as a flight lieutenant to be a flight commander on a Blenheim night-fighter squadron, No.229 being formed at Digby."

I left for Digby in Lincolnshire straight away and as soon as I arrived sent Het a telegram which she received just as she was about to leave for Aston Down. The message was: 'Stop – Ring Metheringham 26'. She found out where Metheringham was by cycling to the post office and they were able to confirm it was in Lincolnshire.

On my arrival at Digby I found that with the exception of the squadron commander, Squadron Leader Harold 'Mac' Macguire – a grand chap, straight from flying boats in Singapore – I was the only other officer in the squadron.

229 Squadron was officially formed (on a one flight basis) on 6th October and on the 14th information was received that a second flight was to be formed.

Over the next week a second flight commander, New Zealander Flight Lieutenant Clouston, and the rest of the pilots and gunners who had come straight from flying training school, where their courses had been drastically curtailed, arrived. The majority were only eighteen or nineteen and they had initially been trained for bombers. One hundred per cent casualties were expected in the first three months.

I was OC of A flight and made my first flight in a Blenheim on Tuesday 17th October. My flight consisted of Pilot Officers Bussey, Simpson, Brown, Linney, Smith, Lomax and Dillon.

The next few weeks were spent training, with lectures and with the pilots getting as much practice as possible on the Link Trainer.

The only difference between the so-called 'night-fighter' Blenheim IF and the standard bomber model was that it had a pack of four forward-firing guns fitted to the bottom of the fuselage. The crew consisted of 1st and 2nd pilots and a mid-upper gunner. The Blenheim, which had two engines, had a bad reputation for single-engine failure just after take-off, often resulting in fatal crashes. They occurred because pilots were not taking proper corrective action. Our first task, therefore, was to demonstrate the proper action to be taken, followed by practical tests. As a result of this exercise we eliminated accidents from this cause.

My log book entries for the next month were brief:

2nd November
The King visited Digby and 229 Squadron, being without aircraft, paraded on the road behind the watch office where they were inspected by HM.

6th November
Four Blenheims were received. Spitfire of 611 Squadron ran into 8722 while it was taxiing towards hangar.
8th November
Three more Blenheims arrive.

10th November
Flying training commenced.

15th November
Three more Blenheims delivered.

24th November
Night-flying by Squadron Leader Macguire and myself.

28th November
Five more Blenheims arrived.

Although the winter of 1939/40 was very bad – cold and with lots of snow – we took every opportunity to train by day and night with the object of attaining operational status as soon as possible. It was during this period that one weekend I met Het at Nottingham station where she had come from Wrexham. On arrival at a hotel called the Flying Horse we signed the register and went to our room. Soon there was a knock at the door – the manager wanted to see us. He produced the

register, pointing out that a Blackwell and a Rosier could not stay together in the same room. Het had absentmindedly signed her maiden
name. She never made the same mistake again!

229 eventually became operational on 21st December and I
recorded in my log book: 'The war starts for fighting 229. Red Section
A Flight carried out first operational duty'.

From then on we carried out patrols over the North Sea, mostly to
protect convoys and fishing vessels. These were known as 'kipper patrols'. On Christmas Eve I was returning from one such patrol when
I lost an engine. With no hydraulic power from the failed port engine
it meant that the undercarriage had to be pumped down by hand – an
arduous and time-consuming job. Choosing to land at Bircham Newton in Norfolk, where the visibility was better than at Digby, my co-
pilot Pilot Officer Brown pumped and pumped frantically and the
undercarriage locked down before we touched down.

Het had arrived that day to spend the Christmas holidays at Digby.
When she arrived at Lincoln station after a slow and tedious journey
across England, she was surprised not to be met by me but by a young
squadron pilot. She said he was a bit inarticulate as, at that time, I was
'lost'. Finally, I was found at Bircham Newton. I was not able to return
to Digby until the afternoon of Christmas Day. We usually stayed together at the Saracens Head, Lincoln, but Het spent that Christmas
night with the station padre's family at the vicarage at Scopwick.

Two days later on the night of 27th December, on another patrol I
was told that a Dornier 17 was in the vicinity. My gunner spotted him
flying east at about 25,000 feet. I gave chase, using full power to climb
from 1,000 feet and managed to get to within half a mile of him before
he saw me and pulled away. I remember the occasion well because I
was not dressed for the extreme cold at night and it took a long time
for me to thaw out. I had never experienced such freezing temperatures; it was a lesson to me.

In January we took it in turns with B Flight to deploy to North Coates
near the Lincolnshire coast where we maintained a state of readiness.
Our role was mostly to carry out convoy patrols. We were rarely called
upon to 'scramble' and when we did the missions were uneventful.

I remember vividly one very dark night that January when it started
to snow heavily. One of our aircraft, captained by Pilot Officer Bussey,

was overdue and radio contact with him was lost. I feared the worst. But shortly afterwards we heard the sound of his Blenheim. It was still snowing and the visibility was poor but he found the airfield and made his approach. Then he spoiled a very good show by landing with his undercarriage up. His excuse to me a few minutes later was, "I'm sorry Sir, but you can't expect me to remember everything."

Coincidentally, Het's brother Stewart Blackwell who had enlisted as an NCO in the RAF at the outbreak of war was posted to North Coates in February 1940 where I saw him on several occasions.

On 24th February 229 had its first casualties when Pilot Officer Lomax crashed and all three crew members were killed while night-flying doing 'search-light cooperation'.

At the beginning of March 1940 the powers that be ordained that we convert from night-fighters to day-fighters, and in our case we started flying Hurricanes. On 7th March I collected my Hurricane (L2141) from 213 Squadron at Wittering. Others were taken over from 56 Squadron at North Weald which had received the new tin-winged version. We said goodbye to our gunners, a stalwart lot, and started to convert our pilots to single-engine aircraft using the Miles Master Trainer. On 15th March the AOC-in-C Air Marshal Dowding visited the station and questioned the squadron leader concerning the re-equipment of the squadron.

Within seven days we reckoned that the pilots were ready to fly the Hurricane but it then took three weeks of hard work to train them up to a reasonable standard before we were declared fit for 'day' operations on 26th March.

During March and April training was interspersed with periods of readiness at our forward base at North Coates where we were some-times ordered to patrol over the North Sea. On 30th March I noted that we intercepted a raid in the early evening. Our early version Hurricanes were fabric covered, and had no armour plate fitted behind the cockpit and no self-sealing tanks intended to minimise the risk of petrol fires. Later Hurricanes had these modifications as standard.

In early April I wrote to Het and told her in great secrecy that 229 Squadron would be moving to a new RAF station at Kirton-in-Lindsey on 15th and 16th May. Little did I know that in fact my next move would be to France.

Chapter 3

A BRIEF TRIP TO FRANCE

MAY 1940

Thursday 16th May was the day when for me the war started. That morning while on early morning patrol from North Coates with part of my flight, I had been recalled to Digby, to be told that a composite flight of pilots and servicing crews was required to leave for France to reinforce 61 Wing, Air Component. Prior to leaving I sent a telegram to Het who had arrived back in Wrexham from the guesthouse in Ruskington where we had been staying for a few days.

POST OFFICE TELEGRAM

Charges to pay
RECEIVED

No.
OFFICE STAMP
WREXHAM
16 MAY

Prefix. Time handed in. Office of Origin and Service Instructions. Words:
119 12.34 METHERINGHAM LI 29 To

From
MRS ROSIER BURNSIDE BELVEDERE DRIVE WREXHAM =
CONFIDENT IN THE JUSTICE OF MY CAUSE AM PROCEEDING TO
ANHILIATE THE ENEMY STOP RING MACGUIRE TONIGHT ALL MY LOVE

Although impressed with my gallant words she told me later that she was worried that my determination would affect my judgement. And maybe it did as I returned from France a week later, a badly burned stretcher case.

At 2.00 p.m. that afternoon six of us from 229 Squadron left Digby and landed at Manston to refuel. In addition to me they were Pilot Officers Bussey, Gower (I think), Dillon and Simpson and Sergeants Johns and Merryweather.

At Manston B Flight from 56 Squadron at North Weald joined us. We knew 56 very well as in those days there was a lot of social interchange between squadrons. They were led by a friend of mine, Flight Lieutenant Ian Soden. I felt very proud when told that I was to command this composite squadron.

While waiting to be refuelled at Manston I wrote to Het:

My Darling Het, I have only a few moments to spare before we go off on our big adventure. I'm afraid I can't tell you the name of the place but it is in the North East near Arras. It came rather as a shock this morning. Poor Mac is very crestfallen. Well my darling wife, keep your chin up – they might let me come home on leave soon. Mac is packing up my kit and it will be stored at the Padre's house. My car will also be there. Tell Dad where I'm off to and tell him I had no time to write. All the love in the world my darling, darling wife. I love you so much.

Fred.

Early that evening we left for France and rendezvoused with a Blenheim which led us to Vitry-en-Artois, near Douai. The aerodrome was a large field with very long grass. There were no obstructions except a crashed Blenheim in the middle.

Landing at Vitry in L2142 at about 6.30 p.m. we were taxiing to dispersal positions when a car speeded up and a wing commander jumped out. Finding out that I was the leader he asked whether we had any fuel left. When I confirmed that we had, he, rather shakily I thought, burst out with, "For Christ's sake keep your engines on and stand by to scramble. There are sixty-plus bandits approaching." I did what I was told.

However, it was not long before our engines started overheating. I told Soden's flight to switch off. Still nothing happened, until one of my pilots, whom I had sent to find out the form, returned saying that the airfield was deserted. We immediately switched off and walked down to the local village where we found the wing headquarters' mess in the only hotel. The wing commander who had given the order to stand by was there. Such was the state of confusion and panic that when I complained about our treatment he said he was frightfully sorry but the events over the last few days had been so tremendously hectic that he was tired out and he had forgotten all about us. I was pretty angry as you can imagine. It was obvious that the events of the previous few days had affected him so much that he was in no fit state to do his job. Two days later he was invalided home with a nervous breakdown.

On asking him where my pilots' accommodation was he told me that we must find our own. Two pilots, who I then sent to find us billets in local houses, returned saying that no-one would have us. Clearly the locals were terrified that the Germans would arrive soon and punish them for looking after British airmen. I told them to try again, this time brandishing their revolvers. The ploy worked and we got to bed at about 11.00 p.m.

The next morning we were up before dawn and at 5.00 a.m., I made the first of five sorties that day leading a flight of six Hurricanes from 229/56 Squadron on a patrol towards Brussels. The sun was well up by then but it was still cold. No enemy aircraft were sighted, but east of Lille we ran into a barrage of AA fire. However, no-one suffered a direct hit and we all returned safely.

At 9.30 a.m. four Hurricanes of 229/56 scrambled in pursuit of raiders who had dropped bombs on Vitry. One of these was shot down by Ian Soden. At 10.30 the alarm sounded again and I scrambled with some of B Flight but returned half an hour later not having seen any raiders.

That afternoon a Dornier appeared over the airfield flying high and out of the sun. It dropped a large bomb on the airfield but did not cause any damage. As it made its second run it was intercepted and shot down by one of the three Hurricanes that had been at readiness and had scrambled.

There was no further activity of note that day but we did not leave the airfield for our billets in Vitry until half an hour after dark, by which time we were very tired and hungry.

The next morning, 18th May, we were again at the airfield by 4.30 a.m. My first action of the day was at 10.45 when I led a patrol of six Hurricanes, three from 229 Squadron and three from 56 Squadron, with orders to patrol between Brussels and Antwerp. Fifteen minutes into the flight we sighted some forty Me 109s at about 8,000 feet. I ordered all the Hurricanes to attack and singled out an enemy aircraft, fired and destroyed it. I then fired my remaining ammunition into another enemy aircraft but did not see it go down. Out of ammunition and with my instrument panel hit by some German bullets, I broke off the engagement and landed at an airfield near Lille where I refuelled.

What I saw there made me livid with rage. Sitting on the ground there were rows upon rows of brand new US fighters, but the French air force had decided not to fly them, nor to participate in the battle. The whole thing was a shambles.

The other two 229 Squadron Hurricanes were shot down in the battle. Pilot Officer Desmond Gower baled out and returned safely to Vitry on foot but Pilot Officer Michael Bussey was taken prisoner when his aircraft crash-landed. Having refuelled, I flew back to Vitry. Having returned to England Gower was to be shot down and killed on 21st May.

That afternoon, with only three aircraft serviceable, as we were in the midst of re-arming and refuelling prior to escorting some Blenheim bombers tasked with destroying the Albert bridges near Maastricht, fifty-plus Me 109s appeared out of the cloud over the airfield. We scrambled and they clearly had us at a great disadvantage and tried to pick us off as we were taking off. It was at this moment that Pilot Officer Dillon was shot down and killed. Somehow I managed to take off, get my wheels up and gain some height. I was at about 4,000 feet on the tail of an Me 109 when my Hurricane's fuel tank was hit by cannon fire from another enemy aircraft that I had

AIRMAN FELL IN FLAMES

WREXHAM PILOT'S ESCAPES

The exploits of a Wrexham airman have just come to light.

Flight-Lt. Frederick Ernest Rosier, after shooting down two enemy 'planes, was himself brought down in an air battle over Belgium and, leaving his blazing 'plane in mid-air, landed by parachute with his clothes on fire.

After his adventure Rosier was taken to hospital at Arras, suffering from severe burns. When the hospital was evacuated owing to the German advance

FLIGHT-LIEUT. ROSIER

he was brought over to this country, and is now in a large military hospital in the South of England.

He had another narrow escape when the train in which he travelled from Arras following the evacuation was heavily bombed.

Rosier's story as told to his wife is that he had his first success while on patrol one day, bringing down one of the latest German 'planes. On the following day he was engaged in a big air battle in which he sent two Messerschmitt 110s to earth.

JUMPED CLEAR

A few seconds later a bullet entered his petrol tank and his 'plane burst into flames. His clothing ablaze, Rosier jumped clear of his machine and opened his parachute. As he fell to earth he was able to beat out the flames and landed safely but badly burned.

Rosier, who is only 24, joined the Air Force in 1935, and last year was granted a permanent commission.

He was educated at Wrexham Grove Park School and was captain of the Rugby XV.

He is a son of Mr George Rosier, of Ramsbury Cottage, Rhosddu, near Wrexham.

not seen behind me. I was soon in a terrifying situation. My plane was on fire with burning fuel coming into the cockpit and my flying suit was in flames. I tried to open the hood to bale out but in spite of pushing with all my strength it was jammed and I could move it only four or five inches. I was trapped and I remember sinking back into my seat and thinking 'well that's that'. The pain was almost unbearable. The next thing I remember I was falling through the air. The aircraft must have exploded. Instinctively I pulled the 'D' ring and my parachute opened. A minute or so later I landed near the aerodrome at Vitry with my clothes on fire. I tried to put the flames out with my hands and remember how surprised I was when my skin began to come away.

Ten years later a friend of mine Teddy Donaldson who was commanding 151 Squadron at Vitry told me that he had saved my life by stopping some Frenchmen taking pot shots at me whilst I was coming down by parachute.

I must have passed out for the next thing I remember was waking up on the ground and being put on a motor cycle by a French civilian and taken to the field dressing station in Vitry.[2] That evening the British Army headquarters at Arras and the hospital were evacuated. Arras was left to the advancing Germans. Therefore, unbeknownst to me at the time, I was put in an ambulance and transported to Frévent where the army had established a hospital in a large chateau. Apparently the journey took seven hours as the roads were covered with army vehicles and the cars and carts

of refugees who had already begun their trek westwards. 229 Squadron
Operations Record Book states on 19th May Pilot Officer Simpson arrived back from France and Belgium. Simpson reported that I was shot
down in flames and later was admitted to hospital seriously burned.
He also stated that I was believed to have shot down two enemy aircraft.

When I woke up at Frévent I found another pilot, a friend of mine from 56
Squadron, Barry Sutton, was in the next
bed suffering from a bullet wound in the
foot sustained during the same battle. He
had travelled in the same ambulance as
me. In his book *The Way of a Pilot* Barry
describes how my neck, face, legs and
lower arms were covered with a black coating
of tannic acid. My hands were the worst burned part and I held
them above my head to keep the blood out of them. The pain was intense and Barry thought I was going to die. Fortunately, he was wrong.
The gods were on my side. I survived and I thus became a member of
the Caterpillar Club, membership of which was exclusive to those
whose lives had been saved by a parachute.

The next morning we were moved again. In addition to Barry, two
wounded army officers joined us in the ambulance. One was a young
second lieutenant, who turned out to be the son of General Sir Alan
Brooke, chief of the imperial general staff for most of the war. After another long journey (the thirty miles on roads cluttered with refugees
took four and a half painful hours) we reached Le Tréport, a large military hospital under canvas where we were cared for by Sister Gutteridge,
of the Queen Alexandra's Royal Army Nursing Corps who hailed from
Yorkshire. Kind and brave, I straightaway christened her 'Sweetie-Pie'.

It was to Sweetie-Pie that I dictated a letter to Het on 19th May as
follows:

My dear Het
You will no doubt be very surprised to hear that I am
now in a military hospital in France. On Saturday af-
ternoon I received a shot in my petrol tank and my ma-

chine caught fire. Luckily I got away by parachute. I am suffering very slightly from burns. There is a possibility that I shall be sent to England to recuperate. My hands are bandaged and I am unable to write myself.

Love and I hope to write myself in a day or two.

Fred.

NURSES DEFIED BOMBS, GUNS TO AID WOUNDED

By STUART FLETCHER

ONE of the girls that soldiers will tell stories about when this bitter war is over is Sweety-pie.

Sweety-pie is just an ordinary girl with a North Country drawl from Stockton-on-Tees. At least she was until a few weeks ago.

Now she is a heroine. Suddenly she was called on to exchange the quiet corridors and unexciting routine of a provincial hospital for the battlefield.

Sister Gutteridge — but the wounded soldiers called her Sweety-pie—took that call. And here is what she found she had to do as she told it to me yesterday, in her own words, a week after her return to England.

Helmet Dented

"My most exciting experience," she told me, "was on the way to the coast when we were evacuating wounded from Northern France.

"For 30 miles I drove in an ambulance with four wounded officers. Those 30 miles on a road cluttered with refugees and Tommies took us four and a-half hours.

"Again and again we were bombed. Again and again the bombers came over low machine-gunning the ambulance.

"At one place I got out of the ambulance to fetch some morphia from a Red Cross. As I was running back

ambulance machine-gun bullets hit and dented my tin helmet."

Sweety-Pie showed me the battered helmet with its tell-tale bullet marks.

"When we at last reached the coast," she went on, "we found that the hospital boat had been bombed and sunk.

"So we went on to the next port and found there that the hospital boat had been attacked.

"At the third port we managed to embark the wounded officers.

R.A.F. Hero

"One of them had brought down three Messerschmitts a few hours before and then leapt out of his burning plane in a parachute."

Sweety-Pie, who under machine-gun fire on the open road tore off her nurse's cap to make emergency bandages for the wounded lying by the roadside, had no admiration for herself. It was all for the soldiers.

"Their calmness and courage were wonderful," she said.

"They had to face bombing again and again and we never saw a sign of a British or French aeroplane."

Another sister told me yesterday how her experience in France and Belgium was that as soon as the Red Cross went up the German planes came over.

"One place we used as an emergency hospital was a lunatic asylum. We ran the Red Cross up and promptly Jerry flew over and bombed us."

Sister Faith Brownhill, an Australian nurse, told me a story of a Tommy pointing out a wounded German prisoner and saying: "He's a brave boy, sister, look after him carefully."

Heroines all, these girls, each with a horrifying story to tell of ceaseless efforts to save life under gunfire and in constant danger from bombing.

But, as you might have expected, they are all going back.

SISTER GUTTERIDGE had been machine-gunned, but returned safely with four wounded.

After two days in Le Tréport, on Wednesday 22nd May, in the face of the German advance, we were again evacuated by ambulance and headed for Dieppe. On the way, I was told later, our convoy, despite the proliferation of red crosses, sustained heavy casualties from repeated attacks by Me 109s. I had no knowledge of the attacks as I was unconscious most of the time. We eventually arrived at Dieppe. There, as the hospital ship the *Maid of Kent* had been bombed while waiting in the harbour, we were put on an ambulance train heading for Brest where the harbour turned out to be mined anyway.

Again, despite its red crosses, the hospital train was dive-bombed and machine-gunned. After a journey that seemed interminably long, we eventually arrived at Cherbourg early on the Friday morning of the 24th of May. Throughout the journey I had been unable to see as my eyes had swollen shut. In addition to tending to my very painful and pretty severe burns, Sweetie-Pie held cigarettes to my lips and fed me with a rough French wine – Pinot. What an excellent compassionate nurse she was. When we eventually reached Cherbourg we were put on board a hospital ship where we waited for darkness to make the crossing to England. Regrettably, Second Lieutenant Brooke (or the colonel as we had christened him) had to be left behind when he was assessed as too ill to travel any further. I later learned that he had died in Cherbourg.

When we reached Southampton we were off-loaded and despatched to Queen Victoria's Naval Hospital at Netley on Southampton Water.

Het received a telegram from Sweetie-Pie, who had left us at Southampton, and was soon on her way by train from Wrexham. She stopped the night at the Paddington Hotel and came on to Netley the next morning. Already worried about what state she would find me in, she was further disturbed by the fact that she was not allowed to go to my private ward until the matron was free to accompany her. Then came another blow for Het, and for me. Outside the door I heard the matron saying, "Don't express surprise at his looks" – or words to that effect – "we are afraid that he has lost his sight". Het came in clearly delighted that I was safe, heard parts of my story, and drank the dregs of the wine while trying to control her emotions. Nothing was said about my sight.

Years later she told me how horrified she was at my appearance. It was early days for the treatment of burns. I was being treated with gentian violet and tannic, something which she said made me resemble a rhinoceros. My eyes apparently were just slits of yellow 'matter'. Forty years later she could still remember the acrid smell which was about me for some time.

From the hotel in Southampton where she was staying Het rang up the CO of 229 Squadron, at Digby, to give him a message from me about the German tactics and how I thought we could counter them. I had learned in two days that much of our pre-war exercise training was useless in practice against this enemy. These tactics were based on the assumption that we would be fighting enemy bombers and not fighters. Our Hurricanes had no rear armour, our guns were harmonised at the 400 yard 'Dowding Spread' rather than the more effective 200 yards, and we still flew in tight Vic formations, which made us vulnerable to enemy fighters, rather than in pairs or fours . We also used the outdated attack system laid down by the *Air Ministry Manual of Fighter Tactics* (1938) which was useless for the type of air combat we experienced in France.

I had also learnt that in combat very few pilots, even those with the very best eyesight, had the ability to scan the sky and take in everything that was happening. These were lessons that I never forgot and continued to emphasise during the remainder of my service career.

Looking back it seemed that there was no way of stopping the Germans who had started their 'blitzkrieg' on 10th May. Their combination of tanks and infantry, plentiful and effective air support, allied to the brilliance of their commanders and the 'press on' spirit of the troops was overwhelming. In comparison the French army and most of its air force lacked the will, and the training, for the fight. I felt great pity for the refugees fleeing from the Germans. They included young and old and travelled in cars with mattresses on the roof. Some were carrying babies, some were carrying all their worldly possessions. Others, less fortunate, were pushing hand carts, wheelbarrows and a few had horses and carts. They cluttered the roads running west.

The British contingent, although small, was resolute and brave, and could not have been expected to stem or even slow down the German advance which was on a very wide front. We had no intelligence, no early warning, communications were nonexistent so we had no idea when we were going to be attacked. It was as though we were operating blind-folded.

'OFF GAMES'
JUNE-SEPTEMBER 1940

After a week at Netley the patients were evacuated. Three of us went to the Cornelia Cottage Hospital in Poole, where we service casualties were treated as heroes. The other two were a Green Howard's NCO who had been badly burned in Egypt before the war, and the marine officer son of Admiral Sir Dudley Pound, First Sea Lord at that time. One day Pound caused great panic by failing to return from an afternoon stroll. He was eventually found asleep on a nearby bench. His behaviour curtailed our freedom of action and alcoholic intake for a time.

Het visited me almost every weekend. She left school in Wrexham early on a Friday afternoon travelling by train as far as Woking where she stayed overnight. She avoided staying in London where we felt that bombing could start at any moment. She resumed her journey the next morning by train to Southampton and onwards to Poole where she arrived at the hospital at about 1.30 p.m. She left Poole by train for London at about 8.00 p.m. on the Sunday evening. She had supper at a cost of about 2 shillings (10 new pence) in the very popular Lyons Corner House in Piccadilly Circus, and then took the 12.10 a.m. train from Paddington arriving at Wrexham at 6.30 in the morning. There were no sleeping compartments on the train so, on my instigation, and against her better principles, she bribed the guard with half a crown to open a first class apartment for her. With little or no sleep she was off to school at 8.30 a.m.

She brought me news about my friends, about the squadron, about the outside world in general and about England during and after Dunkirk. She told me about stepping over completely exhausted Dunkirk survivors asleep on the platform at Paddington, about the newly formed WVS (Women's Voluntary Service) manning the station platforms with food and other comforts for the returning troops. She also told me about the depressing sight she had seen at Southampton harbour of a crowded troop ship from which hundreds of Canadian soldiers were shouting to the folk on the dockside that they had been across to France that morning but had not been allowed to disembark. I guessed that this was most vital (and depressing) news. It was. Two days later Churchill announced that France had fallen.

She told me of the unpopularity of the RAF generated by those returning from Dunkirk. "Where was the bloody air force?" was their constant cry. At one station, when Het's train drew up alongside a troop train, she startled the other occupants of her carriage by jumping up and giving the troops an answer. She told them that she couldn't vouch for the RAF in general, but she did know where one particular pilot was. In fact she was on her way to visit him as he had been shot down and badly burned in France. She was too angry however to register their reaction.

She told me too of the 200 Dunkirk survivors with whom she had travelled on the night train to Wrexham. How, in the early morning light outside Wrexham station, they 'fell in' under the orders of a sergeant major. They were from about fifty different units, each with only two or three men left. She said it was a sad and depressing sight but she was heartened by the smart way they finally marched off to Wrexham barracks.

It was she who encouraged me to get better and who cheered me up.

Most nights the sister on duty, whom I liked, used to visit me for an hour before giving me my next dose of morphine. During this hour she would kindly help me to drink a glass of beer. I kept the crate under the bed. The first time I slept the whole night through was a definite sign of progress but I must admit that I was a little sorry that I had missed the beer and chat with the sister. All the time my sight was improving and I was being allowed to go out more and more and for longer periods.

We had a most lovely summer in 1940. We often sat in the hospital grounds looking down at the flying boats in Poole harbour. Sometimes we went by bus to Bournemouth. The town was crowded with a mixed bag of servicemen who had managed to make it back across the Channel. The colours of their many different uniforms were of great interest. There was a predominance of French sailors. Regrettably, some of these later chose to return to France.

When Het was with me we would have tea at The Royal Bath Hotel and sometimes a meal at Bobby's, a large department store. There we would be entertained by a string quartet of rather drab middle-aged ladies. An incident in Bobby's caused Het such great embarrassment that she threatened never to come out with me again unless I mended my ways. I had done the unforgivable. When a sympathetic old lady asked how I had got my burns, I had replied "smoking in bed". I can only justify such crass behaviour by the excuse that I did not like being an object of pity. I knew I was a most unappetising sight: my face was so horribly scarred that I sometimes saw people turning away in horror. Others seemed to be fascinated with my bandaged arms held almost straight out in front of me. Eating became a long and laborious process. I did not want pity – or curiosity. People actually were very kind. A doctor at the hospital invited us one weekend to stay at his home, a lovely Georgian house in Wimborne just across from the abbey. I remember the joy of his seven-year-old son when I was able to present him with a quite sizeable piece of shrapnel which, with his father's help, had worked itself out of my leg.

When in due course I put in a claim for uniform, shoes, and a watch etc. which had been cut from me after I came down in flames, it was refused. It was pointed out that you could not have a uniform allowance twice. I was given mine when I joined up in 1935. I therefore had to buy myself a new watch upon arriving on sick leave in Wrexham. Later the cost of the service watch lost in the flames was deducted from my pay. Such was the state of the country that we 'took it all in our stride' with no grumbling.

One weekend after I had been in hospital for a month, Het showed me the telegram from Air Ministry stating I was missing and asking her to let them know if she should find me. I doubt she ever bothered to get in touch!

The war news was depressing. The French had surrendered, which had not surprised me; the BEF (British Expeditionary Force) under intense pressure had been forced back to Dunkirk and the beaches; and the RAF losses had been extremely heavy. Then came salvation, which was being hailed as a victory by Churchill. Ships of all sorts of shapes and sizes answered the call to brave the perils of the Channel and they, together with the navy, helped to evacuate thousands of British troops and a considerable number of French soldiers from Dunkirk. It was a brilliant operation, at first seemingly hopeless. RAF fighters, Spitfires and Hurricanes, also played their part, defending inland from Dunkirk, over the beaches and over the armada of ships. Without their support the outcome would have been very different.

In early August I was discharged from hospital and sent on a month's sick leave to Wrexham. We chose to spend part of it staying at a pleasant country pub in Gwyddelwern, close to Corwen and the River Dee. I was just about able to hold a fishing rod and cast a line and despite my amateurism many a pleasant and productive day was spent on the banks of the river and many a pint drunk at the Red Lion. After a few days we moved on to Abersoch on the Lleyn peninsula where amongst other relaxations we were taken out mackerel fishing.

Throughout this time a great air battle was going on over southern England. I hankered for every scrap of news. Although delighted to hear that pilots were saved, I knew how vital the stock of aeroplanes was; I feared they must be rapidly running out. It was at this time, encouraged by Beaverbrook, that the British people gave up their pans and anything made of aluminium ostensibly for new fighter aircraft.

In early September, upon completion of my leave, I returned to 229 Squadron now at Wittering, which at the start of the war had become a fighter station. There were only about half a dozen of the original squadron pilots left. I had lost two of the six I had taken to France – one eighteen-year-old, Dillon, had been killed, the other Bussey, just the same age turned up months later as a prisoner of war. Whilst operating from Biggin Hill over France and the beaches, five had been killed and six shot down and wounded. One, who had been shot down three times, was returning from Dunkirk on a RN destroyer when it was sunk. He eventually reached Dover, where, to cap it all he was booed.

The station was commanded by Wing Commander Harry Broadhurst, whom I had last seen at Vitry where I was shot down. It was he who had asked when we arrived if we had non-armour piercing tanks. When I said "No, it's suicide," he replied, "You mean bloody murder".

The author holding daughter Lis at her christening at RAF Northolt,
5th March 1944.

Het, who became a great friend of his wife Kay, stayed sometimes
at The George at Stamford and sometimes at their residence Pilsgate
House, known to us all as The Pilsgate Arms. This, the Dower House
of the Burleigh Estate, had been taken over from Lord Burleigh, who
had been a well known Olympic hurdler. Later in 1944 Kay was godmother at our daughter Elisabeth's christening at RAF Northolt.

During that month of September my job, such as it was, was helping
out in the ops room. But I also took time off to do some flying at
nearby Sutton Bridge, where my previous CO, Mac Macguire, was now
chief instructor. Officially I was not fit for flying, but in early October
this changed when doctors at Halton declared me able to undertake
further flying duties. It was what I wanted.

On some evenings when no enemy air activity was likely, Broady
would take Pat Jameson, a New Zealander, and a very good fighter
pilot, and me to our favourite pubs in the vicinity. One of these pubs
was the Ramjam, north of Stamford and further up the Great North
Road from Wittering, which had a very good-looking barmaid who
was looked upon with favour by Pat, until his girlfriend, who had

made her way from New Zealand, quickly put an end to 'that non-sense'. Another favourite pub we called the Honky Tonk was on the crossroads where one turns left off the A1 for Peterborough, Stilton and Brampton. On our wedding anniversary 30th September, perhaps somewhat ironically, I sent Het a telegram:

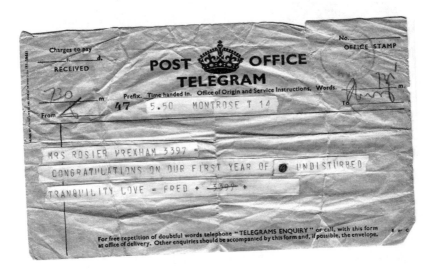

On one of her frequent visits from Wrexham Het came along to a drinks party at the mess, attended by the AOC of 12 Group, Air Vice-Marshal Trafford Leigh-Mallory, who almost a year earlier had told me that, "night-fighters were the thing". During the course of the evening the AOC asked to meet Het. Dismissing me, he apparently said to her, "What do you think of your husband flying again?" On being told, "I suppose it is up to him," he said, "I want him to go as the CO of a night-fighter squadron in a couple of weeks, but don't you tell him, I will." Of course Het told me; I was filled with apprehension and delight.

A week later the AOC contacted me and told me what he had intended. He then went on to say that my old squadron (229), then at Northolt, had lost its CO and if I wished I could immediately go to Northolt and take it over. I jumped at the opportunity and left next day, arriving there on 16th October.

229 SQUADRON
NORTHOLT AND SPEKE
OCTOBER 1940-MAY 1941

At that time Northolt, to the west of London and in AVM Keith Park's 11 Group was one of the most important fighter stations in the south east. In addition to my 229 Squadron, the Northolt wing included the Polish 303 Squadron whose CO and flight commanders were RAF and 615 Auxiliary Air Force Squadron. There was also a large transport squadron. The station commander Group Captain Vincent had been shot down and wounded a few days before my arrival and his place was filled by Wing Commander 'Tiny' Vasse.

My squadron of seventeen Hurricanes still had the same adjutant, Hogan, a First World War pilot who naturally was much older than me and who looked after me like a father. Sadly, there were only a very few pilots who had been with me earlier that year. These were my right hand man Flight Lieutenant Smith, Flying Officer Simpson who had been with me in France, and the loyal and stalwart sergeant pilots: Mitchell, Edghill and Johns, who were founder members of the squadron. During that period, in addition to Flying Officers Salmon, Bright and McHardy, Pilot Officers Dewar and Brown and Sergeants Hyde, Silvester and Arbuthnot, the remainder included two Rhodesians: Flight Lieutenant Finnis and Flying Officer Holderness, two young Poles: Flying Officers Stegman and Poplawski, two Belgians: Pilot Officers Ortmans and du Vivier and the New Zealander Pilot Officer Bary.

My first operational sortie back with 229 was on 19th October, exactly five months since my last sortie in France. Whilst at Northolt, we mostly operated in squadron and wing strength, the squadron commanders taking it in turns to lead the wing. Our most common task was to cover the south-eastern approaches to London by patrolling the Maidstone line at 25,000 feet at squadron or wing strength. Unfortunately, because of the height we were told to patrol at, we often found ourselves below the enemy fighters. Enemy fighter-bombers frequently jettisoned their bombs on sight of us and several of our losses occurred when chasing enemy aircraft back across the Channel.

On 26th October I wrote to Het by then back in Wrexham.

> *We did one patrol of one and half hours and saw several Huns, but could not make contact as they were going back across the Channel. My goodness it was cold up at 27,000 feet. The visibility was amazing, probably over 100 miles and a great part of the French coast was visible.*

It was on that patrol Flying Officer Simpson was killed when he was shot down by a Bf 109 off the French coast.

It was the practice to detail two pilots per squadron to weave behind the formation, their job being to warn of attack from the rear. It was a foolish practice that detracted from operational efficiency because it reduced the speed and rate of climb of the main force. Furthermore, the two unfortunate pilots designated for this task were often the least experienced and the most likely to be shot down. Accordingly at Northolt we fitted rearward-view mirrors to the top of the windscreens of our Hurricanes.

The squadrons took it in turns to disperse for the night on an airfield a few miles away at Heston, which after the war became Heathrow. Whilst there the pilots retired to the Berkeley Arms on the Bath Road for drinks and dinner which we finished invariably with port, courtesy of the manager. Het and I stayed with some very kind people at The Hall in Hanwell, from where we could hear the sounds of the bombing of London. They were paid four shillings a night for billeting us. We have been back there since and in place of The Hall and its grounds is a large housing estate.

At the dispersal airfield early one misty morning that autumn we started our engines and began to take off as a squadron to return to Northolt. About halfway through our take-off run I was horrified to see another squadron coming straight at us. Avoiding action was impossible; but by a miracle there were no collisions. The other squadron, Polish 303, had used a different radio frequency from us and consequently we had no warning of their take-off.

I noted in my log book that on 14th November we had an active day when on three occasions the squadron met formations of Bf 109s scoring three 'probables'. The AOC of 11 Group was keen to take action against the night-bombing raids on London and I spent many nights on patrol. And on 16th November noted that, having taken off at 3.15 a.m., 'on landing my port oleo leg collapsed causing damage to the aircraft'. On one of these patrols Pilot Officer Ortmans' aircraft P3039 was damaged beyond repair in combat.

On another occasion I took off in my Hurricane P3212 one moonlit night hoping that I would intercept and shoot down one of the many German aircraft dropping bombs in the vicinity; but had no luck. To return to Northolt I lost height between two clutches of barrage balloons, found Western Avenue and then requested that the runway lights be lit for my landing. The controller refused because the enemy bombers were still active. I had to come in and land without lights, damaging the undercarriage in the process. The next morning the controller responsible was dealt with severely and an order went out to the effect that the safety of our own aircraft was always to come first whatever the risks involved. Two days after my arrival on 18th October, 303 lost four pilots when a patrol returning to Northolt became lost in deteriorating weather.

One morning the dreaded phone rang but it was not the usual order to 'scramble', but Tiny Vasse asking me to go along to his office. He told me that during the night a Polish officer had smuggled a woman into his room in the officers' mess. At about 3.00 a.m. the bell had rung so persistently in the batman's room that he eventually got up. Knocking on the door of the Pole's room, he was told to "come in". There he was presented with the sight of a naked Pole and a half-naked woman, with the Pole saying, "We would like breakfast for two". The batman, most affronted, reported the incident. In answer to Tiny Vasse's question as to what course of action I would take, I suggested he send for the senior Polish officer on the station, tell him the story and ask him what he was going to do about it.

The senior Pole duly arrived and in answer to Tiny Vasse's question, said without any hesitation, "It is easy, we will shoot him." Vasse, taken aback, leapt from his chair and in no uncertain terms told the Pole that he was in England now, not in Poland. The upshot was that the amorous Pole was confined to camp for a couple of weeks.

During my time at Northolt we had few victories for at the end of October the Luftwaffe gave up their daytime massed-bomber attacks, resorting to wide-ranging attacks by small numbers or even single Me 109s carrying bombs. Their time spent over this country was very brief; they were fast and they proved difficult to intercept. However, during this period 229 had come together as a squadron and morale was high.

On 15th December the squadron left Northolt and returned to Wittering. After a week at Wittering we were posted to Speke, near Liverpool, ostensibly for a rest. On 21st December I flew up to Speke on a recce and the next day the squadron, with its eighteen Hurricanes, arrived two days before Christmas. I was glad to be posted to Speke which was close to Het's and my homes in Wrexham.

Initially there was little activity by day but the heavy bombing of Liverpool by night started in early January.

Having arrived at Speke we concentrated on operational training with our loyal and hard working ground crews: the fitters, the wireless men and the armourers. On one occasion I led a squadron formation over Wrexham with two aircraft weaving about behind the formation. Seeing this, a friend of Het's said to her, "I know it is none of my business but tell Fred that two of his pilots were fooling about at the back!"

Het and I had a pretty thatched house, Bromley Hatch, in the village of Hale, close to Speke. Our neighbour, a Liverpool butcher, was generous and the local pub, The Childe of Hale, was pleasant. Our relationship with the station commander, Group Captain Seaton Broughall (and his girlfriend Poppy) was close and we were not troubled by the other squadron, 312 Czech Squadron, whose officers rarely used the mess. I was given a car, hired locally, but soon damaged it driving as we did with hooded lights. The second sustained similar damage, and when it came to the third, I was warned it would be the last one.

But life at Speke was not the rest we had been promised. Liverpool and its outlying districts came under some heavy night attacks by bombers, and the city suffered. Het spent those nights in a 'command' air raid shelter at Speke, a wise precaution because our house was not far from a Q site, those designed to attract the attention of the bomber crews away from the main target.

When warning of the night raids was received I, usually accompanied by my stalwart sergeant pilots, flew to RAF Squires Gate near Blackpool or RAF Valley in Anglesey. There we awaited the order to scramble and to be directed into the bomber stream. On a few occasions I sighted bombers but by the time I turned to attack I had lost them. We had no radar and relied completely on eyesight. It was most frustrating. To keep up the morale of the heavily bombed Liverpudlians we used to fly around the city just as dusk was falling. One afternoon when Het was at the hairdressers in Liverpool she reported that people had rushed to the windows to see me and my chaps circling the city. They were most heartened thinking they would have protection that night. Little did they know that when we landed they were on their own.

At Speke I lost three valued pilots. The first, Sergeant Arbuthnot, crashed in the Mersey whilst returning to the airfield in thick mist. The other two, Pilot Officers Dewar and du Vivier, were mysteriously lost over the Irish Sea on 30th March. We came to the conclusion that they had collided when being vectored towards a German reconnaissance Ju 88 or Do 17. They were a great loss.

Early in the war I had agreed with Mac Macguire, the CO of 229, that air crew should only be recommended for decorations such as the DFC and DFM if they had performed over and above the normal line of duty. We agreed that the normal line of duty included shooting down one, two or three aircraft depending on the circumstances. That was our job.

As a result by the beginning of 1941 no one in the squadron had been decorated – something that was matched by no other squadron. The point was driven home to me one evening in March 1941 when the three brave sergeant pilots came to my house by arrangement. They had complaints and over a glass of beer I told them to air them freely. The first was that many sergeant pilots junior to them and with less experience had been commissioned. The second one covered the absence of decorations in the squadron. I listened and I realised that I should change my policy. Het too had been pointing out how much such decorations meant to wives, mothers and the general public.

Though I regarded those sergeants as the lynch pin of the squadron, it had simply never occurred to me to recommend them for commissioning – or for a medal. They forgave me for my lack of thought. They and their wives subsequently became great friends of ours for the rest of their lives.

The next morning I recommended the three for immediate commissions. These were celebrated by a squadron pilot's party at our house, where the new officers arrived in borrowed uniforms. When we arrived late – having been elsewhere and given the key to one of the flight commanders, the party was in full swing. The centrepiece was a goat, which should have been cropping our large lawn. They were given a great and well-deserved promotion party. Johns eventually became a group captain, Mitchell a wing commander and Edghill, who was the first in the squadron to get a DFC whilst serving in the Western Desert, retired on medical grounds, as a flight lieutenant.

This kind of life away from the main operational areas could not go on for ever. Therefore, sometime in March I was not surprised to be told the squadron was to move. However, I *was* surprised when I was told that we were destined for the Middle East, most likely for the Western Desert.

During the next few weeks preparations for the move went ahead. The ground crews were to embark on *SS Strathmore* in Liverpool and were destined for a long sea voyage taking the comparatively safe route round the Cape of Good Hope and up to East Africa and thence to Egypt. The pilots were to 'endure' life on an aircraft carrier from the Clyde to the Mediterranean where, at some point, we would fly our Hurricanes off the carrier to Malta and then on to Egypt. Four of my pilots were to take a different route by ship to Takoradi on the Gold Coast in West Africa and then would fly their Hurricanes across Africa to Egypt.

Soon the time came for the farewell parties and a tearful goodbye to Het – and then on 10th May we were off, I by train to the Clyde, and she by service car to Wrexham as 'officer's baggage'.

An overview of North Africa

Chapter 4

SAND IN
MY SHOES

A MEDITERRANEAN CRUISE

On boarding HMS *Furious* at Greenock on the Clyde, I immediately discovered that two old friends were on board, Derek Eyres, then of the Fleet Air Arm, formerly of my flight in 43 Squadron and Squadron Leader Macdonald (Cousin Mac) the CO of 213 Squadron which, along with 249 Squadron, was also on board. That evening we three were enjoying a drink with a friend of Eyres, the captain of a destroyer which had just returned from the successful Lofoten Islands raid, when we were ordered to return immediately to the *Furious*. A drink or two later came the news that the ship was getting underway. By the time we reached her, she was actually moving. We were then faced with a long and somewhat ignominious climb up rope ladders to the flight deck where we were piped aboard, much to the amusement of our pilots and many of the ship's company.

During the voyage to Gibraltar we RAF officers were asked to limit our drinking as there was concern that the gin would run out. In a letter I wrote to Het while on board I said, 'Eyres has a violin which I have played so much (Gin only being 2d per tot) that my fingers are blistered'.

Soon after our arrival at Gibraltar on 18th May the *Furious*, together with other carriers and warships, was diverted to join the hunt for the

German battleship *Bismarck*. Before the *Furious* departed on this mission on 21st May, six pilots each from 229 and 213 Squadron were dispatched from the carrier for Malta and Egypt. There they were attached to 274 Squadron and assisted in covering the evacuation of Crete.

The remainder of us were left behind to enjoy over two weeks of enforced holiday staying in luxury 'in a minor suite' at the Rock Hotel. We were invited to parties every night. One that still remains in my memory was given by the 'Gibraltar Millionaires' for Her Majesty's Forces. There was no blackout at night and food rationing was forgotten. We ate our fill of deliciously prepared food, much of which we had not seen for well over a year. In a letter to Het I told her, 'I had the best sole I have ever tasted with half a lemon, and then a Spanish omelette'. From Gibraltar on 19th May I sent a telegram to Het:

29th May I again wrote to Het, 'I bought half a dozen pairs of silk stockings yesterday, they cost thirty-six shillings altogether, so apart from the fact they are scarce in England they are much cheaper. I made a guess at the size of your feet and legs darling'. I also sent her a bottle of scent.

When the *Bismarck* had been sunk, a slightly depleted convoy – HMS *Hood* had not survived the battle – returned to Gibraltar. On her arrival on 5th June, we rejoined the *Furious*, and, as we left Gibraltar, the two squadron commanders were summoned to a briefing by an admiral who gave us our timings for take-off from the carrier to Malta. We were told that for safety reasons (the safety of the carrier, not ours!) we were to take off in the dark. As not one of us had ever taken off from a carrier, let alone in the dark, this was fraught with danger. We argued against the operational sense of this and during our remonstrations we pointed out that the main object of this exercise was to get us safely to Malta.

Finally, both of us said that we, as individuals, would obey the orders but would not order our squadron pilots to do so. Eventually, the admiral backed down. It was agreed that we should all take off at first light. In the early hours of the following morning, in the middle of the Mediterranean, I climbed into my Hurricane, which was positioned in front of the others and, as dawn broke, saw what a short take-off run I would have. I was sceptical about my ability to get airborne in that distance but the navy were correct in their calculations and I took off safely ahead of twelve aircraft from 229 Squadron. When we were all off the carrier we formed up behind a Fairey Fulmar which was to lead us on the 450-mile journey to Malta.

The last thing we wanted on this two and a half hour flight, which took us close to enemy air bases in North Africa, was to be intercepted. Any fighting en-route would have reduced our chances of getting to Malta because the long-range fuel tanks we needed for the flight had been installed at the expense of fifty per cent of our fire power. The emphasis, therefore, was on accurate navigation and complete radio silence with the Fulmar. It was a long, nerve-wracking flight and I think now that the radio silence was over-emphasised. However, we arrived safely – the first squadron to do so without a casualty.

After our arrival in Malta, I was invited to have dinner with the AOC, Air Vice-Marshal Sir Hugh Pughe Lloyd. During dinner he insisted that the squadron should remain in Malta under his command. I managed to persuade him otherwise by telling him that it would not be in his interests as my best pilots had not come with me but had gone via Takoradi, and he eventually agreed that we could leave. After a day's rest in Malta we took off for an uneventful four-hour flight to Mersa Matruh on the Egyptian coast where we refuelled and flew on to Abu Sueir, some ten miles west of Ismailia. The squadron arrived without loss in Egypt on 8th June where I found the RAF was being criticised by the other services for lack of support in Greece and Crete. I am told that it was the same after Dunkirk, but at that time I was in hospital.

THE WESTERN DESERT
229 SQUADRON JUNE-OCTOBER 1941

My first few weeks in Egypt were frustrating. As the squadron ground crews were still on their way via the Cape, my pilots were sent to re-inforce other squadrons in Palestine and the Western Desert. A Flight was initially attached to 274 Squadron covering the withdrawal from Crete and then to 73 Squadron at Sidi Haneish where they operated as C Flight. B Flight were split between 6, 208 and 213 Squadrons. I was therefore left behind kicking my heels at Abu Sueir in the Canal Zone, the home of 102 Maintenance Unit. I wrote in a letter to Het on 17th June, 'I am depressed darling as I am on my own doing nothing and the rest are more or less split up for the time being. Unfortunately one of the sergeants is missing.'

> *19th June*
> *Darling, Smithie has just arrived here with good news. His flight's score is four-nil, Edghill having accounted for two. I returned to Sidi Haneish and spent forty-eight hours in the desert with Smithie, Ruffhead & Co. It must be difficult for you to realise what the place is like – just miles and miles of nothing but sand – no vegetation – and to the north the terrific blue of the Mediterranean.*

> *29th June*
> *I am still looking forward to the time when I receive some letters or cables from you – it seems such a long*

time with no news. All the other chaps are in the same
boat...Have just heard that Sowrey has departed to a
better land and am cast down about it. Having no con-
trol over the chaps' movements and actions is not likely
to improve my present temper, still, I have tried my
damnedest and am still trying.

Increasingly bored and with the boldness and confidence of youth, I went to headquarters of Middle East Command in Cairo where I asked for an interview with Commander-in-Chief Air Marshal Sir Arthur Tedder. To my surprise, he agreed to see me and I immediately raised the subject of my lack of employment and my dispersed pilots. I told him that in my view it was a silly way to run an air force. For the past nine months I had been training up my squadron to fight as a cohesive unit and had developed a marvellous *esprit de corps* only to find that on our arrival in Egypt my pilots had been sent off to join other squadrons. He not only listened but agreed with my point and, within a few days, at the beginning of July, I left for Sidi Haneish, a landing ground near Mersa Matruh, 300 miles west of Cairo.

Sir Arthur Tedder, was a remarkable man; one of the best senior officers we had in the war. He could be cynical, but had a ready smile and a great gift for putting his juniors at ease. I got to know him well during his overnight visits to the Desert Air Force HQ where Air Vice-Marshal Coningham (nicknamed 'Maori' then changed to 'Mary'), the AOC, would often invite some of us to meet him and have a drink.

At Sidi Haneish, in addition to getting 229 back, following the arrival of the pilots who had come via Takoradi, I was also given temporary command of 73 Squadron to which some of my pilots had been attached. 73 Squadron had not long come out of Tobruk and their CO Pete Wykeham had been sent to the Delta for a rest.

7th July
It is much cooler up here than it is down south but we
are surrounded with miles and miles of desert on three
sides and the blue of the Med on the north.

All I live for I'm afraid is to receive my first letter
from you.

13th July
The past week has been fraught with worries due to foolish accidents and to the loss of five over enemy territory. None of these fortunately were in my squadron although I was in charge of them as well.

After initial success against the Italians in Cyrenaica in late 1940 and early 1941, the situation in the desert had undergone a dramatic change with the arrival of the Germans in the theatre. Rommel's offensive in April 1941 had resulted in our withdrawal to the Egypt/Libya border and Tobruk became a besieged fortress. Operation Battleaxe which began on 14th June, the aim of which had been to push back Rommel's forces and to relieve Tobruk, had failed and the situation was stalemate.

During the next few months whilst there was a lull in the ground fighting and preparations went ahead for the next offensive, our fighter squadrons which by then included 229, were continually engaged in air defence, including night patrols over Mersa Matruh, offensive sweeps and the much disliked job of escorting 'A' lighters to Tobruk where they docked after dark and left before dawn.

The task of defending these slow moving vessels, particularly in the late afternoon, when they were close to the main German landing grounds (LGs) at Gambut was not one we relished. The prospect of Stukas with fighter cover appearing without warning out of the red ball of the setting sun was distinctly unpleasant. On one such patrol I nearly 'bought it' as we used to say. I was firing at a low flying Stuka, perhaps at 100 feet, over the sea when my Hurricane suddenly went into a violent roll to the right. For a moment I thought we would crash into the sea. Fortunately I was able to regain control and by keeping the speed low and using harsh rudder and aileron control I was able to limp back to our advanced base at Sidi Barrani where I discovered that a large piece of metal skin had come adrift from the starboard wing and hit the tailplane.

Later that evening I had a call from Air Commodore Collishaw, the commander of 204 Group (shortly to become Air HQ Western Desert) and was able to tell him that the squadron had shot down six or seven enemy fighters, of which Edghill had shot down three. 'Collie', a Cana-

We are rationed with water here, but it is amazing what one can do with a gallon of water. I can shave, clean my teeth and have a complete bath – rinsing myself down afterwards. During the first week I went for three days without a proper wash, and I began to feel decidedly filthy.

What have you decided to do darling, are you going to lead the life of a woman of slender means or have you decided on a job of work. Whatever you decide darling, if I get back to England before the war is over you will immediately take up house again. I hope you are getting money in your bank regularly.

Mitchell was terrifically excited yesterday, for the last day or two he had been depressed as when landing at night he had swung and killed a soldier – and then he received the first cable from his wife. She had received the parcel he sent from Gib, & I hope that you have received the scent and the silk stockings. It was rather amusing buying the silk stockings there darling. Geo[rge] ...

... and then we realised we had no ... that sizes to buy. I narrowly ... that my guesswork proved right, though in that case George's wife ll have stocking far too small Holderness who is still away from ... unfortunately, not Tubby whom ... in Cairo the other day. I ... bet had who is annoyed after ... having thought they were going to ... settle down for some length of time ... of course am pleased, as it means that a new driving force is getting stronger and stronger. It is very pleasing also to hear that the fighting in Syria has ceased. That and Abyssinia are our victories so far.

Unfortunately we are only allowed to send away one of these letter cards per week – I'm afraid I can't say how long they take to get home. Considering the route they have to follow and the facilities available I wonder they arrive home at all. Will darling remember me to everyone.

All my love sweetheart keep you happy ...

Air Mail Letter Card

BY AIR MAIL — AIR MAIL LETTER CARD

IF ANYTHING IS ENCLOSED THIS CARD WILL BE SENT BY ORDINARY MAIL

R.A.F. CENSOR 124

MRS F. E. ROSIER.
"BURNSIDE"
BELVEDERE DRIVE
WREXHAM
GT. BRITAIN.

WHEN FOLDED THE LETTER CARD MUST CONFORM IN SIZE AND SHAPE WITH THE BLUE BORDER WITHIN WHICH THE ADDRESS ONLY MAY BE WRITTEN.

13/7.

No. 229 Sqdn.
R.A.F.
Middle East Forces.

My Sweetheart

No more cables or letters have arrived during the past week, so since I left England I have only received one cable. The past week has been fraught with worries due to foolish accidents and to the loss of 5 of our enemy territory. None of them fortunately, were in my sqdn although I was in charge of them as well. I have managed to have a couple of bathes in the ... this week – bathing in the nude sweetheart, owing to the absence of my costume, and the absence of females for hundreds of miles around. The water is gloriously warm and so clear that you can see the bottom through about 10 ft. This place is much more healthy than the Delta, and the chaps are keeping very fit. It has been rather unpleasant today however, and the visibility has been limited. Sand in my hair, eyes, in my food – nothing but sand.

dian ace in the First World War, had initially done well against the Italians but when the Germans arrived he was soon out of his depth. His efforts to thwart them were amateur in the extreme and he lacked the professionalism needed for the task.

Life in the desert was tough and demanding. Apart from the stress of continually being on operations, we had to put up with extremes of heat during the day and in the winter months, extreme cold at night. There were also the discomforts of sandstorms, when visibility fell to a few yards and sand got into the food and water. The flies, the shortage of water and the monotony of the daily diet of hard biscuits, bully beef, occasionally tinned fish, tinned bacon and marmalade, only enlivened sometimes by tins of Maconochies 'M & V', tinned meat and vegetables. But there were compensations: the vastness and the beauty of the desert, the night sky full of stars, the sunrises, and the silence. During the first few months, until it was lost, I had a violin and in the late evenings, when in the mood, I would scrape away under the night sky and the sound would come back to me, transformed. However, at Sidi Haneish where we bathed in the warm Mediterranean and had parties with the other squadrons, living conditions were more bearable.

16th July

In a way I am enjoying life up here darling, I am especially struck by the terrific camaraderie amongst the pilots, I suppose it is a natural consequence of being isolated from civilisation. The mess consists of a shack with a wooden partition across the centre. On one side we have a miniature bar, some camp chairs and a wireless set, and on the other, our so-called dining room. The food quite naturally lacks variety, but one develops such a terrific appetite that any food tastes good. We had a most successful fracas with the common horde yesterday evening and the resulting score was certainly seven to their two, probably nine to two. We have not seen Lauder since the game. Smithie, Edghill and Johns distinguished themselves, but your amazing husband met with a slight reverse right at the beginning, which necessitated his limping back to base.

On 27th July I wrote to Het: 'We are having a very slack time of it today and I have sent some of the chaps to Alex so that they can have a night out. Most of the others are out bathing this afternoon.' I mentioned in a letter on 2nd August that I had not yet received a letter from Het but finally received a second cable that day.

> *6th August*
> *My time has been occupied during the last few days writing letters of condolence to relatives of chaps who are either missing or have been killed. It is a shocking job. At the moment I have about ten of these on the go.*

There was always plenty of work to do. I often flew at night hoping to intercept the odd German bombing Mersa Matruh. On the night of 7th/8th August on one such patrol at 3.25 a.m., I shot down a Blenheim of 113 Squadron. It had just dropped its bombs on Mersa Matruh and was illuminated by search lights, when, as it did not show IFF (identification, friend or foe), I shot at it from fairly long range. Fortunately, the crew managed to bale out and were found in hiding the next day. I wrote to Het about this incident: 'I also achieved a bitter success. I shot an aircraft down in flames but the aircraft should never have been there. Luckily the pilot was rescued. You can probably guess what happened.'

In the subsequent Court of Inquiry the senior air staff officer 'SASO', of the Desert Air Force Group, Group Captain Freddie Guest found the crew guilty of a 'gross error of navigation' but he also attached some blame to me for the shooting down. I was certain he had never been placed in a similar situation.

> *8th August*
> *Nothing exciting happened yesterday darling, but this morning another game took place and we wounded a couple of players on the opposite side. I was a non player however as I had been night-flying until an early hour this morning.*

On 27th August having received my first letter from Het since leaving England in May – a batch of four letters with photographs – I wrote:

> *Mitchell, Ruffhead and Russell are spending a few days in Alex and the rest are still up in the desert. I am trying to organise things at my base landing ground so that very soon we will all be together again. Horniman is missing after a brush with the Huns last week – so now I am rather depleted having very few of the originals left.*

The 73/229 partnership, which had been a very happy one, came to an end on 27th August. 229 Squadron, again complete with the ground crews who had come via the Cape, again began to operate as an independent squadron. 73 went back to the Delta for a rest. At a party to celebrate this where we all got 'rather merry' their CO, Squadron Leader Peter Wykeham, recently returned from a well-earned rest, presented me with a silver tankard inscribed 'from the CO and officers of 73(F) Squadron in memory of 73/229 June-August 1941'. I still have this tankard and it has quite a story to tell!

> *2nd September*
> *I am writing at my base whilst the others are finishing their lunch. I then have to fly back to our operational aerodrome. I have been at sixes and sevens trying to get night-flying organised. We started it last night – pretty unsuccessfully as Penny damaged his A/C when landing.*
>
> *There are two small oases near our base – plentifully provided with figs, dates, wild tomatoes and prickly pears. The pears grow on a kind of cactus tree and taste something like a pomegranate. The figs are ripe, but the dates are green.*

On 13th September 229 Squadron pilots left for Cairo en-route to Takoradi to collect Hurricane MkIIs.

24th September
It has been completely impossible to write as since my last letter there have been great changes; first we moved to about three different landing grounds within just over a week. I then arranged for the pilots to go and collect their own aircraft [Hurricane IIs from Takoradi] which meant a trip of several thousand miles, and then I was posted to 204 Group to become fighter liaison officer. It means that I shall be promoted (to wing commander) and within a month or so will probably control at least four squadrons. Naturally I feel sad at leaving the squadron but I had a pre-sentiment that I was about to go up in the world.

So in late September I left 229 for Maaten Bagush, on posting to HQ 204 Group, shortly to become Air HQ Western Desert, where Air Vice-Marshal Coningham had just taken over as AOC. I was very sad to leave for, apart from spending a few months in hospital and in convalescence, I had been in the squadron continuously from October 1939 when it was formed at Digby, as a flight commander and then CO. Bill Smith, my senior flight commander since our days at Speke, took over from me as CO a day or two before the squadron's second birthday celebrations, with Johns and Mitchell as the flight commanders.

STEALING A STUKA
262 WING AND OPERATION CRUSADER

One evening a few days after my arrival, Wing Commander Al Bowman, the chief training officer of the Western Desert Air Force, and I discussed the possibility of finding and flying back a Stuka dive-bomber. A number had reportedly forced-landed due to fuel shortage in the forward area close to 'the wire'. The next day we put our proposal to the AOC Air Vice-Marshal Arthur Coningham. To our delight he agreed.

The next morning Bowman, who was a big, bluff and determined Australian, and I took off in a Wapiti with a captured Italian Stuka pilot, hoping that he would be of some help.

The Stuka. September 1941.

By midday we had reached Thalatta where we found a Ju 87 which had crashed on landing and flipped on its back. Continuing the search we flew to Al Hamra, twenty-five miles away where we made contact with a South African armoured car unit. As they had seen nothing we decided to fly further west towards enemy territory and landed at Fort Maddalena on the Libyan frontier where the 11th Hussars were based.

At this stage as dusk was approaching, because our aircraft was making us vulnerable to enemy air attack we we decided to send it back, with to his delight, the Italian prisoner on board.

That night we dined with the 11th Hussars. The officers were most friendly and having heard what we intended to do entered into the spirit of the adventure with enthusiasm. At dawn next morning loaded with rations and water for three days we set out to resume the search in a couple of their trucks with an escort of an officer and several troopers. After a few hours of nothing but sand we came across a British patrol who had seen a German dive-bomber intact. It was clear from the increase in enemy aircraft activity around us that they were also seeking their lost Ju 87.

We soon found the German aircraft standing on a patch of firm sand next to which reclined a very young British Army officer who was delighted to hand over his charge to us.

By now it was late afternoon and we were anxious to get the Stuka refuelled and to fly it back whilst it was still light. We had several cans of petrol with us and whilst our army friends were pouring this in under the direction of the wing commander, I was fiddling about in the cockpit. Suddenly there was a commotion and everyone started running away. I had mistakenly pressed a switch or moved a lever which had jettisoned the bombs. Reacting to their shouts, I was out of the cockpit in a flash, but it was not long before common sense prevailed: the bombs could not have become armed in the short distance they had fallen. So back to the Stuka we went to continue the preparations, which seemed to be going well when two CR42s came over at about 5,000 feet. Convinced that we must have been spotted we decided to try to start the engine and to get away as quickly as possible. After a few attempts with the starter handle the engine fired and within a few minutes we took off and set course towards the east. The wing commander was at the controls and I was in the rear cockpit.

After some twenty minutes cruising in a north-easterly direction the engine suddenly spluttered and stopped. We were forced to land but after a little tinkering the engine came to life and we set off again. However, again we were unlucky as the hydraulic gauge burst and we had to make a forced landing in the gathering gloom. In the process we suffered a burst tyre and damaged the undercarriage in a shallow wadi. As the light was failing we decided to set up camp for the night next to the Stuka. It was only then we realised what trouble we were in as, in the excitement of getting the aircraft to start, we had left behind our rations, water reserves and maps.

That night we slept in the folds of our parachutes. At dawn, with only our water bottles and with the prospect of at least a forty-mile walk back to Sidi Barrani, we spelled out a message with stones and then set off heading north. Around midday we saw dust clouds on the horizon. Confident that this was a friendly patrol, we streamed a parachute which fortunately was seen and our walk was soon over. We were rescued by a South African officer with a long-range desert patrol. I then returned to air headquarters to await my posting order whilst Wing Commander Bowman, with a repair team, returned to the Stuka and subsequently flew it back to our lines. Sadly, Al Bowman was killed a few weeks after he returned with the Stuka. Making an approach to a remote desert landing ground in a Blenheim with Group Captain Dearlove aboard, he was shot down by our own AA in a tragic case of poor aircraft recognition.

A few days later I flew another Stuka from the same formation which had also been flown back to our lines. I was not impressed with the Stuka. It was very slow.

In early October I was delighted to be told by Air Vice-Marshal Coningham that, in order to support the army's anticipated advance to Tripoli – Operation Crusader – a second fighter wing was to be formed (262) and that I was to be promoted to wing commander and take it over. Operating in conjunction with the senior 258 Wing which was to be commanded by a group captain, we were to be responsible for the detailed operations and control of the desert fighter force. 262 Wing consisted of six squadrons, three each of Hurricanes and Tomahawks, and was organised so that it could control the whole fighter force of twelve squadrons and both wing headquarters. In many respects the wings, which were fully mobile and self-contained, corresponded to the group control centres later in the war. As mobility and good communications were vital for effective air support the wings would be responsible for sifting requests from the army, deciding on bomb lines and on ground-to-air signals.

> *6th October*
> *Mersa Matruh*
>
> *I am now a wing commander and am fulfilling the functions of this position. I am starting the whole wing from scratch – a big undertaking as you will probably gather from other sources in the immediate future. The fighting 229 is only going to be one of six with Frederick as the big white chief. Truly sweetheart mine, the job is terrific.*

At this time in the desert we had twelve squadrons of Hurricanes and Tomahawks plus a naval squadron of Hurricanes and Grumman Martlets from the disabled carriers HMS *Illustrious* and *Formidable*. As we had numerical superiority we decided to operate over the battle area in formations of two squadrons, a total of twenty-four aircraft, which made up for the inferiority in performance of the Hurricane and Tomahawk against the Me 109F.

In late October the CO of 258 Wing 'Bull' Hallahan who was almost twenty years my senior, was replaced by Group Captain 'Bing' Cross, an old friend from Digby days.

20th October

Things seem to be freshening up out here. Hardly a day goes past without an aerial combat over the forward areas. Sandstorms are the only things which interfere. Still I hope to have my HQ in Benghazi or even Tripoli by Christmas. Group Captain Bing Cross is now my sparring partner in charge of the other fighter wing. I think we will have a pretty fine combination as I get on extraordinarily well with him. There is only one thing I am afraid of. The establishment for the CO of a wing is group captain. I hope one doesn't come along and take over from me.

On 21st October I flew back to Alex for a day and while there bought Het half a dozen pairs of silk stockings.

1st November

I would like you to visualise darling what I am doing and where I am at the moment. It is 6.15 in the evening, quite dark and I am sitting in my office – a three-ton truck. It is illuminated by a small oil lamp. I have some chairs and a table. Within two or three days I shall make this truck my complete home, have my bed in here, and rig it up with electric light. At the moment I sleep in my tent about 20 yards away.

4th November

I went to bed fairly late last night, tired out having been working continuously since early morning. The trouble was caused by the unexpected activity of the Huns last night. They're getting quite cheeky. That co-incided with the fact that when our fighters were up, thick fog developed, causing us some anxious moments.

If I can manage it I intend getting down for a swim today. I get a very good view of the sea from my tent.

In my wing I now have two wing leaders, Johnnie Loudon being one of them. [Wing Commander Pete Jeffries was the other.]

On 14th November, in preparation for Operation Crusader, our squadrons moved to our forward battle airfields (LG110 and 111) about forty-five miles south of Sidi Barrani and then on the 18th moved forward again to Fort Maddalena (LG122) and I located my wing headquarters close to them. In the days before the start of the operation we tried to achieve a measure of air superiority by conducting fighter sweeps often of wing strength. As Bobby Gibbes of 3 RAAF Squadron wrote in his diary on 16th November:

Did a patrol this morning with 112 Squadron and 8 Squadrons. [Actually 3 RAAF.] *Went in north of Bardia and came out at Madelina* [sic]. *Passed two Hurry squadrons patrolling over our forward troops. A dashed nice sight to see so many of our machines on the job.*

We also escorted bombers and tactical reconnaissance 'Tac-R' aircraft with the aim of impeding the enemy build-up of supplies and of establishing enemy armour locations which we then strafed. In the event, we proved remarkably successful in preventing the Axis air forces from observing the movement and concentration of our ground forces immediately prior to Crusader.

The aim of Operation Crusader, which began on 18th November, was to push back the Axis forces and lift the siege of Tobruk. It began with XIII Corps, which included most of the armour, moving boldly round the enemy's open flank, aiming for Tobruk. The operation got off to a good start and for the first few days there was a complete absence of enemy aircraft as their airfields at Gambut and Gazala were waterlogged by the rains that had hit the coastal strip. However, this soon changed as the ground dried and Me 109s began to operate from the airfields west of Tobruk. The enemy fighters sometimes surprised us by putting in an attack on our fighters and then using their superior performance to climb away before we could reply. There was a radar listening post in Tobruk which should have been passing us news about the approach of enemy aircraft from the west but in practice we got very little information of use from them.

Accordingly, on Saturday 22nd November, I decided to fly to the besieged fortress of Tobruk to organise the airfield facilities for fighter operations and to find out why the post there was failing to give us early warning of the approach of aircraft from the west.

That afternoon, with an escort of two Tomahawk squadrons, 112 (Shark) Squadron and 3 Squadron of the Royal Australian Air Force, I set off in my Hurricane II for Tobruk. We were well on the way when at 4.15 p.m., south-east of El Adem, we were intercepted by a group of perhaps twenty Me 109s. Bobby Gibbes again wrote in his diary that day: 'They straight away climbed up into the sun and came down onto us and started to dogfight. Soon got sick of that and formed a big circle about 2,000 feet above us and came down in twos and threes from all directions. The wingco, Pete Jeffries came back, "Rosier and 112 bloke are safe".'

After about twenty minutes, on breaking away, I saw a Tomahawk of 112 Squadron diving down streaming white smoke. I followed it down. He lowered his undercarriage and forced-landed, only a few miles away from an enemy column which I had noticed. In order to prevent the pilot falling into the 'bag' I decided to try and rescue him. I landed my Hurricane alongside the Tomahawk and the pilot, Sergeant Burney, an Australian, ran across to me. I jumped out, discarded my parachute and he climbed into my cockpit: I sat on top of him, opened the throttle and started to take off. Then disaster struck. Just as I started my take-off run my right tyre burst. I accelerated but the wheel dug into the sand and we ground to a halt. There was nothing to do but abandon the plane.

At that time it was nearly dusk and, as there was an Italian armoured column about two miles away, we ran to the shelter of a nearby wadi. After some time as there was no sign of the enemy, we returned to the aircraft and I quickly removed all my possessions from the Hurricane, including my wife's photograph and the silver tankard I had been given by Pete Wykeham, and hid them under some nearby brush-wood. Taking some food and water we returned to our hiding place where we planned to spend the night. A little later, trucks arrived and Italian soldiers began to search for us. They found all my possessions but although they came within yards of where we were hiding behind some rocks, they did not see us.

The next morning, anxious to get as far away as possible from the scene of our landings, we set off in an easterly direction to walk the thirty miles or so back to our lines. That night, using the Pole star to navigate, we found ourselves in the middle of some German tanks and lorries. We started crawling on our hands and knees and I thought the game was up when lights came on and we were twice challenged by sentries. Eventually, when all became quiet we continued walking. As dawn was breaking we found ourselves still close to the enemy force who were searching for us on motor cycles. We therefore made for the shelter of some brushwood surrounding a dry well which was the only bit of cover for miles around.

At about 8.00 a.m. that morning (24th November) we found ourselves in the middle of an artillery battle with shells falling on and around the enemy force close to us, which immediately began to disperse and withdraw. We then heard unmistakable orders being barked out in English. I decided that the best thing to do was to make a dash for it, so we ran until we eventually reached the artillery unit. We were at first greeted with suspicion but were soon given some tea and food and sent on to an armoured brigade headquarters not far away.

They welcomed us and provided us with a truck and driver to take us to Fort Maddalena. En-route, as we approached a South African armoured car unit, shells started falling around us and a number of enemy tanks appeared about two miles away coming straight towards us. The enemy force which we had encountered had broken through and was heading east towards the Egyptian frontier. The South African major's last words to us were, "I think we are the last line of defence before the 'wire'". So we turned round headed east and went like the wind. Later on we were strafed by 110s but our fighters appeared and shot down four or five of them. Again we passed a most uncomfortable night not knowing the position of the Hun tanks but got back to Maddalena the next morning – the 25th.

When we reached Maddalena we were given a heart-warming welcome by Bing and others. The last thing they had heard

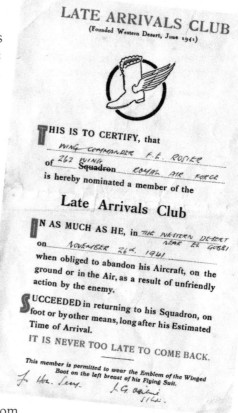

about my whereabouts was from one of the Tomahawk pilots who had seen 'the wing commander going well on the tail of a 109'. I had been reported 'missing' and Wing Commander H.A. 'Jimmy' Fenton had taken over the wing in my absence. On my return Jimmy left to return to Sidi Haneish where he was in charge of our reserves. As a result of this escapade I became a member of the Late Arrivals Club.

In retrospect, I doubt whether I could have coped for nearly three days in the desert on my own. It was Sergeant Burney who gave me the will to continue for I felt responsible for him and I could not possibly have let him think that my confidence showed signs of wavering. Burney was a brave, resourceful and determined chap who never lagged behind or complained, in spite of his raw feet caused by ill-fitting flying boots. I was wearing my suede desert boots. He was an ideal companion, a typical down-to-earth Australian. Unfortunately,

soon after being commissioned, on 30th May 1942, less than six
months later, he was shot down and killed.

It was not until thirty years later that I learned it was the Guards
Armoured Brigade that had befriended us. Colonel John West, from
my personal staff at AFCENT, remembered their astonishment at seeing two bedraggled men walking into their camp from the wrong direction. As a twenty-year-old lieutenant in the Royal Corps of Signals,
John West had been attached to the recently formed Guards Armoured
Brigade. Poor old John, I saddled him with the responsibility for what
I deemed were the deficiencies of army communications at that time.
However, I had the grace to tell him that I still remembered the marvellous reception we were given and thanked him for the army's first
class help and hospitality.

Back in harness there was no respite as, after some initial successes
the 8th Army suffered heavy tank losses as the counter-attacking German armour penetrated our scattered defences. Our LGs at Maddalena
were threatened and we had to take immediate action to safeguard our
fighters from the approaching German armoured column by sending
most of them back to the rear bases at Sidi Haneish. My wing HQ also
'retired as a precautionary measure'. Most fortunately for us, the German tank force turned north when ten miles away from our airfields.

On 28th November I wrote: 'Our air force is doing magnificently
and we have at the moment unquestioned air superiority.'

The next day I flew to Tobruk. This time the trip was uneventful.
On 1st December I wrote: 'Had my first party last night. One of the
squadrons here was celebrating its 100th victory and the award of the
DSO to their CO.' That day I again flew to Tobruk returning two days
later.

3rd December
*I got back this morning from the stronghold and thor-
oughly enjoyed myself there, other than for the discomforts caused by spasmodic shelling. The accommodation
there was extremely good, everything below earth. The
dugout I slept in had an Italian wardrobe and dressing
table and even had a tiled floor.*

I hope quite optimistically that we shall clear up the

Huns during the next few days and then we shall have
a clear run through to Tripoli.

It's 8.45 in the evening and I'm comfortably sitting
down in my office tender, with the wireless giving out
sweet music, and my nightly glass of whisky and water
in front of me. The only thing I am annoyed about is
the absence of your photograph in front of me. How I
hate the thought that a blasted Italian has probably
put it in his bag as a keepsake.

We have moved about 150 miles west since mid-Oc-
tober when we were known as the Matruh Wing. The
climate here is quite different – quite warm during the
day but intensely cold at night.

In the confusion of battle it became clear that our army commanders and their staff were uncertain or probably entirely ignorant of the position of some of their units. Afraid that our air forces would be unable to differentiate friend from foe, the army established bomb lines far in advance of the calculated position of their troops. This greatly limited the assistance we could give them. Other than in special cases we were not allowed to attack any units within this bomb line. This often seemed ridiculous to us for more often than not we knew far more than the 8th Army about the position of their own units and of the enemy. What is more, we had passed this information on to them in the first place.

In early December, after a week of heavy fighting, the tide turned and by 7th December Rommel's forces began to withdraw and Tobruk was relieved. In this, the second conquest of Cyrenaica the RAF was well to the fore. The positive effect of air action cannot be over-estimated. Offensive fighter action had limited enemy air attacks on our army. Attacks against enemy airfields at Gambut and El Adem and on supply columns and dumps had inflicted much damage and our light bombers had been most effective. In addition, from our armed reconnaissance sorties we were finding and attacking many more targets than we received from army calls for support.

On 8th December Bing Cross was injured when his Hurricane

crashed on landing following a sweep with 274 Squadron over the Gambut airfields. While he recovered in hospital he was replaced by Jimmy Fenton and I became the senior wing commander or as I wrote to Het, 'Since then I have been running the whole shooting match'.

> *11th December*
>
> *The war here is going well and within two hours I hope to have my HQ functioning where the majority of the German air force functioned a fortnight, or even a week ago* [Gambut]. *Today is in point of fact most difficult. If you can visualise a bus owner at Newcastle trying to control a fleet of buses operating between London and Brighton, attempting to prevent them being shot at or bombed every hour and also trying to take a personal interest in all of them, then you have the position in which I am working today.*

During our advance across Cyrenaica that December, in order to speed up communications, rather than encrypted signals the AOC often used voice radio to speak to me, using language that we were confident would not be understood by the enemy.

After Gambut, east of Tobruk, our next move on 15th December was to Mechili and it was whilst there that we had a visit from a female reporter from the American magazine *Time & Life*. We threw a party, which was also attended by Buck Buchanan, the CO of 14 Squadron, a Blenheim squadron. He was a fair-headed, good-looking chap who was exceptionally brave. A few weeks later I landed at Buck's airfield very early one morning. On enquiring about his whereabouts I was told that he would be along shortly but, as time went on, I began to lose patience. At last he arrived, with apologies. I heard later that the reporter, Morley Lister, had been staying with him in his tent for the last day or two and that she had accompanied him on the odd operational flight.

It is hard to believe it but his squadron thought so much of him and were so loyal that they kept it all quiet. However, it was not long before Mary Coningham got to hear of it. Buck was promptly removed from his squadron and posted to a ground job in the Delta. Buck's next posting was to Malta to command a Beaufighter squadron. One day he was shot down over the Mediterranean but he and his crew, who were un-injured, got safely into their dinghy. Eventually rescue came but by that time Buck seemed to have lost the will to live and had died. This seemed unbelievable in such a dynamic character. He was a great loss.

> *15th December*
>
> *We are now based fairly deep in Hun territory, the bat-tle not far away from us. Our fighters are still doing extraordinarily well – score day before yesterday was fifteen-three.*
>
> *I've just been outside to see the gallant 229 pass over on their return from patrol, Johnny Loudon is the wing leader of that and one other squadron. I saw the 229 chaps yesterday. Up to date their losses have been few and they are in fine form. An Me 109 was shot down here the day before yesterday and I interrogated the pilot – he was twenty-seven years of age. I was not impressed and was thankful that I was British.*

On 22nd December I moved the wing HQ and fighter squadrons to Msus about sixty miles south-east of Benghazi. During December con-tinuous daily operations supporting the advancing army took its toll on the squadrons and many were temporarily withdrawn to regain their strength. Bing Cross returned to duty on the 29th and a few days after his return he and I took the opportunity to visit Benghazi where, at the invitation of the Middle East RAF Press Unit, we sat down to an excellent lunch with plenty of good Chianti and cigars. It was a wel-come change from our normal fare.

We stayed there for about ten days before moving again in early Jan-uary to Antelat, near Agedabia, about forty miles south west of Msus. Here three landing strips had been constructed and XIII Corps had established its headquarters. During these moves I, together with those of my wing HQ who had not been sent to Benghazi to control the fighters, joined Bing Cross's 258 Wing. Operating from Antelat allowed our fighter force to range over the enemy's troops south of

Agedabia, where Rommel had decided to halt his retreat, and to strafe
El Agheila airfield further west.

> *6th January 1942*
>
> *I am sorry that this is the first letter I have written for
> three weeks, an awful long time I know but conditions
> have been such that letter writing has been impossible.
> I've had about ten weeks in the desert now without a
> break and I feel that I deserve forty-eight hours leave,
> so I shall fly the odd 600 miles to Alex. Then I shall
> return for the advance to Tripoli.*

Little did I know!

The fighter sweeps from Antelat provoked little opposition from the
Luftwaffe but the flak from the enemy ground troops was always heavy.
Having returned from forty-eight hours leave in Cairo, other than it
being very cold, I remember that on 17th January we had a visit from
both Air Marshal Tedder and Air Vice-Marshal Coningham who spoke
to our squadron commanders.

Bing and I were at Antelat when, on 20th January, it started to rain
heavily. Our landing strips rapidly turned to mud and became unfit
for taking-off and landing. The situation was serious in the extreme,
for it meant that our fighter force of over 100 aircraft would certainly
be destroyed on the ground by the Luftwaffe fighters if they became
aware of our predicament. Our only defence was a Bofors gun unit.
That afternoon Bing and I, having discussed the problem with the
squadron COs, decided that every effort must be made to make at least
one of the strips serviceable.

That night it rained again and although it had stopped by the morning, we began our attempt to get the aircraft away. At a meeting with
the squadron COs, one said his strip, though pretty bad, was better
than the others because it had been built on a slight ridge. After ex-
amining it, we decided to try to make it usable by filling the holes with
stones and scrub bushes. Soon, 2,000 officers and men of the two
wings were working on the strip and by early afternoon, when it

seemed marginally satisfactory, we decided to try it out.

A Hurricane was manhandled through the mud and, much to our relief, took off safely. By nightfall three squadrons had got away, flying east to Msus. The remaining three followed the morning of the 22nd.

That morning Bing went to XIII Corps HQ where he was told that Rommel's forces had advanced towards Agedabia during the night 'but it was probably just a reconnaissance force and wouldn't get far'. After briefing me on the situation, Bing instructed me to remain at Antelat with a skeleton wing HQ, to keep in touch with XIII Corps HQ and to do what I could to assist our fighters by giving them the latest information by R/T on the enemy movements. He then left for Msus.

Later that day I heard that Rommel's forces had actually broken through our defences. It was the start of an advance that took him back to the Gazala line of defence and seven months later to El Alamein; so much for a 'reconnaissance' force.

For me and my wing HQ, it was only a matter of hours until it was too dangerous to stay at Antelat. So, along with XIII Corps HQ on the night of 22nd January we moved back to Msus, some forty miles away. On arrival we found that 258 Wing HQ, together with the fighter force, had that morning moved back to Mechili, a further eighty miles east.

I decided to stay at Msus whilst I could continue to act as a forward information post for our fighters, having done so previously in Antelat. But a few days later I was told by XIII Corps HQ that they were moving back due to the proximity of the enemy and that I was to do the same. I ignored this and stayed on, I think, for another couple of days. I felt safe because at first and last light I was informed by our reconnaissance aircraft of the forward position of the enemy troops who had not advanced from Antelat. Consequently I was able to assess the risk of staying. When I did move again on 26th January I joined up with Bing's wing HQ at Mechili. As a result of the German counter-attack and our hasty withdrawal, I was unable to write to Het until this date:

> *26th January*
> *It seems an eternity since I last wrote to you and the news I have accumulated during that time is tremen-*

dous, but most of it concerns movements which are secret. Anyway everything is most depressing at the present time. I myself do not like progressing with my back to the enemy.

The army seem to have excelled themselves in this theatre of operations by displaying bone-like ignorance at all times. I have a shave every morning which comforts me into thinking that we are carrying out an organised withdrawal rather than a disorderly retreat. But still our air force, working sometimes like today for example under almost impossible conditions, is roaming round the sky maintaining air superiority and destroying enemy troops and transportation on the ground.

I think that after the war, unless I have lost interest, I shall go into politics and press for an air force army and air force navy.

I spent forty-eight hours in Cairo a few weeks ago (12th/13th January) – a glorious time of complete abandon and bad headaches which has done me the world of good. On my way I landed near Alex and telephoned for transport. Wing Commander Grant-Ferries MP picked me up and took me to the home of a wealthy cotton grower where I arrived, unshaved and in my desert suiting, at a cocktail party. After summoning up my courage (after three drinks), I craved a bath and strangely enough they said yes to my odd request.

27th January
Two o'clock in the afternoon amidst a raging sandstorm feeling still depressed because we, under these weather conditions, are so utterly useless. Actually nine enemy fighters have just passed close to us but obviously failed to sight this place.

28th January

Had no further opportunity of writing yesterday as a general flap developed and I was up most of the night making decisions about movements. I expect we shall move from here during the course of the day.

Rommel, having caught the British XIII Corps off balance, now made a sudden turn northwards and on 28th January Benghazi fell.

Having six squadrons on one airfield at Mechili was too much of a risk so 258 Wing HQ and the fighter squadrons withdrew a further sixty miles east to Gazala where three landing grounds had been prepared next to the coast road. Since 2nd January we had moved our fighter force of over 100 aircraft four times, one move forward and three back. Apart from the six unrepairable fighters we had left at Antelat, we had lost nothing – not even a vehicle.

We were on the move for the following three days. On 1st February, because the enemy's advance made our airstrips too far forward for safety, we moved back from Gazala and I set up my wing HQ at El Adem, fifteen miles south of Tobruk. Bing's wing and nearly all the fighters then moved to the Gambut group of landing grounds further east.

1st February

And now darling I think you must have some idea of what our life consists of. We arrived at this place yesterday and we are operating today. Quite a number of my chaps including the adjutant have not yet turned up so I presume that they have been cut off and captured on the way from Benghazi. This is a major blow as he was a very good adjutant.

Luncheon interval – there are talks of an impending move.

1.30 p.m. Yes we have to move because of the presence of the enemy. It will mean another night move, blast it.

10.30 p.m. We have done the journey better than I anticipated darling and the chaps have already dug themselves in here and we start operating at dawn tomorrow.

> *We had to move again last night and we are now*
> *settled at an aerodrome we were at two months ago.*
> [El Adem]

Once settled at El Adem and Gambut the primary task of our fighter force then became the air defence of Tobruk, our main supply port.

The enemy air force was constantly active during this time, carrying out frequent bombing raids against Tobruk and strafing attacks by fighters, which now included the superior Bf 109F. With good tactical information from the Y Service and a radar unit at Gazala we were able to intercept many raids but the strafing attacks were difficult to counter and they destroyed many of our fighters on the ground.

One day, much to my delight, part of a detachment I had sent to Benghazi for fighter control duties many weeks before and who I thought had been captured turned up. With the exception of a very brave RAF chaplain, who was wounded and captured, they had managed to evade the enemy patrols and under the most stressful conditions had walked over 200 miles from Benghazi to Gazala. It was a tremendous feat.

> *7th February*
> *Since I last wrote we have had a particularly active time.*
> *Our ground strafing has been so very successful that the*
> *Huns have been trying to fix our fighter force by bomb-*
> *ing and ground strafing our airfields by day and night.*

> *8th February*
> *Having a most exciting day darling. The 109s have*
> *reappeared and dog fighting seems to be the order of*
> *the day. We put on a big show today and the chaps*
> *are just arriving back in dribs and drabs which means*
> *they have had a fight.*
>
> *We have not had a very good day unfortunately.*
> *Valour does not always make up for inferior equipment.*
>
> *I've invited some Hussars over for dinner tonight.*
> *We can give them some gin but that's about all.*

9th February

At 5.00 a.m. a stick of bombs fell right through our camp and rather disturbed the peace of mind of 262 Wing. Still, we had a good dividend with the CO of the joint squadron I had last July shooting down an He 111. Then to cap everything we shot down a Ju 88 in flames – breakfast was a cheery meal. It is now mid-day and half an hour ago we shot down a 109 close to the aerodrome.

10th February

I am sending a truck all the way back to the Delta to-morrow, darling, so I shall send all these letters with it. (26th January to 10th February).

I have a new adjutant arriving today thank good-ness. My camp commandant has absolutely no idea and as I have been so busy with operations I've had no time for administration.

By mid-February the front line had stabilised between Gazala and Bir Hacheim and it was at this time that Bing and I received a signal in-forming us that we had both been awarded the Distinguished Service Order (DSO). I remarked that had we been advancing rather than re-treating we might well have got VCs.

The citation in the *London Gazette* on 13th February 1942 read:

'The King has been graciously pleased to approve the following award in recognition of gallantry displayed in flying operations against the enemy:
  Distinguished Service Order
  Flight Lieutenant (Acting Wing Commander)
  Frederick Ernest Rosier (37425)

This officer has commanded a fighter wing since the commencement of operations in Libya both in the air

*and on the ground. His courage and efficiency have
been inspiring throughout. On one occasion, when one
of our fighter wings was being attacked by a large number of aircraft, Wing Commander Rosier joined in the
engagement. When breaking clear he observed one of
our pilots who had been forced to land in enemy territory and, in an attempt to rescue him, Wing Commander Rosier landed his aircraft. He was unable to
take off again owing to the close proximity of enemy
forces. Nevertheless, both pilots eventually got away,
and, after many narrow escapes, succeeding in regaining
base after a period of three days. Wing Commander
Rosier is an outstanding fighter pilot and leader.'*

13th February

*I met some old friends of mine last night at Tobruk
and Freddie, having just been awarded the DSO, got
horribly tight. I am amazed darling and so proud.
The AOC had a telephone message from Middle East
HQ yesterday morning saying that both Bing Cross
and myself had got DSOs. I didn't think so before
but now I know that it means a hell of a lot to wear
that little bit of ribbon.*

Later that month Air Commodore Thomas Elmhirst arrived at Air HQ
to take charge of administration. One of his first tasks, with the help
of Bing and me, was to plan the reorganisation of our two fighter wings.

4th March

*From now on darling address letters to 262 Wing or
239 (Offensive) Wing. I don't know why they've
changed our numbers unless it's an attempt to fox the
enemy.*

*Had lunch with the AOC two days ago. There was
a real, live woman there. I was so shy that after one
beer I told the story of the elephant and the mouse be-*

*cause she told a foolish (funny) American story. I be-
lieve she was the journalist wife of a well known US
politician.*

19th March

*I'll soon have a new job my dear, and will probably
become a deputy group commander. I've heard rumours
for some time that I might get further promotion but I
stayed with the AOC last night and he mentioned
nothing about it.*

23rd-24th March

*After the party I finished up by playing the violin for
a couple of hours. I managed to get the violin from
Benghazi. It's quite good and belonged to an Italian
officer…I've built a magnificent ops room here, along
the lines of those at home. It's all below ground.*

*What an awful day. The worst we've had since the
terrific rains. We had a gale 'kamseen' all night and
now it is blowing the most awful sandstorm and it is
also bitterly cold.*

26th-27th March

*A Hurricane has just crashed on the aerodrome. Pilot
is OK but he's a fool. Of course I told him so.*

*I'm going to tell all my officers today about the fu-
ture of the wing. I'm rather depressed about it…*

*Had the most awful party last night. It was a
farewell party. I made a speech – a magnificent
drunken speech. You see darling, the wing was my baby.
I created it, I trained it and I hate to leave it. I'm told
that we were all trying to stand on our heads at 2.00
a.m. What a fine relaxation!*

31st March

Well darling mine the fighting 239 has gone, and I am left. No longer do you address your letters to 239 Wing but to 211 Group.

Since last November we have only lost three bombers from enemy fighter action, when we have provided fighter escort. It's very, very pleasing.

My tent is still surrounded by a carpet of flowers. They smell beautifully in the evenings.

Chapter 5

EL ALAMEIN AND WESTWARDS

211 GROUP AND THE WITHDRAWAL TO EGYPT – 1942

On 2nd April 211 Group was formed with three new mobile fighter wings. They each controlled three or four fighter squadrons equipped with the same type of aircraft, Kittyhawks and Hurricanes; all based where possible, on the same airfield. I became second in command of the group with Group Captain Guy Carter taking over as OC from Bing Cross, who was posted back to Egypt. Guy had fought in the First World War but had no operational flying experience in the Second. He was a delightful man and a great character, and left me with my team of wing commander controllers to cover the detailed planning and execution of operations. He then devoted most of his time to maintaining close contact with the wings and squadrons. I shared his caravan and sometimes during 'quiet' evenings we had a glass of Zibib together. We became firm friends. In an article of 17th February 1943 headed 'Salute to the Tacticians of the Desert Air Force', Richard Capell, special correspondent of the *Daily Telegraph*, wrote of Guy: 'His command was then that of the principal fighter group (No.211) with Wing Commander Rosier as his second in command. It was an admirable combination…'

The next few months were difficult as we tried to maintain air superiority by offensive action while defending our LGs at Gambut and

Tobruk with a depleted force, as many of the squadrons had been with-drawn for rest and re-equipment and some had been posted to the Far East. The remaining squadrons fought with great courage but the Hur-ricanes were no match for the 109s. We needed better, and more fight-ers – Spitfires and Kittyhawks.

The HQ of Group 211 was situated with the fighter wings at Gam-but while I and a team of controllers and operations personnel stayed on at El Adem.

> *2nd April*
> *It poured with rain yesterday afternoon giving fresh life*
> *to the carpet of flowers round my tent. I'm told it is*
> *the last drop of rain we shall see for about nine months.*
> *Libya – Oh my Libya!*

From my operations room at El Adem I had direct communication with a radar unit at Gazala which had been withdrawn from Benghazi just before Rommel's attack on the port. This radar proved to be most useful as it could detect and track aircraft which had taken off from an important German air base at Martuba. For example, using this information we were able to intercept some of the Luftwaffe raids on their way to Bir Hacheim where Free French troops were based. We were also able to see the build up of Stukas and escorting fighters set-ting off for attacks against Tobruk. This allowed us enough time to try to intercept them en-route.

Another valuable source of information was a tactical intercept Y Service unit, situated close to my HQ. It had German and Italian speakers who listened in to enemy transmissions, ground-to-air and vice versa, and informed us of what the enemy air forces were up to. They became so expert that they were able to recognise the identities of some of the enemy formation leaders.

On one particular day, when rain had made the Gambut landing grounds unusable and our aircraft were grounded, the Y Service in-formed me that there was a build up of enemy fighters and Stukas from Martuba and that there was a strong possibility of a raid on To-bruk. Knowing that the Germans also had their equivalent which mon-itored our transmissions, I decided on the spur of the moment to try to hoodwink them and to see what happened.

As the Italian Stukas, escorted by German 109s, set off to attack To-bruk and were tracked by our radar at Gazala, I scrambled two squadrons of imaginary fighters telling them by radio to keep low so that they would not be seen by the enemy radar. I then heard from our Y Service that the enemy had picked up my transmission and was relaying it to the force, telling them that they could expect to be inter-cepted by British fighters. My next order to the 'fighters' was to main-tain radio silence, to climb to a certain height and to fly on fixed compass headings, continually updated by me, which should lead to an interception. My last transmission was to inform our mythical fight-ers that they should soon see the enemy raid approaching from a cer-tain direction. As the incoming raid got closer I thought that my ruse had been unsuccessful, and then the telephone rang. It was our Y Serv-ice with the news that on receipt of my last transmission, the Stukas had jettisoned their bombs south of Tobruk and were heading for home. I was told by the Y Service that the German leader of the fighter escort had told the Italian bomber leader in no uncertain terms what he thought of him! The ruse had worked; the enemy had been com-pletely hoodwinked and there was much joy in our camp.

Unfortunately as the enemy reached and then broke through the Gazala defences west of Tobruk in late May, the radar had to be with-drawn and we could no longer track enemy raids and therefore our ability to make planned interceptions came to an end. Fortunately the Y Service continued to tell me when enemy raids were building up over Martuba, the size of these raids and their composition; e.g. Stukas and the 109s. This enabled me to position our fighters where they had a reasonable chance of engaging the enemy on their way to Tobruk.

16th April
Things are very static out here at the moment, but it won't be long before one side or the other takes the of-fensive.

3rd-5th May
Dearest, my promised leave was only forty-eight hours. I went to Cairo first which was awful, to see about

*pay, and spent the rest in Alex, which I thoroughly en-
joyed. I even played a game of squash. I went to a
cocktail party and had three or four baths a day and
was made much of by 'Alex' society.*

*Did I ever tell you darling that I am second in com-
mand of the group. I have the three wing commander
controllers, all of them proper whereas I am only acting.
Normally I don't do any controlling but if a large
enemy force is about either the group captain or myself
is brought in.*

*I had a case the other day where there was a formation
of over thirty Huns going down to attack one of our army
positions. At that time we had seven fighters in the air
and there was no time for our striking force at readiness
on the ground to intercept them. I had to decide whether
to leave the Huns alone or attack them with the aircraft
available. It was a dreadful decision to make. I decided
to attack. The initial result seemed awful and caused
some remorse – only two of our seven came back, but it
got better. Our casualties eventually were one killed, one
missing, two wounded and the enemy had four shot
down and some damaged. I think it was worth it.*

*Just had lunch darling with the GOC in C, AOC
and our guest was the King of Greece.*

7th May

*Last night I went along with the group captain to 73.
We drank rather a lot of beer but I went on duty at
about midnight. I feel fine this morning however.*

8th May

*I forgot to tell you in my previous letter that I met
Dickie Bain* [the CO of 43 Squadron when the author
was at Tangmere] *in Alex. I had two or three drinks
with him for old times sake. He had been burnt in very
nearly the same places as I have. An aircraft crashed on*

the same ship that got me away from England and set fire to some others. Quite a number of people were killed so Dickie was probably very lucky. I think my short leave in Alex did me the world of good darling. Although I had very little leisure time, being too occupied playing squash, going to cocktail parties, speaking French and even playing three games of billiards, and feeling awfully tired it was a terrific change.

11th May

The Hun has been fairly quiet all day but he might come over with his Stukas later as there is shipping in Tobruk. At least I anticipate an attack.

We had an extremely good result two days ago when one of our squadrons knocked down two 110s and thirteen Ju 52s. The Ju 52s were full of troops and they were shot down about forty miles out to sea.

The good weather hasn't lasted. I never want to see sand again. There is enough of it in my hair even now to provide amusement for a child making sandcastles.

The offensive will soon start again darling. It will be so much better than this static warfare. Whether the Huns will start it however is in the lap of the gods.

17th May

Billy Drake (do you remember him at Tangmere?) has just arrived up here as a supernumerary squadron leader. Met him at a conference we had this morning. He still looks as young as ever.

We're being fairly active this morning bombing the Hun with our fighter bombers. We get up too early for them.

Rommel's next offensive started at Gazala on 26th May. The battle started well for the allied troops but, after nearly four weeks of fighting, the Axis forces broke through and Tobruk fell. With the 8th Army by then under General Auchinleck's leadership, defeated and virtually out of tanks, we withdrew over 300 miles in an orderly manner to behind the El Alamein line where we held firm, reaching there in early July.

30th May

The battle has started again and I am no longer bored with the state of static allied troops warfare. I think we are doing well. For the first time since 1939 the army seems to have come into its own. The other day I went to Alex for a conference with the navy. I stayed down there for a day and brought back with me 200 eggs, five crates of beer, some gin and enough dinner – Coq au Vin – for four which, in its earthenware dish, was still warm when I arrived up in the desert the same evening.

2nd June

The battle has started again and we have won the first round.

As far as the air force is concerned the squadrons have been hard at it, strafing and bombing enemy transport. Our losses have been fairly high, quite naturally. I should have liked to have seen our force used differently. First of all I should have gained local air superiority by using our air force for its own purpose and not as army coop squadrons. When this had been achieved, then we could have switched over to ground strafing and bombing with much fewer losses. Still – can't be helped. The desert is not what it was.

Had the worst storm I have ever known this evening darling. The wind came up to 70-80 mph, an awfully hot wind, 120° from the south. Visibility was without exaggeration about a yard. It then started to rain and the mud came down.

4th June

The battle is still on. The Huns lost the first round, but they are coming back for more. It is so important that we win this battle, much more important than is generally realised.

It's about 11.00 p.m. and I'm sitting in the ops room waiting for the Huns to come over. I did some night-flying two nights ago by the way.

On 17th June operations reached a crescendo as, following the fall of Bir Hacheim on the 11th, the Gazala position had become exposed, resulting in the withdrawal of the 8th Army. By 14th June the retreat was in full swing and two days later I was forced to move back from Gambut, first to Sidi Azeiz and then on the 18th to Sidi Barrani.

A few days before Tobruk fell on 22nd June I had sent a small team including a controller, Squadron Leader Young, there. The job of this outpost codenamed 'Blackbird' was to provide forward control of fighters, and I anticipated that they would return if or when Tobruk was evacuated. It was not to be, for one afternoon I had a call from the controller saying that German troops were approaching him and his team. He just had time to say goodbye before the line went dead. The thought that I had sent them there only to become prisoners of war was disturbing, but there was no time to dwell on this because an approaching enemy column was not far away and I had to organise a hurried withdrawal from El Adem to the main HQ of the group.

During Rommel's advance his columns came under frequent air attack, whilst our withdrawing army units, often moving bumper to bumper along the coastal road, saw little of the enemy air force. There is no doubt that action by the fighter-bombers of the Desert Air Force, the light bombers, the Malta-based squadrons and the Royal Navy had weakened Rommel's forces to such an extent that he was unable to penetrate the Alamein defences and advance further.

During the retreat, which lasted for seventeen days, I was kept busy all day and most of the night planning the next day's operations and keeping a close watch on the number of our casualties, on the numbers of reinforcements we were getting and on the availability of aircraft and pilots.

It was exhausting moving backwards. The wings and squadrons were moving by night and attacking Rommel's forces by day. Every time a squadron pulled back to a new LG the fuel bowsers and ammunition lorries were waiting. There was no panic. Unserviceable aircraft which could be moved were towed behind three-ton trucks: the ground crews kept up an amazing serviceability rate of eighty per cent most days. The ground and aircrews deserved the highest praise.

During the withdrawal we were operating at extreme range, which meant that we were unable to escort the light bombers. The army were fixing bomb lines too far ahead of our army formations, and this severely limited close support; and the problems of getting fuel up to the forward airfields were immense. In addition, the prolonged and intensive operations had so weakened our fighter force that the twelve remaining squadrons could barely muster 100 aircraft. Despite this, we had overrun the enemy air force – no mean feat.

The withdrawal ended in early July with the 8th Army in a defensive position of strength between the Mediterranean and the Qattara depression, 211 Group continued to operate in support of the army until we reached a clutch of landing grounds at Amariya, twenty miles or so from Alexandria.

8th July

Sweetheart darling mine. How you must have worried about this campaign. I hate this retreating. After the first week I could visualise what was going to happen. Our retreat has been terrific and we have left our bases on occasions when Hun tanks have been within fifteen miles of us (and nothing to protect us). Darling mine things have been so disrupted and we have all been so tired that letter writing has been out of the question.

We are not so very far away from Alex, and I'm going in tomorrow. But of the future – we either defeat him and go forward, stay as we are now, or withdraw into Egypt.

I don't think that there is any doubt that the RAF has saved the day. The chaps have worked harder than

in the Battle of Britain under conditions ten times as
bad. Eleven different sets of landing grounds in seven-
teen days, darling, and we operated continuously.

On one occasion during the withdrawal AOC Coningham accused me
and Guy Carter of lying about not having received his orders to intercept a raid with Kittyhawks rather than Spitfires. He was livid and so
were we. He refused to see me. Some two years later in May 1944
when he had become C-in-C of the Second Tactical Air Force he invited me to lunch at his farmhouse near Uxbridge. During lunch he
apologised. It transpired that many months after the incident he had
found that his wing commander ops, concerned about security, had
not passed on his orders in full deciding that it would be more appropriate for 211 Group to decide for itself which particular aircraft to
use. I thought at the time that it was a great pity that Guy was not
around to receive this apology: he had been killed in Italy when he
was hit on the head by an axe which had been dislodged during a
bumpy landing.

By the time we arrived at Amariya in early July I was dog-tired for
I had been on the go, with no more than four hours rest a night, for
over six weeks. Now was the time for relaxation. Our fighter squadrons
were able to concentrate on training for there was little requirement
for active operations, and their personnel as well as ours in the group
HQ were able to take some leave. Other than the odd weekend in
Alexandria and Cairo, I had taken none since leaving the UK more
than a year previously. There I enjoyed the pleasures of the fleshpots
but always the first priority was a haircut, shampoo and bath at the
Cecil Hotel in Alexandria or the Continental in Cairo. On my return
to the desert from these weekend breaks my overloaded Hurricane
was filled with fresh fruit, canned beer and large dishes of Coq au Vin
and the like supplied by the best restaurants in those cities.

20th July
I went down to Cairo last Friday afternoon, to have a
medical board on the Saturday morning. Do you know
darling the board was for a permanent commission.
[Technically I still had a short service commission as I

had not completed the engineering course at Henlow in
1939.] *I was rather angry about it as I have already
done two for the same thing. However, I was AB
which pleased me.*

*The group captain has been rather ill for the past
fortnight with sandfly fever and consequently I have
been extremely busy.*

On 31st July, somewhat reluctantly, knowing I would miss Winston
Churchill's morale-raising visit to North Africa, I set off for Palestine
on my long leave in a halftrack, with a V-eight engine, which had been
given to me by grateful sappers in Tobruk.

> *10th August*
>
> *I've just arrived back from ten days leave and I'm feel-
> ing as fit as a fiddle. I set off from here on the 31st at
> dawn and drove down to Cairo where I had breakfast
> and a shampoo in the Mena House Hotel near the
> pyramids. I had lunch at the French Club at Ismailia
> and then started an awful drive over the Sinai desert
> to Beersheba, then on to Gaza, arriving at Tel Aviv
> about 8.30 p.m. That same evening I walked into a
> hotel and ran into MacDougall who was in 43 until
> 1937. He promptly invited me to stay in his house (he
> is station commander at Ramleh). I went to Beirut and
> Jerusalem, played squash every day, drove back and
> finished the last two days of my leave in Alexandria.*
>
> *I did the journey in a most wonderful car darling,
> which was made by engineers in Tobruk. It's got an
> open body and a new 30 HP engine, and it does 85
> mph.*

Whilst we were at Amariya I made a few overnight visits to Alexandria,
usually starting at the Cecil Hotel, then going to the Union Bar or Pas-
troudis to eat, before visiting one or more of the night clubs. I remember clearly one of these visits made with a friend of mine, Wing

Commander Johnny Loudon. Having removed our badges of rank, I managed to borrow a violin from the band and to the delight, or otherwise, of the guests, I serenaded them whilst my friend followed me around with his hat. I think we handed over the money we collected to the band.

20th August

One of the Spitfire squadrons did well yesterday destroying four 109s and probably getting eight more with no loss to themselves. We will shake the Hun one of these days.

As you may have gathered from the newspapers Winston Churchill had lunch in our mess but unfortunately I was away. I should have liked to have spoken to him. He made a speech, full of confidence.

Things are still very quiet out here sweetheart – the lull before the storm. By the time you receive this I imagine that the issue will have been decided. A quiet air of confidence reigns. If we can defeat his main forces, especially his armoured forces, in this area, then we shall have a clear path to Tripoli. I think I know most of the way blindfolded.

I wonder if you ever gathered my whereabouts during the advance and retreat – Maddalena, El Adem, Gazala, Mechili, Msus, Antelat and then a place just south-east of Agedabia.

During the last part of this advance I pushed Dakin and part of my wing to Benghazi. I spent Christmas Eve at Mechili. On the way back we did the reverse but in addition went to Martuba and Tmimi. You remember I told you about my tent being surrounded by a carpet of flowers. That was at El Adem where we stayed for about three months. Then off to Gambut for a month or so. The sandstorms there were terrible. And then the retreat.

In that late summer of 1942 both sides were intent on building up their forces. We began to receive more Kittyhawks to replace the inferior Tomahawks and, thankfully, Spitfires. We were also reinforced by the Kittyhawk-equipped American 57th Pursuit Group. The 8th Army too was strengthened, not least by Lieutenant General Bernard Montgomery who arrived in August to replace General Ritchie following the sacking by Churchill of Claude Auchinleck as C-in-C Middle East. Montgomery's arrival prompted enormous change in the army. As the new commander 'Monty' was able, in a very short time, to instil fresh heart into his men and a confidence which had been lacking.

Montgomery also made it clear that he and the RAF would work closely together. He believed in joint planning of operations. In doing this he was putting into action what had long been advocated by our brilliant AOC, Mary Coningham.

No longer was the ground situation allowed to become so confused that air support was limited. We knew where the enemy were and were able to attack them in relays of light bombers and fighter-bombers. In addition we had been reinforced, so that by the time the El Alamein battle began, the Desert Air Force had some dozen wings containing forty-eight fighter and fighter-bomber squadrons – almost 600 aircraft in all.

Towards the end of August the group was called upon to return to intensive operations, for it was expected that Rommel would soon attempt to break through our defences at Alam Halfa: he tried and was driven back. The battle of Alam Halfa officially lasted from 31st August to 3rd September but our air forces were committed from the 21st August. The victory showed what could be done when land and air forces co-operated closely in the planning and execution of operations – a sensible development which was to be followed in the forthcoming Battle of Alamein and indeed, in the rest of the war. Rommel was defeated and our success marked a turning point not only in the desert war but in the fortunes of the allies.

Alam Halfa was a battle in which our air forces: bombers and fighters, played a major part by taking the offensive. The 8th Army's role was strictly defensive. During the battle I was again hard at work organising fighter escorts for our bombers, and providing air support for the army (mainly by ground attacks on the enemy forces, and by

attacking the enemy air force, both in the air and on their airfields).
By day and night the Axis forces attacking the Alam Halfa ridge were
bombarded continuously from the air, with our squadrons flying two
or three sorties per day against them.

As we were about to start the offensive aimed at, once and for all,
driving the Axis forces out of Cyrenaica, I should mention the state of
our armed forces compared with those of the Axis. In numbers both
our army and RAF had superiority over the enemy, e.g. in tanks and
aircraft, but in other respects we were inferior. For example, German
leadership (Rommel) was incomparably better than ours; German
troops were better led and better trained and the German tanks and
their six-pound anti-tank guns were far in advance of ours. If I remember correctly, our anti-tank guns were two-pounders.

As if this was not enough, army communications were poor; orders
from the 8th Army headquarters would sometimes be taken merely as
subjects for discussion; and some senior commanders in the army still
believed that they should have their own RAF squadrons to 'play with'.
This would have been a recipe for disaster.

20th September

*I have been quite busy darling. Guy has just got over
his monthly attack of sandfly fever, and has gone into
Alex to have lunch on the beach. He is going off on
sick leave tomorrow for a week.*

*I went down to Cairo on Wednesday evening to lec-
ture to about 400 army officers. The last battle (Alam
Halfa) resulted in quite a victory for us, army and
RAF, and the Hun had to withdraw. Funnily enough
there was no feeling of blind optimism.*

22nd September

*On my own again this week. Garvin, the other wing
commander, is in hospital with malaria and Guy
Carter has gone on leave for seven days. Things are
very quiet on the ground and in the air. This will not
last very much longer. There will be the most terrific*

battle. I am always confident.

Then darling, when we defeat him here, the end of the war will be in sight. I am certain of that. Three years is a long time.

I'm going to try to persuade people that for England to launch an offensive on the continent without my knowledge of mobile warfare would be a catastrophe. I want to live with you again.

Received a letter from you yesterday in which you enclosed the small snapshot. It was a wizard photograph of you.

I shall go into Alex fairly soon to do some Christmas shopping. The price of things has gone up considerably since the Americans arrived out here. An American colonel friend of mine gets, with pay and allowances, 900 dollars a month. It seems so foolish that there should be any disparity.

I've put all the news in another letter which Paddy Dunn, an old friend of mine, who is wandering around at the moment with Lord Trenchard, will be taking to England. In it I mention how I met Cedric Masterman in Cairo. He has a Beaufighter squadron in Malta and had come over here for a week's leave. I have also heard that Broady is on his way out here.

Do you remember me telling you that 73 Squadron presented me with a silver tankard. I lost it together with a lot of my kit last November. Three days ago a South African major arrived here with the tankard which he gave to me. He said he had found it in the front of a truck last January when the armoured cars he was commanding shot up an enemy column south of Benghazi. It is now in Cairo being repaired.

This tankard had been given to me by Pete Wykeham in August 1941, as related earlier. It had been found with my possessions by the Italians in November and 'liberated' from them by the major in January 1942.

EL ALAMEIN AND ADVANCE

Following the defeat of the Afrika Korps at Alam Halfa, Montgomery and Tedder began to plan the break out from the El Alamein line. I spent September and October at group HQ planning the air support for the Battle of Alamein which started at 10 p.m. on the night of 23rd October with a thunderous barrage of 456 guns from the British artillery which could be heard back at our base at Amariya. From 19th October our air force had been busy preparing the way. Our bomber force, which had been augmented by ten US Air Force squadrons, attacked the enemy's landing grounds by night and day, whilst our fighter force, now reinforced by three US Air Force Kittyhawk and three RAF Spitfire squadrons, provided escorts and attacked enemy LGs, lorried infantry and transports. Our main objective had been air superiority and it had been achieved. We had also played havoc with Rommel's supply lines.

During the battle which lasted until 3rd November when Rommel started his withdrawal, I was on the go most of the time. As the enemy retreated it seemed to me that our advance was much slower than it should have been. For this, we in the RAF, and many others, criticised Montgomery as it appeared to us that he was unwilling to take risks.

> *31st October*
>
> *The battle has started. This time we should really clobber the Hun. We have almost complete air mastery and the army have done well so far and I expect our long trek to Tripoli to start fairly soon.*
>
> *I'm well equipped for the journey. I have a new Hurricane and a magnificent Chevrolet saloon car.*
>
> *The group captain has promised me that when we get to Tripoli and the campaign is over we shall go back to England together.*

From 4th November the withdrawal of the Axis forces began to turn into a headlong retreat, harried all the way by the RAF. The tempo of our fighter operations depended on the supply of fuel and on the range to the enemy airfields. When it was quiet I used to take the opportunity of spending more time with the wings and squadrons, sometimes attending their parties and flying back to my 'home' in the dark. At one such party at Martuba I am told I gave a 'spirited rendering' of Do You Know the Muffin Man on my violin.

Tobruk was taken on 12th November and by this time the RAF had complete air superiority, making the Axis convoys easy targets for our ground-attack aircraft.

> *24th November*
>
> *At last I get an opportunity to write. Until now it has been impossible as the rate of advance has been so terrific. We have now stopped for a breather before carrying on with the second phase. It will start with the Battle of El Agheila, and I anticipate several days of tough fighting.*
>
> *Broadhurst is out here. He's got a very important job as number two to the AOC. He sends you his regards.*
>
> *Looking back on the past eighteen months I can say I've enjoyed it. It's meant hard work under rather hard conditions, with very infrequent visits to Cairo or Alex when one spends a lot of money and wakes up with an awful head next morning.*
>
> *All the love in the world my dearest. Look after yourself. I love you so much.*

The advance westwards continued relentlessly and on 24th January 1943 the 8th Army entered Tripoli. Guy Carter was determined that he and I would be first to land at Castel Benito airfield. When we were reasonably confident that it would be safe to do so, we set off in our Hurricanes only to find to our intense annoyance that a party of war correspondents had beaten us to it!

Tripoli, with its splendid curved promenade, had suffered little damage from our night bombing, the port area having been the main target. An officers' club was soon set up in a large house in the town centre, and very good it was too. After the monotony of desert rations it seemed like heaven.

Soon after Rommel had been driven out of Libya, General Montgomery paid this tribute to the RAF:

> *'On your behalf, I have sent a special message to the allied air forces that have co-operated with us. I don't suppose that any army has ever been supported by such a magnificent striking force. I have always maintained that the 8th Army and the RAF in the Western Desert together constitute one fighting machine and therein lies our strength.'*

A few months earlier I had been told by the C-in-C of the Middle East Air Force, Sir Arthur Tedder, that on reaching Tripoli I would be posted back to the UK, and it was not long before my posting came through. On 4th February, in the absence of Guy, who was stricken low by a bug, I handed over the group to Group Captain 'Batchy' Atcherley, one of the well-known Atcherley twins.

During this period I paid a farewell visit to 3 RAAF Squadron. This was one of the two squadrons escorting me when I failed to get to Tobruk in November 1941. When I landed they were having lunch. Bobby Gibbes, their renowned CO, jumping up on his chair, announced: "The wingco is leaving, give him a cheer." This they did, following up with a special, rather bawdy, rendering of Waltzing Matilda.[3] Whilst waiting in Tripoli for a lift back to Cairo, AVM Keith Park, who had been my pre-war station commander at Tangmere and who, with Lord Dowding, had masterminded the RAF operations during the Battle of Britain, came over from Malta (where he had taken over from Hugh Pughe Lloyd) to visit Mary Coningham. He invited me to spend a few days in Malta, before returning to the UK. I felt rather sad saying my goodbyes to the many friends I had made in the desert but I was ready to go.

A Mosquito, piloted by Pete Wykeham, arrived to take me to Malta. I was most impressed with the place, with the people of the island for their resolution in the face of almost continuous bombing and with the efficiency of our forces, both in the air defence of the island and the offensive action taken to stop men and supplies reaching the Axis forces in North Africa. As usual, the hospitality was excellent. After three days the visit came to an end and I was flown back to the Continental Hotel in Cairo.

About 8.00 a.m. on my third morning in Cairo I was surprised to get a phone call from Guy Carter, "Rosie, how are you feeling?" His answer to my reply of "terrible" was to come along with a bottle of Zibib, a potent Egyptian drink similar to Pernod and Arak. It was said that drinking it cleaned your teeth. After a few of these we had breakfast at Groppes, a favourite spot, and then went on to the Gezira Sporting Club for drinks and lunch and a visit to the races. After a few hours rest we were ready for a round of the nightclubs. This programme was repeated daily and nightly for a further four days.

On the seventh and what proved to be my last night in Cairo, I was found in some nightclub and told that there was space for me in a Liberator leaving for the UK in a couple of hours. Swiftly collecting my belongings I rushed to the airfield and with a couple of minutes to spare got on board. I fell asleep immediately on the cold cabin floor. Waking up in the morning, stiff, cold and with a hangover I made my way to the cockpit. There the captain told me that we would soon see Gibraltar.

On leaving the aircraft I was recognised by an old acquaintance of mine, a major in the Devons, who remarked that I could not have arrived on a better day as the Gibraltar Millionaires were again giving a party. Coming on top of the alcoholic few days with Guy in Cairo, this was the last thing I wanted. I craved sleep and more sleep. Nevertheless, I was easily persuaded. I spent the day drinking and eating and drinking again – my stamina must have resulted from nearly two years of deprivation in the desert. Wherever it came from, I certainly needed it as the flight back to the UK was delayed for twenty-four hours and the next day I found myself again at a lunch party, which went on until late afternoon. That night we flew back to the UK, landing in Cornwall early next morning.

Thus came to an end a fascinating part of my life. At the age of twenty-six I had been given a position of high responsibility in the Desert Air Force which had not only been successful but which had provided the blueprint for future army/air force co-operation. Working hand in glove with the 8th Army in Cyrenaica, in spite of the inferiority of our fighters, and in spite of the high casualty rates suffered, mainly as a result of our emphasis on offensive action, the pilots of the Desert Air Force operated with unfailing determination and spirit. And gradually gained ascendancy over the Luftwaffe. They were some of the bravest, cheerful and likeable chaps I have ever known and with whom I have been privileged to serve.

The Desert Air Force was also very well led; the combination of Tedder and Mary Coningham could not have been better. We all looked up to them and especially to Mary who was an excellent tactician and leader. He was also very charming. His staff at Air HQ included George Beamish who, as SASO, was succeeded by Harry Broadhurst. And Tommy Elmhirst, the AOA was a brilliant administrator who stayed with Mary Coningham until the end of the war. I knew him well and much later I gave the address at his memorial service at St. Clement Danes. We middle ranking officers who were younger than our opposite numbers in the army, were encouraged to use initiative, and a general spirit of togetherness prevailed.

But all was not perfect. We were not as well trained in tactical operations as we should have been; our air firing was moderate at best, and our armament of .30 and .50 guns was effective only against aircraft and soft-skinned vehicles. What was even worse was that the performance of our Hurricanes and Tomahawks was second rate compared to that of the Me 109.

Basically, air support should entail the air defence of our own troops from air attacks and assistance to those troops by attacking enemy ground forces. Early on we had concluded that offensive action would be the only sensible method of defence. Trying to get some measure of air superiority became our aim.

In a short article in the 1992 *Air Mail*, I wrote:

> *'Life in the Western Desert fifty years ago was tough and precarious. We had to put up with the extremes of heat and cold, the flies, the sandstorms, the shortage of water, the muddy tea, the almost daily diet of bully beef and lard biscuits, the awful-tasting cigarettes, the fear and the never-ending losses of friends and com-*

rades. Yet, with the passage of time most of us tend to dwell on the brighter side, the camaraderie and the cheerfulness which existed among all ranks, the uplift which came with the arrival of the beer ration, the fun of the squadron parties, the joy of the occasional dip in the sea, the tonic effects of a weekend in Alexandria or Cairo, the sing-songs at Air HQ with Air Vice-Marshal Mary Coningham and Air Marshal Sir Arthur Tedder joining in, the elation of winning, and that great feeling of being alive.'

On leaving the desert I was appointed an Officer of the Order of the British Empire (OBE) the citation for which read:

'This officer is a brilliant controller and has been second in command of number 211 Group since March 1942. His outstanding personality and great knowledge of operations in the Western Desert were largely responsible for the successful fighting retreat and subsequent advance of the group over an approximate distance of 2,500 miles. Wing Commander Rosier, by his cheerfulness, understanding and popularity with all branches of the service has been a source of inspiration to all with whom he came into contact.'

Chapter 6

PRE-INVASION PLANNING AND D-DAY

HOME LEAVE

Landing back at Perranporth in Cornwall on a dull, cold and wet Sunday afternoon in February, still suffering from the after-effects of over-indulging in Gibraltar, I phoned Het and told her to meet me in London the next morning, and to bring some money. We met and stayed at the Savoy for a few days, where we made up for an absence of twenty-one months. I then reported to the Air Ministry to find out what fate had in store for me. It was a job in Army Co-operation Command, which was the last thing I wanted.

During the meeting I was handed a note which to my surprise I found to be from the C-in-C Fighter Command, Air Marshal Sir Traf-ford Leigh-Mallory. It was he who in October 1939 had told me about his plans for night-fighters, and who told Het at the party at Wittering in September 1940 what he had in mind for me. His message was simple: 'Come and see me'. This I did. He told me that he was aware of what I had done in the desert and now I was to take some well-de-served leave. When I told him that I had already been told that I would be going to Army Co-operation Command, he said, "Forget that, I will tell you what you will be doing when you return from leave." Het and I spent that leave in London and Wrexham.

After about ten days Het returned to her job as a teacher at Gwersyllt Church of England school whilst I lazed my time away. The leave, which lasted a month, came to an end when, returning from a fishing trip with an old school friend who was also on leave from the RAF, I was told that a telegram had arrived for me from the ADC to the C-in-C of Fighter Command. The telegram, which came on a Thursday, said that Leigh-Mallory would see me at Chester on Saturday where he was taking the salute at a Wings for Victory parade. He was there in the role of 'the local boy made good' as he was the son of Canon Leigh-Mallory, Vicar of Doddleston near Chester.

The alternative was to see him at his HQ at Bentley Priory on the Friday. Being an extremely keen type, within a couple of hours I was on the midnight train to Paddington. I was ushered in to see the C-in-C the next morning. He came straight to the point, saying that he wanted to introduce fresh blood into his OTUs and that I was to become station commander of Aston Down and the commander of 52 OTU with the acting rank of group captain. I was twenty-seven. Overjoyed, I asked him when I was to start, to which he replied, "Now, straight away, and you will be there for six months".

I immediately went into London where I bought a 'scrambled egg' hat (so-called because of the gold braid around the peak) at Gieves the tailors and had a fourth stripe put on my uniform before returning to Paddington to catch a train for Stroud in Gloucestershire. It was a journey I had last made on 2nd October 1939 but that time my posting was cancelled and my stay at Aston Down was limited to two days.

On the afternoon of 20th March I presented myself to the station commander, who was probably twenty years older than me, who greeted me by saying that he had only just heard that I was taking over. I was most embarrassed. He wished me luck and departed.

ASTON DOWN
MARCH-SEPTEMBER 1943

The station was now mine. It all seemed so simple. That night I stayed in the mess.

The next morning I met my subordinate commanders, amongst whom were my right hand man, Wing Commander John Lapsley (soon to be relieved by Peter Brothers), the chief flying instructor, Squadron Leader Dafforn, the chief ground instructor, Squadron Leader Crusoe, the officer in charge of administration, Squadron Leader Whittle who, in addition to his normal duties ran the thriving station pig farm, and the head WAAF officer Flight Officer Haggerty (known as 'The Hag'). She was soon to be relieved by Mary Boyd, who remained a close friend of Het until she died in the early 1970s. My last two meetings were with Wing Commander Taylor, a very high-powered ex-civil engineer, who was in charge of the maintenance and service unit on the station and to the civilian head of the air transport auxiliary unit which was also on the station. This was composed of male and female civilian pilots who did much of the ferrying of aircraft from the units to the squadrons.

The main job of the OTU was to take students who had completed basic flying training and to turn them out operationally fit for front-line Spitfire squadrons. We also had responsibility for the Fighter Leaders School at Charmy Down near Bath, and South Cerney, a satellite airfield near Cirencester. That April while on a short course at Wittering I managed to fly solo in a Mosquito and on 2nd May made my first solo flight in a Mustang – which in my log book I described as 'delightful'.

Life on the station was almost too good to be true. Het, now showing signs of pregnancy, resigned from her job and in April came down to live with me in the Cotswolds. I had rented one of two cottages known as the Nook and Cranny, in the village of Amberley, about three miles across Minchinhampton Common from Aston Down. Ours, the Cranny, she refused to live in. This, despite the fact that I had already paid a deposit of £20 – a large sum in those days. We stayed for the next three weeks in Field End, Amberley. This was a lovely Cotswold house, converted into a guesthouse by Phyl Mould, the widow of 'Boy' Mould, who had been in 1 Squadron at Tangmere. He had survived whilst with them in France in 1940 with the Expeditionary Force but had been killed in Malta in 1941. We eventually found a place nearby which was part of a house (Dial Cottage) owned by Sir Fabian Ware, head of the Commonwealth War Graves Commission.

The arrival from Tangmere of Peter Brothers, who took over from John Lapsley, made life even better. He was accompanied by his wife

Annette and we remained close friends thereafter. One of the important jobs I gave to Pete was to increase the throughput of students
without sacrificing operational efficiency. This he achieved with great
success.

My personal aircraft was initially a Spitfire Mk2 No.8132 and latterly
a Spitfire Mk VB – No.262. On occasions, Pete in his Mk V and I would
fly away to visit chums at other stations. I still recall one night when
we had flown to Charmy Down for dinner or a drinks party – I forget
which. Around about midnight I said to Pete, "Time to fly back". Quite
rightly he remonstrated with me saying that we had had too much to
drink, but I insisted. We started up our Spitfires and then with the aid
of a lorry's headlights on the opposite side of the airfield we took off –
and what is more surprising landed some minutes later at Aston Down.
After that I vowed never again to fly whilst under the influence and,
apart from one other occasion, I never did.

On Sundays we often invited members of the local Home Guard,
largely comprising senior retired army officers, to the mess for lunch.
Music was provided by the all-star station band led by Sergeant Felix
King, famous for many years as a noted London band leader. The CO
of the Home Guard unit Brigadier Jock Campbell – the 'Tally Ho' VC
of the First World War – was now a corporal.

Often there were pleasant diversions from normal station life; for
example, I made speeches to local communities in small towns around
Gloucestershire and took the salute at Wings for Victory parades in
Stroud, Wotton under Edge and Dursley. On the twenty-fifth anniversary of the founding of the RAF on 1st April 1943 I took the salute
near Minchinhampton Church at a march past of most of the personnel of the station.

On 9th June I flew in my Spitfire to Biggin Hill to attend the '1,000th
Hun Party'. (They were celebrating 1,000 claimed combat victories.)
Later in June, for my desert service, I was awarded the OBE or, in the
long form, I became an Additional Officer of the Military Division of
the Most Excellent Order of the British Empire.

My six months at Aston Down soon came to an end with my posting
on 14th September to be station commander of Northolt and CO of
Northolt Sector. Pete Brothers was also posted as chief flying instructor
to another OTU, Rednal, near Shrewsbury where Station Commander

Don Finlay was an Olympic hurdler.

My time at Aston Down had been a most welcome break for me but winning the war was still uppermost in my mind and I was keen to get back to active service. Often at dusk, which was about 11.00 p.m. as we then had double British summertime, we would see or hear the droning of bomber formations overhead doggedly making for their target somewhere in Europe. Next morning we would learn where they had been making for and how many of them had not made it home.

The Dam Busters raid, which took part during that summer, improved our morale no end. Unfortunately, it did not cause as much devastation as we had hoped. I had great admiration for those Bomber Boys.

NORTHOLT AGAIN
SEPTEMBER 1943-MARCH 1944

Northolt was a station with three Polish squadrons 303, 306 and 308 and one RAF squadron, all flying Spitfires, a large VIP transport squadron for domestic and overseas flights, and an operations room at Eastcote House near Ruislip.

It took time to get to know the Polish squadrons but gradually I began to like them and began to understand them in spite of the language difficulties. Their behaviour and code of conduct was very different from ours. Their obsession with chasing women (and catching) took up a lot of my time. It frequently resulted in a Pole and the mother of the girl involved appearing before me. Once indeed, I had both mother and daughter claiming that the same Pole was responsible for both their pregnancies!

The Poles were subject to rapid changes of mood. One moment they would be on the crest of a wave following a good operational mission. The next, worrying about the future of their beloved Poland, they would be sad, doleful and dispirited.

The senior Pole was Group Captain Tadeusz Rolski, 'Rolski the Polski', a polite, quiet, undemanding officer who wielded very little influence. The wing commander flying was Aleksander Gabszewicz, a different man altogether. One day, having asked Rolski to come to my office, I told him that it would not be long before the invasion and that the Polish squadrons comprising 131 Wing would participate in it and then move to France and on to Germany. For him it was an emotional moment and he had difficulty keeping back his tears. I then got down to business and told him that his Poles would from now on have to learn to fend for themselves domestically and for a start, I wanted them to take on the responsibility of doing their own 'cook-house' chores. They would have to manage without the WAAFs doing the dreary work for them. I argued that the sooner they started the better. A date was fixed. Late afternoon on the appointed day, although I had heard there was trouble, I just sat back and waited. Eventually Rolski himself arrived saying, "We have great problems. The Polish men will not wash up their plates." I told him that to make it easier for him I would stop their food until they started washing up their plates. Naturally it worked. To me it was further proof that Rolski was far too weak to command the Polish wing. Only Alek Gabszewicz, a strong character in all respects, would be suitable. He was 'tailor made' for the job.

The comments I made to the Polish air force HQ were listened to. A big parade was held where Alek was presented with the highest class of *virtuti militari*. It was the first time that this medal had been awarded other than to a general victorious in battle. The way was now clear for him to be promoted to group captain and to take over 131 Wing. I got to know Alek well. I respected him and our friendship lasted until he died in 1994 following which I gave the address at his memorial service held in St. Paul's Cathedral.

Of the two other units, the first was an RAF squadron equipped with unarmed Spitfires, and engaged on high altitude reconnaissance. Apart from station services and administrative support, they operated mostly as an independent unit coming under the operational control of our parent group, 11 Fighter Group. Their squadron leader CO, a little ball of fire, maintained a very good squadron. They were no trouble to me.

The second, an air transport unit, was very large. It served as a general air transport provider, having small and medium aircraft for domestic flights and large aircraft including Liberators and a York, for the increasing number of overseas flights by VIPs. The York was mainly used by Prime Minister Winston Churchill and other cabinet ministers. The crew of the York were hand-picked men of vast experience.

When flying to North Africa or points east the PM, who invariably stopped to have a word with me, would arrive just after midnight with his retinue and the take-off would be an hour later. He was particularly interested in the reaction of the Poles to events in their homeland. I was able to reassure him that in spite of their changing moods, their offensive spirit and hatred of the Germans and Russians had not diminished.

Whenever the York returned from North Africa it would be laden with fruit. This was most welcome. Oranges were generally in very short supply, bananas were unobtainable and had never been seen by those born during the war. I used to meet all VIPs, both service and political, returning from across the Atlantic. I particularly remember my talks with Anthony Eden.

The sector operations room was in a converted squash court in Eastcote House, some five minutes away from Northolt. It functioned twenty-four hours a day and was manned by army and RAF personnel. It was mostly active at night when enemy bombers were around and the fighters and anti-aircraft guns had to be controlled. The plotting of aircraft, hostile and friendly, was done by WAAFs who had clearly been chosen for their good looks as well as their intelligence. And good plotters they were too.

The chief controller, an RAF wing commander, was in charge but when night-bombers were likely to be active a brigadier was normally present but I was in overall charge. Occasionally, I spent the night there in a most luxurious bedroom.

It was while I was at Northolt that our first child Elisabeth was born on 26th November.

PRE-INVASION PLANNING

In March 1944, just after the departure of the Poles from Northolt (by then formed into 131 Wing), I was posted to 84 Group as CO of 23 Mobile Sector, one of the units recently formed by the newly established 2nd Tactical Air Force (TAF).

Preparations for the invasion had been in full swing since the end of 1943. Most of the planning was done at the 21st Army Group HQ in St Paul's School, Hammersmith. This was directly across the road from Latymer Court (in which Monty and Eisenhower had flats). [Coincidentally where we had a flat since 1973.]

The 2nd TAF was part of the Allied Expeditionary Air Force (AEAF) which had been established to control the tactical air forces consisting of: fighters, fighter-bombers, light bombers and reconnaissance squadrons. For specific purposes, the strategic bomber forces of the USAAF and RAF came together under command.

AEAF was commanded by Air Chief Marshal Sir Trafford Leigh-Mallory, who had done much to shape my career in the war for which I was most thankful. But few senior air force officers, British or American, liked him or considered him fit for the job. He was considered to be pompous, overbearing, over-ambitious and did not take kindly to advice. But Monty liked him, which may not say much for Monty, but was all that mattered as they were to work closely together.

Mary Coningham was head of 2nd TAF, which comprised of two fighter groups: 83, commanded by AVM Harry 'Broady' Broadhurst, and 84, initially commanded by AVM 'Bingo' Brown, and subsequently by AVM 'Teddy' Huddleston, and a light bomber group commanded by AVM Basil Embry. As CO of 23 Mobile Sector, I was part of 84 Group. I had a small HQ staff consisting of five officers and a few airmen. The HQ was located close to Selsey, near Chichester, one of the many landing grounds on the south coast which had been built expressly for operations prior to and during the invasion.

In the sector I had two fighter wings, both with Spitfire IXs. These were the Hornchurch Wing and the Free French Wing at Predannack in Cornwall. I had two very competent wing leaders and two equally competent station commanders in Pete Simpson and Tony Linney (ex 229) at Hornchurch and Roy Marples (who sadly disappeared in mysterious circumstances whilst flying with the Free French) and Cam Malfroy, a notable New Zealand tennis player, at Predannack. When weather permitted I visited them daily in my personal Spitfire.

It soon became increasingly clear to me that Pete Simpson was 'operationally tired' so I arranged with Bingo Brown for him to spend three or four months lecturing in the USA before returning refreshed for operations. On landing from his next sortie I told Pete that he was finished with operational flying for the time being and explained what we had in store for him. He argued and argued until tears came into his eyes, a sure sign of complete exhaustion. When he asked whether he could see the AOC, I agreed. To my astonishment Bingo very foolishly agreed that he could continue flying. This convinced me that Bingo, a First World War ace, was too old and out of touch to understand such things.

The mobile sectors were disbanded after a few weeks – not surprisingly, as in my view they were serving no useful purpose – and I was given the excellent posting of group captain operations of 84 Group replacing a much-liked more senior chap, for whom I felt great sympathy. The war had taken its toll and he had practically become a nervous wreck.

Little is known of the great influence that Montgomery had on the invasion plans. The initial planning for Operation Overlord (code for the invasion) had started in London in May 1943. It was envisaged that the attack would be made by three seaborne divisions, with two more to follow, and two airborne brigades. The limit on numbers was dictated by the availability of landing craft and transport aircraft. At the end of 1943 Montgomery, who was chosen to command the allied assault forces, realised that the planning was poor. The assault forces were too small; the beachhead was too narrow and an airborne assault was needed with three divisions, not two brigades. Whatever criticisms are levelled at Monty, and I had many, there is no doubt that his decisions at that time made the difference between success and failure. In comparison his faults in other matters were minor. Had the original plan been actioned, the result would have been disastrous.

On Christmas Eve 1943 General Eisenhower was appointed supreme commander for Operation Overlord. He was the obvious choice. The Americans were supplying the majority of the attacking forces. He chose Tedder as his deputy with Montgomery commanding the British and Canadian ground forces and Leigh-Mallory, the allied air forces.

The AOC of 84 Group, Bingo Brown, did not seem to fit the part of commanding a tactical fighter group. He was certainly not as knowledgeable or experienced as Harry Broadhurst, the AOC of 83 Group. Thank goodness Bingo had a good SASO, Air Commodore Theodore 'Mac' McEvoy. I had known him as a flight commander in 1 Squadron

at Tangmere in 1936-7 and his wife was a godmother to our daughter
Elisabeth at her christening at RAF Northolt in March 1944. The AOA
was a chap named Spencer. My most vivid memory of him was his
booming voice, punctuated by expletives, on the occasion when he got
tangled up in the camouflage netting over his caravan when he was in
a hurry to get to a shelter during a night-bombing raid.

The HQ of the group was in a large country house close to Leather-
head, called Headley Court which after the war was to become the
RAF Rehabilitation Centre. We lived there in some comfort but this
soon came to an end when, in preparation for the invasion, in late
April we moved to Goodwood Park, about one and a half miles from
my pre-war airfield, Tangmere. There we lived, and sometimes
worked, as we would have to do all the way up to Germany. I was
amongst the few senior chaps to have a caravan (or trailer); the rest
were in tents.

One of those on the group planning staff was Tom Dalton-Morgan
who had commanded 43 Squadron towards the end of the Battle of
Britain. I was later to write of Tom, 'it would be impossible to overstate
Tom Dalton-Morgan's importance and influence on the conduct of
fighter operations for and beyond D-Day'.

By May it was clear that the invasion was imminent. Visitors were
barred from large areas of southern England where troops were being
assembled. 'Where' and 'when' was uppermost in the thoughts of every
serviceman, woman and civilian.

At this time visiting HQs, wings and squadrons was mostly done
using an Auster, a two-seater, short take-off and landing aircraft. The
open space at Goodwood Park was just big enough for the operation
of these aircraft. We had three of them.

During this time, the Duke of Richmond invited me and a chap
called Peggy O'Neill, whom I had known well in the desert, to dinner
at Goodwood House. During the evening we drank a huge amount
of a whisky called Red Hackle, the after effects of which (a monumen-
tal hangover) persisted well into the next day. I made sure that I never
drank Red Hackle again.

During the pre-invasion period the fighter and light bomber wings
were kept very busy attacking flying bomb sites, airfields and road and
rail junctions in northern France.

Churchill and the chiefs of staff had been under considerable pressure from their counterparts in America and Russia to agree to the launching of the invasion up to two years before it actually took place. Had they given in, the result would almost certainly have been catastrophic. Their resistance was based on logical arguments: on the practical experience gained from the complete failure of the Dieppe raid; on the desirability of first invading Sicily and Italy and on the absolute necessity of achieving air supremacy. The latter was partly brought about by the withdrawal of German fighters from France, both for the defence of Germany and for the Russian front.

The eventual successful outcome of the invasion owed much to the measures that were taken to hoodwink the Germans about the location of the assault. Thanks to very clever misinformation put out by the BBC, by the daily newspapers, by 'double agent' German spies unknowingly working for us and by signals traffic, the German leadership was completely taken by surprise. Rather than Normandy, Hitler and his generals expected us to land on the Pas de Calais beaches or even Norway and regarded Normandy purely as a diversion. Throughout the British intelligence services proved that they had no equal. It was an exciting time.

D-DAY AND THE INVASION OF FRANCE
JUNE 1944

At the supreme commander's meeting on 3rd June the weather expert, a group captain, forecast very poor weather for the next few days. At the next meeting early the following morning Eisenhower, normally so calm, exploded saying that for months he had been told that air support was essential, and now he was being told by Monty and Admiral Ramsay that they were prepared to go on the 5th even if bad weather prevented air support. He then postponed Overlord for twenty-four hours until 6th June.

On the night before the invasion my opposite number from 83 Group, Tap Jones and I, who for the previous few days had been attached for planning duties to the 11 Group HQ at Uxbridge, were invited to dinner by Marion McEvoy, with whom Het was staying. That night Tap and I arrived at the house very late for dinner. Marion at first appeared a little annoyed and subjected us to a barrage of questions about why we were so late. Tap and I found it difficult trying to co-ordinate our answers. She sensed we were not telling the truth and said, "I know why you are late, the invasion has been postponed". Seeing the horror on our faces and realising that Tap and I would have concluded that Mac (her husband) had told her the date of the invasion, she went to great trouble to tell us that her hunch was merely guesswork – which I am certain it was!

The night of 5th June was rainy and windy. I wish I had been there to see the armada of ships streaming towards their appointed beaches (two streams were American and one each British and Canadian) and to have seen and heard the bombardment of the enemy guns covering the sea approaches to Normandy by the navy and by allied bombers.

The success of the invasion was secured by our complete air supremacy. On D-Day plus one, our air superiority was such that the enemy could not reinforce their forward troops in daylight. All the Typhoons of 83 and 84 Groups were targeted at the armour to the rear of the main battle. They roamed far and wide and strafed, rocketed and bombed everything that moved. However, there was a huge cost to this as on that day, seventeen Typhoons were shot down by flak.

On D-Day plus three, 9th June, keen to see what was going on, I flew across the Channel, landing at St. Croix sur Mer, the first airfield to be liberated. Apart from the hundreds of ships close to the beaches, and much evidence of fighting, the Normandy countryside appeared unaffected. It seemed that many of the locals were afraid that their peaceful existence had come to an end. Admittedly, some greeted the allies with open arms but others seemed to take no notice of them.

I returned to England the same day with butter and Camembert cheeses which I gave to Het when I flew up to Wrexham on the Friday. I was hailed as very much the local hero.

In mid-July, when Broady's 83 Group was established in Normandy, it was arranged that I should be attached to it. My brief was to keep 84 Group, which was still based at Goodwood Park, informed of what was going on. I reported on such things as the operating conditions, methods of control, the working of the link between the group and its GCC, the relationship with the British 2nd Army, and so on. This information was of critical importance when 84 Group eventually moved to France as, from day one, we were fully prepared to start operations supporting the Canadian 1st Army.

During that June and July in support of Operation Goodwood, 84 Group's UK-based squadrons of rocket-firing Typhoons and light bombers continuously pounded the enemy's positions around Caen in support of the allied armies which were gradually establishing a larger and larger bridgehead in Normandy.

By 25th July General Bradley's army group, supported strongly by the USAAF, had broken out from the Cherbourg peninsula and began a major offensive from St. Lo towards Avranches. By the 30th, when he had reached Avranches he decided that General Patton's army would lead the drive eastwards. The German forces fought with tenacity and fell back in an orderly fashion until Hitler gave the order, one of the many which proved disastrous for the Germans, to counter-attack against the US force at Mortain. He refused to permit a withdrawal to the Seine. The German counter-attack failed and led to a retreat through the Falaise Gap and on to the Seine, which was reached towards the middle of August. It was here the defeated remnants of the German armies in Normandy took a severe mauling from our air forces as they struggled back across the Seine.

It was on 8th August, during the German withdrawal to the Seine that 84 Group HQ finally moved to France. Following this move across the Channel, we set up our headquarters at Amblie, a few miles from the beachhead. 84 Group consisted of five fighter wings: 35,123, 131,145 and 146, and was designated to support the Canadian 1st Army. The group HQ was therefore co-located with the Canadian 1st Army HQ.

The GCC was originally conceived as the group's mobile operations room with the staff work and planning being done by the Group HQ. As such they were situated close by. However, as the campaign developed it became clear that 'planning' could not be divorced from 'operational control'. This was exacerbated by the fact that the location of the GCC was dependent upon that of the wings and airfields, which were often many miles from the group HQ. As a result the GCC was soon delegated the main responsibility for the detailed planning as well as the execution of the group's operations.

Due to our proximity to the Canadian 1st Army HQ I was invited by General Crerar to use the senior Canadian officer's mess but, in common with most of my colleagues, soon elected to return to our own as we disliked the formality of the army mess.

In the five days up to 16th August the group concentrated on attacking the enemy endeavouring to escape through the Falaise Gap. Nearly 1,000 sorties were flown and a total of 260 motor transport and tanks were destroyed.

I believe that it was at this time that air power really came into its own. Rocket-firing Typhoons from both 83 and 84 Groups began operating in 'cab rank', where a squadron patrolling over the front line would be directed on to the targets by controllers on the ground who were attached to forward army formations. In addition, the light bombers of the USAAF and RAF and American fighters and fighter bombers created havoc amongst the German forces. By the end of the first day of the enemy retreat it was clear that air history was being made. The destruction of men and machines by the Tactical Air Forces was greater than had ever been achieved before. This continued throughout the retreat until the Battle of Normandy was over. The allies had complete air superiority.

During the Battle of Normandy the German 7th Army lost 10,000 killed and 50,000 taken prisoner and was left with only 100-120 tanks and assault guns out of their initial force of 2,300. However, this was at some cost, as in the same period the allies lost 4,100 aircraft and nearly 17,000 aircrew, divided almost equally between the RAF and USAAF, while 21st Army Group suffered 84,000 casualties.

On 14th August, during a massive daylight bombing attack on Caen, I received a call from the army asking for the operation to be stopped as British and Canadian troops were being bombed. I immediately got on to Bomber Command to be told that there was nothing they could do because the bombers were using their own discreet radio frequency during the actual attack and consequently could not be contacted. It transpired that the lead aircraft of a Canadian bomber group had dropped it's coloured target markers on positions held by our own troops. The immediate response of the troops was to display their 'colours of the day'. Unfortunately Bomber Command had not been told that the army's colour of the day was yellow, whilst the target markers dropped by the lead bombers were also yellow. I was told that the C-in-C of Bomber Command placed the blame entirely on the

o left: The author wearing a
ove Park school blazer, 1934.

o right: The author (back row,
· right) taken at Bristol Flying
hool in 1935.

ove left: The author's Hawker
·ry, named 'Queen of North
South' which he flew
tween 1936 and 1939.

ove right: The author as flight
mmander of B Flight with an
·craft fitter, taken in 1937.

ght: The author on the right,
·tside B Flight office of 43
·uadron, Tangmere 1936.

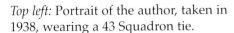

Top left: Portrait of the author, taken in 1938, wearing a 43 Squadron tie.

Top right: 43 Squadron reunion dinner at the Savoy Hotel in April 1937.

Above: Aerobatics in a Fury, 1937.

Above right: 43 Squadron final squadron formation in Furies, January 1939.

Right: The author and his wife Het on their wedding day, 30th September 1939. There was no time for a wedding dress!

Above left: A wing briefing in the Western Desert, 1942.

Above right: The author with Wing Commander Pete Wykeham, Western Desert 1942.

Middle: Posing in the officers' mess of 262 Wing, 1942.

Left: 211 Fighter Group HQ, Western Desert 1942. (Left to right) Group Captain Guy Carter, AVM Mary Coningham, the author, others unknown.

Above left: Relaxing in the officers' mess of 262 Wing, 1942.

Above right: Air Vice-Marshal Si Keith Park, Air Vice-Marshal Mary Coningham, and the author, Tripoli, February 1943.

Left: The author joking with Gu Carter and Mary Coningham, Western Desert 1942.

Below: Senior RAF team, Tripoli, February 1943. The author is back row, second from left

Top left: The author as group captain at RAF
Aston Down, 1943.

Top right: Olek Gabszewicz, Polish 131 Wing
Leader, and his wife on being awarded Virtuti
Militari, Northolt, 1943.

Above: The author inspecting Polish troops,
Aston Down 1943.

Right: The author now station commander of
RAF Northolt, 1943, wearing Polish flying
wings.

Above: Portrait photo of the author taken in 1944, clearly showing his burn scars.

Above right: 84 Group operations room, 1944.

Right: Visit of HM King George VI to 84 Group HQ, Belgium (the author on the left), October 1944.

Below: General Montgomery visiting 1st Canadian Army (the author far right), autumn 1944.

left: Portrait of the author by William
ng, 1944.

right: Devastation caused by bombing
ls on a German city, 1945.

Above middle: Time for celebration! 84 Group,
May 1945.

Above: Denys Gillam's wedding at the Savoy,
June 1945. (Left to right) Zulu and Audrey
Morris, Al Deere, the author and wife Het, and
Joan Deere.

Above: Crowds at the Victory Air Display taken in The Hague, September 1945.

Left: Victory flypast, The Hague, September 1945.

Below: 84 Group summer party, Celle, 1945.

p left: Het presenting Sports Day prizes at orsham St. Faith, 1947.

p right: The author now station commander RAF Horsham St. Faith, 1947.

Above left: Class photo at the Armed Forces Staff College, Norfolk, Virginia, USA 1948.

Above right: The author and his wife, looking glamorous at Mitchell Field, New York, 1949.

Below: The author, now group captain flying, CFE, getting ready for take-off at RAF West Raynham, 1952.

Top: HRH Duke of Edinburgh with the pilots of West Raynham, 1953. The author is second to his left.

Above left: The author flying a Desford Trainer in prone position, West Raynham, 1953.

Above right: Nicholas' christening, West Raynham 1953. Back row centre is 'Birdy' Bird-Wilson and second from right is 'Ricky' Wright

Below: The author in flying kit at West Raynham, 19

Top left: The author greeted by son David on his return from a trip to Australia and New Zealand, West Raynham, 1953.

Top right: The author getting into his suit before flying a Meteor, West Raynham, 1954.

Above left: The author with Ricky Wright, Eglin AFB, Florida, November 1954.

Above right: The author playing cricket for Imperial Defence College, Burton Court, 1957.

Left: The author on promotion to air commodore in 1958.

Below: Chiefs of staff, Middle East Command, 1962. Clockwise from back left: Major General Robertson, the author, Rear Admiral Fitzroy Talbot, Air Marshal Sir Charles 'Sam' Elworth (C-in-C), unknown.

Above right: The author on becoming ADC to HM The Queen, 1958.

Left: Family photo of the Rosiers taken in 1958 Nicholas and David are at the back, and Lis is seated with her parents.

Above left: Group shot at the Chiefs of Staff conference (the author, now director RAF plans is back row, second right), Air Ministry, 1958.

...left: With Air Vice-Marshal Ralph Bentley, AOC ...desian Air Force, 1962.

...ve left: The author performing his 'party trick', ...en, 1963.

Above: The author with HM The Queen inspecting Royal Observer Corps, RAF Bentley Priory, 1967.

Below: The author playing the 'fiddle' at a party in Aden, 1963.

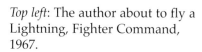

Top left: The author about to fly a Lightning, Fighter Command, 1967.

Top right: The author with Sir Robert Watson-Watt, the inventor of radar, at Bawdsey Radar Station, Suffolk, 4th August 1967.

Above left: Flypast over the Fighter Command disbandment parade.

Above right: Battle of Britain veterans at the disbandment parade of Fighter Command, April 1968. (L to R) Johnnie Johnson, Peter Townsend, Bob Stanford-Tuck, the author, Al Deere, Douglas Bader, Peter Brothers.

Above left: The author inspecting Winchester College CCF, son David Rosier, head of the RAF section, is beside him on the left, June 1968.

Above right: The author flying a Harrier with Wing Commander Le Brocq, RAF Wildenrath, 9th March 1972.

Middle: Group shot taken at the CAS conference, 1973; the author is on the front row 6th from left.

Left: The author unveiling the Polish air force memorial at St. Clement Danes, 1968.

Top left: The author, now wing commander, with Group Captain 'Bing' Cross, Western Desert 1942.

Above left: The author again with Air Chief Marshal Sir Kenneth 'Bing' Cross, 1992. They haven't changed a bit!

Above: Flypast over St. Clement Danes by 43 Squadron Tornadoes after the author's memorial service on 14th December 1998.

Left: The author installed as Knight Grand Cross of the Order of the Bath, Westminster Abbey, 1993.

bomber group for its appalling navigational error. He sacked its CO and reduced the rank of the squadron commanders. Our army suffered over 400 casualties that day.

20th August

The last three days have been extremely hectic. I've been getting up between 6 and 7 and getting to bed just before midnight. Our chaps have done magnificently, saved thousands of army lives. I often wish I had my own unit rather than being a staff officer in a group.

21st August

It's pouring with rain and the clouds are right down to the ground. Although it means we can't fly it's probably a good thing as everyone was in need of a rest. I myself was so tired out that I stayed in bed until 10 this morning. I've only been away from this HQ once since we started operating, so I think I shall drive round to some of the wings this afternoon.

We shall probably have a different change of scenery soon, and I hope to manage a day off before that takes place. I must choose it carefully as I need to ensure the weather will be good enough for me to fly back the next morning. I hope I can manage it soon!

24th August

Took a few hours off yesterday and drove close to Deauville and then on to Lisieux where I saw some of the fighting. The news is good, we're fairly rushing ahead.

In early September, shortly after Paris had been liberated, I took the day off to drive the seventy-five or so miles to Paris from Evreux where our HQ then was. The celebrations were still going on with an intensity and fervour that one would expect from the French, free again after four years of occupation. However, I also saw quite a lot of chas-

tisement of collaborators. Paris seemed to have suffered little damage
and I was able to obtain a bottle of Chanel No.5 and of Schiaparelli
Shocking. These I despatched to Het by the hand of a friend. It was
a great luxury – no French perfume had been obtainable in England
since 1940. In fact I think it was the first she had ever had.

> *7th September*
>
> *At the moment our advance is so rapid that one can't
> grumble at all. Two days ago during one of our moves
> I drove down to Paris from Brionne and spent half an
> hour there buying you some perfume. It looked mag-
> nificent. From there I went up as far as Chantilly,
> then northwards. I was driving for about twelve hours.
> More moves again soon and everything is so good I
> can't see ourselves becoming static for some time.
> Never been to Brussels...*

The early part of September was marked by very poor weather which
limited the support we could give to the Canadians, who nevertheless
managed to overrun the V1 sites in the Pas de Calais area. Compared
with the rate of advance by the American and British armies after the
decisive victory in Normandy, that of the Canadian 1st Army on the
left flank was slow due the stubbornness of the enemy resistance in
the French Channel ports of Le Havre, Boulogne, Calais and Dunkirk.
The Belgian ports of Ostend, Zeebrugge and the island of Walcheren,
which dominated the sea approaches to Antwerp, similarly hindered
our progress. It was essential that these ports should be cleared as
quickly as possible because the supply situation of our advancing
armies was becoming increasingly desperate.

Le Havre eventually fell on 11th September, Boulogne on the 22nd
and Calais on 1st October.

84 Group's role of supporting the Canadian 1st Army in the Pas de
Calais led to constant close support sorties by our wings. As the intelligence summary of our GCC put it, these consisted chiefly of, 'a steady
hammering of enemy garrisons, strong points, and gun positions and
in close support of the Canadian troops whose progress at this stage

was necessarily measured in yards, rather than miles, against an enemy who was prepared to defend every ditch and dyke and to hang on to every watery foot of this dismal terrain'.

16th September

Managed to get away from here [St. Omer to where the group HQ had moved] *for the evening two nights ago so flew to Johnnie Walker's place (135 Wing was based at Merville with Desmond Scott's 123 Wing) and went into Lille with him and Ray Harries. The place appears very little affected by the war and we were able to buy champagne quite cheaply and drink it with zest. I also visited one of the big storage dumps (underground) which the Huns had been trying to construct with thousands of men for well over a year. Bomber Command had fixed it beautifully.*

Well sweetheart mine I hope to get off for a day during the next fortnight. I hardly get a moment to write. In addition to controlling current operations I am planning future attacks. There is a big one tomorrow.

19th September

Managed to get away yesterday afternoon so visited Ypres (was only there for about ten minutes, but it looked a marvellous place), Menin Gate, Menin, Courtrai and Ghent. I went with Sandy, Sailor Malan and Bill Compton. It was dark unfortunately when we got to Ghent as there was a curfew, but we managed to get the odd bottle of wine. Stayed the night with Sailor and got back this morning. Mac is in England for a day's leave. I'll try and get away as soon as I can, probably on 25th or just after that. But I do want to receive a letter from you before then.

Chapter 7

THE END IS NIGH

THE LOW COUNTRIES – AUTUMN 1944

In the early part of September Monty started planning a complex operation designed to leap frog forward and to establish a bridgehead over the Rhine. It was to involve the British 2nd Army, with three divisions of General Browning's 1 Airborne Corps with the 82nd US Airborne Division under command. Before joining in the Canadian 1st Army would concentrate on opening up the port of Antwerp.

D-Day for Operation Market Garden was on 17th September. That morning vast fleets of aircraft and gliders converged on their landing areas close to the Arnhem bridge meeting light opposition. However, two days later the weather was so bad that the air lift programme had to be halted and our tactical fighters could not provide support. These factors were to have a serious effect on the whole operation.

Sadly, on the night of 25th September 2,400 men, including some of the Polish Parachute Brigade, had to be evacuated across the lower Rhine and Arnhem was lost to us, as was Nijmegen which was still in German hands. In his book *From Normandy to the Baltic* Monty claims that the battle of Arnhem was ninety per cent successful. On the ground we thought otherwise. It seemed a sad end to an ill-conceived and ill-fated operation. It should be noted that we in 84 Group were not included in its planning. Had we been, we would have had the necessary 'crystals' in our radio sets to communicate with our ground forces during the first few days and to give direct support to them.

20th September

Mac got back today and told me I could take a day off. Unfortunately, it's impossible this week, as you will have probably gathered from the news (Operation Market Garden/Arnhem), but I hope to get away next Monday or Tuesday. I'll probably be able to bring back the odd pair of stockings.

It's been a tiring day. I held a conference at 8 this morning, AOCs conference at 9. Army conference at 10, a quick lunch, tea in my office, conf at 5.30, half an hour for dinner and it's now well after midnight.

22nd September

Flew to Brussels yesterday afternoon and had to stay the night because I had been delayed. It's just like peacetime there – but terrifically expensive. I went out with Tom Morgan, Derrick Walker and Killy. But believe it or not I was so tired I left them and went to sleep.

On 22nd September Boulogne had fallen to the Canadians after the last strongpoint received a final 'rocketing' from our Typhoons. Cap Gris Nez and Calais soon followed. In the south the Americans, after a spectacular outflanking drive, reached the German border. Le Havre finally fell, brought to its knees by a mass Lancaster raid, and Ghent was captured by the Polish Armoured Division (within the Canadian 1st Army). Hence, in late September our group HQ was able to move in their wake to Ghent. From Amblie in France, 84 Group HQ, alongside that of HQ Canadian 1st Army, moved three times in six weeks before setting up shop in Ghent in late September.

I liked Ghent. The people were friendly and occasionally we were invited out by them. The Polish wing based on the local airfield was commanded by a great friend from Northolt days Group Captain Alek Gabszewicz. There was a story that the wing was accompanied by a lorry load of women. I didn't investigate – but think it was probably true!

For 84 Group the early days of October were mainly occupied with operations against the coastal batteries at Breskens in support of the troops storming the island of Walcheren. The docks had been captured almost intact and the battle was on to clear the estuary for shipping. It was during this period, on Friday 13th October, that His Majesty the King, accompanied by Field Marshal Montgomery and Air Marshal Coningham visited 35 and 146 Wings at Antwerp-Deurne. I made a brief presentation about our operations during this visit.

> *15th October*
>
> *Received Cecil Beaton's book from you today. It is very good isn't it? I had forgotten all about my birthday* [13th October] *until I was in a room with various people including Monty and Mary. Mary turned round to me, seeing the date up on the wall, and said Friday 13th looks ominous. And only then did I realise it was my birthday!*

On 20th October the 84 Group squadrons attacked the HQ of the German 15th Army at Dordrecht and caused huge loss of life including seventeen officers of senior rank – two of them generals.

That autumn it rained almost non-stop for weeks on end considerably interfering with operations and often preventing the RAF from flying from sodden airfields. The inability of many in the army to understand how much the RAF was contributing to their support caused frequent friction, especially in pubs.

One Sunday morning when the low cloud again made flying impossible, three wing commanders and I went out to a pub in Ghent called the Falstaff. Deacon Elliot was one of my HQ chaps whilst Al Deere and Johnnie Baldwin were planners in the GCC which at the time was also based in Ghent. Almost as soon as we arrived an army major came up to me saying, "Where is the bloody RAF?" It was pretty clear that he had been drinking so I said, "If you keep quiet I'll tell you where the RAF is and what it's doing." He didn't listen and his ranting continued until Deacon intervened saying, "Go away, you're annoying my group captain". Away he went but soon returned and continued to harass me. Deacon once more told him to go away and his response was to throw a punch at Deacon. Then the fight started. It was the army versus the RAF. The two barmen hid behind the counter as bottles on the back of the bar were broken. Al Deere, once a champion RAF boxer, was in his element and Johnnie Baldwin, who, as an airman waiting for flying training, had once knocked a corporal flat on the parade ground at Uxbridge, dealt with the rest. Deacon saw the major off. It was just like a scene from a Wild West film. Despite my concern that it had happened, it was a Sunday that I always remember with some pleasure.

> *30th October*
>
> *Fifteen minutes to go before the 5.30 p.m. conference. Got a letter from you yesterday my sweet in which you mentioned place names – two big bangs just happened (naughty Huns). You were quite right but don't bother to mention them in future as security might accuse me of telling you. The army has been doing quite well the last few days. Makes all the difference in the world when things become fluid and positions on the maps are constantly being changed.*

Breskens had fallen on 22nd October but the Hun, well aware of what was at stake at Walcheren, clung on doggedly to their positions. Finally, after a week of murderous fighting, which included the last great amphibious operation of the war in Europe by British commandos and Canadian troops, the Walcheren garrison surrendered on 8th November and we moved our group HQ from Ghent to Antwerp. Even then, until the approaches to the port were cleared of mines we remained short of essential supplies.

During my time at Antwerp V1s and V2s fell on the city every day and the task of depriving the enemy of his V2 supply routes became a priority for our wings as London was also being targeted. At this time the enemy had established his front line on the River Maas beyond which he showed every intention of staying put.

After a short stay in Antwerp, the group HQ moved to Breda in Holland, where I stayed with a most charming woman, Madame Hoedkop, a friend of Queen Wilhelmina. When I had a few days leave that November I took a letter from her to London addressed to Queen Wilhelmina, care of the Netherlands government in exile. I was given a very warm welcome by them and was told to tell Madame Hoedkop that they would get the letter to Her Majesty as soon as possible. Queen Wilhelmina had left Holland in May 1940 for England and eventually Canada. I returned to Breda with the message and a present for Madame Hoedkop of 2lbs of coffee beans which my mother-in-law had managed to inveigle from her regular coffee supplier. During the occupation of Holland real coffee was unobtainable and they had to make do with ersatz made from acorns. Madame Hoedkop was so delighted that she gave me an old piece of Delft – a teapot. This I looked after carefully for some months until I could deliver it to Het. Sadly, in 1961 it was stolen.

November ended with the Canadians struggling eastward in line with the Maas. We continued to support them by carrying out continuous low level operations called down by the forward controllers.

In early December, the group HQ moved again from Breda to a school a few miles away in Tilburg, with our GCC based at Turnhout.

9th December
I hope to have some silk stockings for you by Christmas. One of the chaps is going down to Paris this week. I hope he can get some reasonable ones. On Wednesday night I went to a performance of 'Blithe Spirit' with the army commander and the AOC. Dorothy Edwards was in the cast. She had seen Challoner two or three days previously at Tilburg. On Thursday I had dinner with Loel Guinness (the MP relief for Sailor Malan), Bill Compton and a merchant captain on board his ship at Antwerp.

On 17th December after days of rain the Germans, supported in strength by what remained of the Luftwaffe, began a bold but desperate major counter-offensive along the American front in the Ardennes. Their object was to drive a wedge between the American and British forces and strike at Antwerp, our main supply base. Another of Hitler's fatal mistakes was about to be made – Von Runstedt was told to make a bid for an eleventh-hour victory.

> *22nd December*
>
> *I wonder what you have thought and what you are still thinking about the turn of events out here. We are not unduly perturbed as if the cream of the German army can be defeated west of the Rhine our final task will become even more simple and can take place much sooner.*

> *25th December*
>
> *Thought of you all day today. Working fairly hard yesterday, but managed to get away after supper and had a most enjoyable party with the AOC at one of the wings. Have got six pairs of silk stockings for you, I'm told they are quite good. Cost £2 per pair.*

For some days bad weather prevented us from giving air support to our troops as our squadrons were grounded, but on 27th December the weather improved enough for us to make a few perilous sorties which were in general frustrated by an impenetrable layer of mist and low cloud. This was not as much support as we would have liked to have given. However, on the 29th our Tempests destroyed sixteen enemy aircraft in air combat over the battle area. The American army fought magnificently in ice and snow and before the end of the year the tide had turned, in no small measure due to the refusal of the garrison commander at Bastogne, General Macaulay, to surrender. This operation resulted in German losses of 120,000 men, 600 tanks and assault guns, and their retreat to the 'West Wall'.

Von Runstedt's failed offensive was followed on the morning of 1st January by widespread attacks on our airfields by German fighters. These occurred at a time when most of our squadrons were grounded by ice-bound runways and mist. Only the Polish 131 Wing at Ghent was able to intercept this raid, claiming to have destroyed twenty enemy aircraft in the ensuing combats. Overall, these raids caused little damage and of the eighty-plus Typhoons at Deurne only one was destroyed.

I remember these raids well as a few days earlier I had received an invitation from a family I had met in Ghent to spend New Year's Eve with them. On 31st December I drove from Tilburg, where we had our HQ, to Ghent, drank and dined, probably to excess, and left early the next morning on New Year's Day. On my way back I decided to call on Denys Gillam and his Typhoon wing at Deurne. When I got there he was still in bed in his caravan, but his batman was around and brought us coffee. Suddenly all hell let loose. We were out of that caravan in a flash with Dennis, ahead of me, jumping into a slit trench. I jumped in on top of him from which position I heard, but did not see the enemy attack. A great pity, as we had not seen attacking German fighters for weeks.

One morning in late January, I was surprised to get a phone call from occupied Holland. The caller told me that the records of several hundred young men were kept in a particular house in The Hague and unless the records were destroyed within three days these men would be sent to a forced labour camp in Germany. He gave me details of the position of the house and then pressed me to have it destroyed. I told him to contact me later that day.

I discussed this with Zulu Morris, the new SASO who had just taken over from McEvoy. As the house was in a terrace and damage would inevitably be caused to the houses on either side, we decided to say no. But we changed our minds on receiving a later call informing us that two men with lights or signals of some sort would be on the roof of the house to give its exact position. Clearly, the Dutch considered it terribly important that the job should be done. I therefore told the Dutchman that we would do it but that there would be no need to have the two brave men on the roof.

The job of planning and execution was given to the GCC. Denys Gillam's Typhoon Wing 146 was selected. Two Typhoons circled the area to attract AA fire, flying just above effective light flak height. The target marking was spot on and the attack achieved the desired result. Much later in the war I heard that a Dutch telephone engineer had 'jumped' a line in the Nijmegen exchange allowing communication from occupied Holland to the outside world. The line remained secret so far as I knew.

It was in early February whilst 84 Group HQ was still at Tilburg that I summoned up the courage to tell Teddy Huddleston, who had taken over from Bingo Brown as AOC in November, and Zulu Morris that I had been unhappy for some time with our GCC. It was responsible for the detailed planning of our operations and I was particularly unhappy with the methods used to make decisions about what force and which wing should be detailed for each operation. I thought that, for other than routine operations, the wings themselves should play a part in deciding on types of attack and the numbers and types of the aircraft needed. The outcome was my posting a month later to take over the GCC, and the posting of Denys Gillam to take my place as group captain ops in the group HQ – he was an excellent choice.

On 6th February I was invited to dinner by the CO of a Canadian Scottish regiment. Their mess was in woods just west of the Reichswald Forest. My welcome by the officers, who were a merry bunch, particularly after the alcohol took effect, was most warm. At the end of the evening I was escorted back to my transport by the CO and his pipe major who piped me aboard.

Twenty-four hours later, on 8th February, the regiment was in the thick of the fighting, as the battle for the forest had begun. This long awaited offensive by the Canadian 1st Army and the British 2nd Army's 30 Corps, known as Operation Veritable, was intended to clear enemy from the country between the Maas and the Rhine. It started after a night of intense bombing and one of the heaviest artillery bombardments of the war. Air support for the offensive was provided by nearly all the available resources of 83 and 84 Groups, together with the RAF light bombers of 2 Group and the 9th USAAF. [4]

8th February 1945

Have been unable to write to you for several days. By now you will have heard most probably the reason why. Things are progressing quite well at the moment. I hope we can carry on and knock the Huns for six. The planning for this has been going on for some time and we have been extremely busy. We've had numerous visitors including my old friend Tedder. He was on very good form.

During the first day of the battle twelve pre-arranged targets were attacked and a total of 520 sorties flown, nearly all in direct support of the army. Excellent initial progress was made through abominable terrain. In the following days the weather again turned against us and our air operations were reduced to a fraction of our total capacity. On 14th February when the weather improved the group flew nearly 750 sorties. A total of 180 tanks and MTs were destroyed or damaged.

17th February
The pipe arrived two or three days ago, since when any cigarette consumption has gone down by at least half. As you'll notice I am still at group and likely to remain here for the next week or so. Did I tell you in my last letter that Mac's successor is Zulu Morris — you'll remember him — an admirable choice.

Pete, Hugo and I went to Brussels the day before yesterday and had quite a good party — including champagne and pâté de foie gras.

25th February
I often wish I had my own unit. I probably convey that I'm a little depressed but it's the reverse really. We're doing quite well.

26th February
A busy and trying day in that the weather has been terrible — we had laid on such a comprehensive programme to help the army. Still they're doing quite well.

Denys Gillam arrived today to take over but I shall have to stay here with him for another two or three days until he knows the ropes.

Last night I went down to the GCC for two or three hours to meet some of the chaps there. I believe I'm going to enjoy it. Nine months as a staff officer was long enough for me.

As far as leave is concerned it should be possible in about a month. Don't worry darling I'll do my damndest to get away as I could do with a clear seven days. It's now well over three months and I want to see you and Elisabeth. She won't remember me. Wish I was with you – by God this Hun takes some beating.

At the end of February, after one of the toughest slogging matches of the war, some fifteen German divisions, hammered by the British and Canadians from the north and the Americans in the south withdrew to the Rhine and into Germany. 84 Group supported the army as it worked slowly south by sending successive waves of Typhoons to batter enemy positions. Von Runstedt had no option but to withdraw the remnants of his force (he had been losing an average of 10,000 a day) across the Rhine. In the meantime, the Russian army was still pressing ahead westwards, it looked like disaster for the Germans.

8th-10th March

The fight still goes on – and the general feeling is that the Hun will be defeated within a matter of weeks. As soon as we can get across the Rhine in strength nothing can stop us. Let that time come soon.

Going to GCC in a few days. Had the most interesting time two days ago. Set foot in Germany for the first time. It gave me quite an amazing feeling of self-satisfaction. I spent the whole day going round army formations. The countryside was quite pretty although the towns and villages were heaps of ruins from the terrific shellfire. The only untouched or rather undamaged building I saw during the whole day was a church. The Rhine was in the distance. Won't it be marvellous when we can wander at will (if we wanted to) through that foolish country? Won't be long now. We've had a good day today, should have helped quite a lot in cutting down rockets on England.

On 12th March I finally took over the GCC which was still based at Turnhout. We soon moved to Hatert, a few miles south of Nijmegen, which was within shelling range of the German lines. The location of the GCC was dictated by the necessity to be able to maintain contact at all times with both the wings and the group HQ. It was a happy place. I had four very good wing commander planners including Peggy O'Neill (of Goodwood House and Red Hackle fame) and Al Deere. They readily accepted the new policy I introduced to devolve responsibility for the detailed planning of operations to the wings.

> *14th March*
>
> *I'm now, as you've probably noticed, in my new job. I've been here for only two days and I feel better already. I've brought my batman A/C Ford along so that all my personal needs are well attended to. I think the main reason I feel so much better is that I am no longer tied to my office. If I want to go out I go out. Yesterday I flew forward to one of our units (I have my own Auster strip).*

It was for my minor part in the liberation of the Netherlands that I was made a Commander of the Order of Orange Nassau by Queen Wilhelmina. The citation read:

> *'For his excellent services from 20th April 1944 until 28th February 1945 conducting operations of number 84 Group RAF during the liberation of the Netherlands, showing initiative, courage and perseverance.'*

THE BEGINNING OF THE END
MARCH 1945-MARCH 1946

On 9th March Monty issued orders for Operation Varsity, the crossing of the Rhine north of the Ruhr, with the longer term objective of isolating the Ruhr and moving on quickly into the northern plains of Germany. In the final line-up on the Rhine, the 9th US Army took up positions from Düsseldorf to Wesel, the British 2nd Army from Wesel to the Dutch frontier with the Canadian 1st Army covering the remaining ground to the North Sea.

During the three days before the Rhine crossing, sustained bombing attacks caused tremendous damage. RAF heavy bombers flew over 5,000 sorties, dropping nearly 25,000 tons of bombs, whilst the 8th and 9th USAAF, flying over 11,000 sorties, dropped over 24,000 tons. 83 and 84 Groups had also a pre-arranged programme of air operations in support of the assault crossings. These included the maintenance of air superiority, the neutralisation of flak, fighter protection for the airborne forces and close support to the assault and airborne troops.

> *20th March*
>
> *Well darling I was all set to jump into an aeroplane to fly home this morning but the fates have destined otherwise. You will probably be able to sense whether I shall be able to get away by study of the news.*
>
> *Had lunch with Tedder two days ago and yesterday I was visited by our service 'father' Lord Trenchard and later had dinner with him. He is an amazing man with the most active brain. We could do with some more like him. We're remaining rather quiet at the moment although you have probably just heard of the activities by our Typhoons.*

On the night of 23rd March, bridgeheads were made over the Rhine and, as I had missed viewing the great Armada on D-Day the previous June, I decided that I must see the crossing of the Rhine, led by the airborne forces, from the air. Accordingly, on the next morning I took off in our Auster with Al Deere as passenger, reaching the Rhine at about 9.45 a.m. Its width at this point varied from 400-500 yards and up to 1,200 yards at high water. We flew up and down at about 300 feet. Just before 1.00 a.m., in perfect weather we saw the aircraft of the first parachute serial arrive. They flew just over us.

For the next three hours wave after wave of aircraft came to the dropping and landing zones in a thrilling demonstration of air power.

Dakotas carrying paratroops were followed by Halifaxes and more Dakotas towing troop-carrying Hadrian gliders. Over 1,500 aircraft and gliders delivered 14,000 troops to the battle area. The losses of only forty-six transport aircraft were much lighter than we had expected and were a testament to our total domination of the air and to the success of the anti-flak patrols by 84 Group Typhoons.

I shall never forget what a tremendous sight it was and thinking how marvellous that we had 'got it together' at last. I should have mentioned that the actual bridgeheads across the Rhine had been made during the previous night.

On returning to our Auster strip I remarked to Al, who had not flown an Auster before, that had we not used it we would never have seen that wonderful sight. I suggested he should go solo on one. He readily agreed, making his first flight that afternoon. Unfortunately, whilst making his approach to land he hit a high hedge damaging the aircraft rather badly. In the accident report, later published in *RAF News*, I attached no blame to the pilot, but said the blame lay on the Ministry of Aviation for allowing an aircraft with such a muddled control system to enter service! The throttle, a pull and push affair, worked in a reverse manner to those of all other aircraft.

Al Deere was in good company as some of the best-known fighter aces would not fly the Auster; Sailor Malan, Bill Compton, and Desmond Scott had all also crashed them on their first attempt. Des Scott, a most competent New Zealander, was famous in RAF circles as, within two years and five months, he had been promoted from sergeant to group captain.

Following the crossing of the Rhine, the British forces drove north of the Rhine towards the north German plain threatening to trap the enemy forces in Holland. In early April, the Canadian 1st Army pushed north-west towards the Zuiderzee while the British 2nd Army drove north towards the Baltic.

By mid-April our fighter wings, which had continued to give direct and indirect support to the 21st Army Group forces by attacking the enemy's retreating columns, were operating from the superb permanent airfields in the Rhine area, and the GCC moved to Brogbern close to Lingen, its last location in the war.

21st April

Time has flown the last few days and darling no letters have been written. We have been working hard. I thought it would be strange having a site well inside Germany, but everything is, superficially at any rate, peaceful and we have a lovely site in the country.

I was out most of yesterday looking to the future; found a place and told the locals to build an Auster strip for me within two days. They actually like being ordered about and the jobs will be done. Eggs are plentiful. I have a feeling that I might be able to get away for a few days before you get this letter. It depends upon the AOC.

My batman Ford is priceless. All through the moves he has arranged things perfectly. I'll try and keep him after the war, he cooks my breakfast, provides my coffee at 11.00 if I'm in and produces afternoon tea.

For the next few weeks the destruction of enemy road and rail traffic went on and the most important enemy airfields were battered by our newly arrived squadrons of Tempests. In early May, the Typhoon wing crowned a long list of spectacular achievements with strikes on enemy shipping trying to escape to Norway from Kiel and Lübeck, sinking ninety-six ships.

For the record it should be noted that from 17th April to 6th May 84 Group flew 4,672 sorties, 1,674 on close support and army targets. During this period our squadrons destroyed and damaged 1,097 MT, and tanks, 221 enemy aircraft in the air, and on the ground and 898 railway engines.

From 12th August 1944 when 84 Group arrived in France its squadrons flew 69,294 sorties – over 270 per day. During this time it destroyed 9,398 enemy tanks and MT and 439 enemy aircraft while losing 479 of its own aircraft and 371 pilots.

On the ground progress was swift. By 17th April General Patton was in Czechoslovakia and the Ruhr was passed through. On 22nd April the Russians started their assault on Berlin and it looked as though the war in Italy would soon be over. Nine days later the Americans and Russians had linked up. The 21st Army Group had reached the Baltic and North West Germany, and Holland and Denmark surrendered. On 4th May Montgomery accepted and signed the 'Instruments of Surrender' at Luneburg Heath.

After six years of war, which in my case had included three years outside the UK, the fighting in Europe had come to an end. It had been a long time.

A few days previously I had been back on leave in England with Het. When it became obvious that the war would soon end, I decided that I must get back to the GCC straight away. I was trying to summon up the courage to tell Het when she forestalled me by saying, "I know you're dying to get back to your chaps, I think you should go." I left that afternoon. I felt that Germany was where I should be celebrating the signing of the peace treaty. After my personal effort over the previous five-and-a-half years I thought that I had earned the ultimate in celebrations. This could only be by celebrating victory in Germany with those magnificent men in their flying machines.

I was delighted that I managed to arrive back in time to celebrate VE day with my chaps at the GCC. I cannot quite remember what we did, but I know I spent the next few days with Teddy Huddleston visiting the three 84 Group airfields in an ambulance. We were driven round to the different messes on each airfield where we celebrated with the men. In each mess, no matter what the time was, we drew the curtains and 'declared a guest night'. I think the party lasted for about three days.

10th May

We have had one or two good parties over here but in the main it has been moderate celebrations. We gave the troops a good party on Wednesday night. It's awfully strange coming back to a peacetime basis especially with so many bodies: four wing commanders, lots of squadron leaders – I'm racking my brains to make work for them to do.

I'm going to Winschoten, Groningen and to the North Sea coast today to see some of our units. It means staying away the night.

A few days later I moved the GCC close to Dudeldorf, an airfield east of Celle and within a few miles of what eventually was to be called the 'Iron Curtain'. My old friend from flying training and Tangmere days, Johnnie Walker, was commanding a Spitfire wing on the airfield. We celebrated well and often. We made the most of the services of local people. When I needed a haircut the local barber would arrive posthaste and the local farmers would meet our requirements for eggs, pork, chickens and such like. It was a case of 'to the victor belongs the spoils'. But we did no looting. In general, we behaved well towards the local population; we paid them in cigarettes. The fact that they were so subservient however did not impress me.

> *21st May*
>
> *Sweetheart, I've managed to get a Spitfire again, that coupled with Denys Gillam's marriage means that you can go ahead and book a room in London for 8th and 9th June. I'm afraid you've received very few letters in the past fortnight. The reason is that I've been doing so much travelling to the various attached units − in the north of Holland, and then far east into Germany. Last week I was staying in Wildeshausen and visited Bremen and Hamburg. It's a terrific eye opener darling. The damage is so fantastic that it is quite incomparable with anything we have seen in England.*
>
> *I heard yesterday that I might have to write an official history of the campaign. What a book it would be.*

In late May Al Deere, Peggy O'Neill and I went on a two-day trip to Amsterdam taking our drinks and food. While there we gave a party for some locals at which we gave them bully beef sandwiches. As I said in my letter to Het, 'The joy they caused was terrific as it was the first time for months they had tasted white bread'.

In early June I returned to London for forty-eight hours with Zulu Morris where I met Het, stayed at the Savoy, and attended Denys Gillam's wedding.

20th June

My Spitfire has arrived and I'm getting back into trim. Should be all set to take me to England pretty soon. I've been working on the AOC for the last few days and I'm pretty certain that I shall get at least a fortnight's leave probably beginning of next month.

Work here at the moment is far more tiresome than in wartime.

27th June

Had quite a good party for the C-in-C last night. It was held in the open – good food, drinks, band, lots of guests. Mary Coningham made a magnificent speech. He mentioned four names: his own SASO and AOA. Then came on to 84 Group, mentioning his long and happy association with Teddy Huddleston whom he first met at Cranwell etc and then came on to speak of Rosie, of mobile warfare fame, who blazed his way through Africa, complete with fiddle and has never looked back. I thought it was rather nice – and so did lots of other people.

In late June I managed to get a week of leave in Wrexham returning to Germany from Lasham.

In early July I flew up to Denmark and on my return wrote to Het on paper taken from the Hotel Terminus in Copenhagen.

This paper is typical of the place. No suffering, plenty of food (I'm enclosing the "Bill of Fare" from a place where we had lunch). It seems rather strange that Holland, Belgium, France should have suffered whereas this country appears quite normal. Makes one quite cynical.

25th July

As I anticipated I am being posted to group from the 31st to do group captain ops. Apparently TAF or BAFO as it is now called wanted me but the AOC pressed for me to stay.

Denys Gillam has just given me the most marvellous photograph of Zulu, his wife, Al Deere and Joan and ourselves taken outside the church.

Peggy O'Neill is posted as wing commander flying at North Weald with Bader as his sector commander.

Ford's release group has just come up but he doesn't want to return to civil life yet. Wanted to stay with me. I dissuaded him from staying in for a further twelve months so he has asked for a six months postponement of release. I hope it is granted so that he can continue.

At the end of July I was posted back to 84 Group HQ at Celle to take over from Denys Gillam, once again as group captain ops. The SASO, Zulu Morris, remained a close friend. We played tennis, and went hunting and gliding in our free time.

Our HQ was in a large cavalry barracks just north of Celle which, for obvious reasons we renamed Trenchard Barracks – the name which the now British Army barracks retains today. Although Celle was an attractive town undamaged by war, when I first arrived our officer's mess was in a large tent in a nearby field.

When it became clear that the group HQ would stay in Celle for some time, Teddy Huddleston, the AOC, and his AOA Bill MacDonald, did their best to ensure that the personnel lived in reasonable comfort and that provision was made for them to enjoy their time off duty.

In August we moved our HQ 'A' mess into a house in Celle with grounds sloping down to the river. Food was good and I still maintain that the smoked eels from Steinhuder Meer near Wunstorf airfield were the finest I ever tasted. Wine and spirits were no problem to obtain. In Celle itself the officers' club was well stocked and well patronised whilst the orchestral concerts at the Schloss were of a very high standard.

7th August

*I wish you could have been here this weekend. If you
had been it would have been the perfect holiday! On
Saturday I managed to buy a racquet (Dunlop Max-
ply) from welfare and so after bathing on Saturday afternoon I went up to the country club with Zulu where
we played tennis (I beat him), had a magnificent dinner, played skittles and then drank. On Sunday we
had a repeat performance and stayed the night at the
club. On Monday morning we went out riding for two
hours, bathed in the afternoon and then returned here
to have dinner with the inspector general.*

*And what of the atomic bomb? The possibilities are
immense. What a world.*

15th August

The war's over [Japan had surrendered]. *Strangely
enough I have a feeling of contentment but not of elation.*

*What I really wanted to do was to jump into a Spit
and fly home and spend a few hours with you. The
AOC said I could go providing I could guarantee getting back tomorrow in time for a visit by the C-in-C.
I was annoyed when I saw the Met forecasts. I had to
cancel it.*

*Last Sunday I went gliding with Zulu. We each
flew three times and I was thrilled. It gives one a marvellous feeling of freedom. I shall not be happy until
I can soar and stay up for the odd hour or two.*

*Tomorrow we move out of our tents and start living
in complete luxury in one of the best equipped and
furnished houses I've ever known. The house is in
Celle and it has lawns stretching down to the river
about 200 yards away.*

Well Sweet, the war is over. Knowing what weapons

[the atom bomb] *will be available in future I can't say that I am terrifically enthusiastic in doing my normal day's work. What I want is to lead a family life. Soon.*

1st September
I've been scouting round this week in search of the odd present. I've managed to get a little silk, a black suede handbag, some scent and possibly next week a pair or two of silk stockings. What a fortunate woman you'll be.

We are putting on a display at The Hague on 15th and I've been put in charge of it. I hope the weather keeps fine so that we can really get down to practising. The show is going to be on the lines of the old Hendon Air Display.

Zulu and I went to a party at 145 Wing last Thursday night – Loel Guinness is just being released. We got to bed very late.

Next week is being known as 'Celle' week. Various entertainments have been organised – sports, cricket, various shows etc. It should be quite successful.

We'll lead a family life fairly soon – Elisabeth as well, even if it means going to staff college.

Whilst in Celle we sometimes visited the nearest Malcolm Club at Hanover from where, on one occasion, we took the club head and deputy on a day trip to Berlin. Driving fast along the autobahn in a black Mercedes coupé, which had been acquired from a wealthy German, we soon arrived at the outskirts of Berlin. There we stopped to ask for directions from a woman, who immediately ran away, having taken us for Russians. We then spent a long time looking around, driving down streets cleared of rubble and noting the devastation everywhere. We soon tired of this, and found our way to the officers' club which was full of Americans, Russians and others of our allies.

After a few drinks Zulu and I decided to do what we called the 'The

Volga Boat Man'. With shirts outside trousers and ties as belts we could have been taken as Russians by a very drunken man. We then proceeded to circle the room treading on furniture and without touching the floor whilst singing the song. Not surprisingly, we were soon joined by others thinking it was fun. After a few circuits we noticed a group of Russians who were definitely not amused. At that point we thought it wise to leave and find our way back.

Coming across an autobahn, assuming it was the right one, we set out on our way. Suddenly, we saw that the road ahead appeared to be barred by a mass of Russian transport. Somewhat perturbed – in fact, jolly frightened – we managed to turn around without any reaction from the Russians. This quickly sobered us up. Returning to Berlin, we were able to find the right autobahn for Hanover and the welcome of the Malcolm Club. It had been quite a day!

When Zulu left the group in the autumn on posting back to the UK, I took his place as SASO. In that job I remained a group captain but had it been a littler earlier I might have been made an air commodore.

One evening that autumn, during a drinks party the C-in-C, Mary Coningham, told me of his concern for the future of the RAF. The drift of it was that we had taken chaps, many of them straight from school, taught them to fly and ordered them to go out and 'break windows'. They had been thought of as heroes by their ground crews. Now they had finished their 'window bashing', they had little to do and most of them wanted to return home. As for the ground crews, they also had little work to do. They no longer had their flying heroes to worship and no longer did they have that incentive to do their best to win the war. They too wanted to return home. Mary went on to say that this was a recipe for trouble and it wouldn't surprise him if loyalty and discipline were affected. "Everything should be done to try to avoid such a state," he said.

Fortunately, although there were occasional rumbles of discontent, 84 Group was not affected but we heard of many cases of indiscipline, even mutiny, in other parts of the RAF.

During our time in Celle I got to know Teddy Huddleston well. We took every opportunity to visit the wings and squadrons and often dined with them. That winter, we occasionally drove to the Harz Mountains for some skiing, staying at the 84 Group Rest Centre in Bad

Harzburg and we went gliding at the club we had taken over from the Germans at Salzgitter.

14th January 1946

On Saturday we went along to Broady's place. He has a magnificent mess. I was greeted with black velvet and oysters and afterwards we went along to their officers' club. It's run perfectly. Saw Bitmead there, Pat Jameson, Tap Jones etc. Bitmead (ex 43 Squadron) has just been posted into the group after returning from India. He was on very good form.

It's quite good fun in our new mess. The AOC and AOA are quite young – thirty-six – and the AOC particularly has a very good brain and a very fine sense of humour. Actually, I'm getting a little fed up with this job. I've had it now for about eight months, I'd like my own command again.

It was during this time at Celle that on 25th January 1946 I was 'Mentioned in Despatches for distinguished service'. I was also told that my next posting was to be to the RAF Staff College at Bracknell.

18th February 1946

Joe Holmes came in to see me this morning. Told me he'd just received a rocket from his wife for having wished her a happy birthday on entirely the wrong date. With a start I realised that I too had committed the unpardonable crime of forgetting your birthday. I humbly apologise sweetheart and promise to make up for it.

I'm anxiously awaiting word from you about accommodation. I'll be overjoyed if you have managed to get something. It's time we started living together. I long for it. If you haven't had any joy we'll try together when I arrive home.

I should arrive home on 4th or 5th March which

The author skiing in the Harz Mountains, January 1946.

should give us a full month's holiday before the course starts.

Went skiing yesterday and even though there was a blizzard most of the time, I thoroughly enjoyed myself. Noel Smith and I did about eight miles cross-country before lunch. It's so enjoyable that I'm bringing a pair of skis home for you.

Darling, I do hope you have succeeded in this house hunting game. If not, will you put an advert in the local papers? Only fourteen days to go. Give Lis a big kiss for me.

23rd February
I think that I shall remain in the UK after staff college
– probably at Air Ministry. The chaps due for overseas
service are going to Haifa. Therefore, it's a good gam-
ble to think of a car as a long-term measure.

AOC and I are going skiing this afternoon.
Farewell party for us at Hildesheim tonight. There's
a farewell party for us on every single evening next
week. The whole thing seems fraught with danger!

The Air Staff have just given me an electric train
for Elisabeth. She's a bit young for it yet but I'll enjoy
it.

In early March the time came to say goodbye to Germany. By a happy
coincidence Teddy Huddleston was posted at the same time so we
travelled back to England together. As the weather was unfit for flying
we took the 'services special train', drank a bottle of Teddy's champagne and eventually arrived at Dover delighted to be home at last.
We then went our separate ways – mine led to Bracknell to begin the
staff college course. Where, having been a group captain since 1943,
I arrived as a wing commander.

Chapter 8

POST-WAR
SERVICE LIFE

RAF STAFF COLLEGE, BRACKNELL
APRIL-OCTOBER 1946

The RAF Staff College had moved to its permanent home at Bracknell in Berkshire in 1945. The pre-war staff college had been sited at RAF Andover because of its proximity to the army at Salisbury Plain and Aldershot. However, at the start of the war the airfield at RAF Andover was needed for operational purposes. During the war the two-year course was reduced to three months at either Bracknell or Bulstrode House, near Gerrard's Cross. However, for some years the name of a graduate in the RAF list was still followed by the letters PSCA (Passed Staff College Andover).

In early April 1946 about 100 of us assembled at Bracknell. We RAF officers were leavened and strengthened by a dozen from the army and half a dozen from the navy. We were inevitably the most decorated course ever.

Amongst us we had had an immense amount of operational experience in every theatre of operations. We were the 'types' who had resolutely avoided the safety of staff college whilst there was a war to be fought. Most of the directing staff (DS) were older, and had much less battle experience than us. We doubted their knowledge of tactics and strategy; we certainly questioned their ability to mould us into a peacetime military shape. This they believed could be accomplished by un-believably petty rules. We tidied up our dress by buying new uni-forms, adhered to sensible RAF service rules; but in no way adhered to local staff college rules as drawn up by the DS. Women, including wives of long-standing (Het and I had been married nearly seven years), were not allowed in the ladies room after 10.00 p.m. I well re-member her being pushed through the window by a couple of my friends, whilst I nonchalantly walked in through the front door. Some-time later she was discovered by the duty officer, a young, pompous wing commander DS, one of those we thought was lacking in both operational experience and humour. After pointing out these defi-ciencies we threw him out of that self-same window.

We had frequent outside lecturers. Those we judged good were ap-plauded. Others we subjected to relentless questioning, but we always tried to introduce some humour into the proceedings. The jester-in-chief was Cedric Masterman, who had been our best man back in 1939. He dedicated himself to getting a laugh wherever and whenever possible. I well remember the roar of laughter greeting his shout of "Bingo" when our commandant, 'One-Armed Saunders' appeared with the lecturer of the day, a similarly disabled senior army officer.

In May came the Victory Parade for which we were determined to tear ourselves away from our studies. It still amazes me that it took such an enormous amount of agitation, culminating in threats, before the commandant made what he called 'a concession' and allowed us to attend. We did not envy those who had been chosen to be on pa-rade that day. We sympathised and felt we should be there to give them a friendly wave.

At 4.00 a.m. we left a party at RAF Blackbushe, near Yateley, in Hampshire for London. On the way there we stopped at Lightwater Court to pick up our friends, Peggie and Jock Henderson, who had come down from North Wales for the occasion. Jock was still recov-ering from the privations of the Burma campaign. At 6.00 a.m. when we arrived there were already people lining the route. We chose a van-tage point on the Embankment which gave us a view up Northum-berland Avenue, down which the parade would proceed.

This spot proved to be an excellent choice as we were able to shelter under Hungerford Bridge from the heavy downpour which started about noon and went on for the rest of the day.

We had a long wait. Although we had been the first to arrive and found seats in the front row, as time wore on Jock and I found that we were back in the tenth row. Het's friend has never let us forget this. She loves telling the tale of how, "those two fools kept giving up their places to any woman who fluttered her eyes at them". We knew that we were not fools but perfect gentlemen!

The parade itself was a feat of organisation. I remember it chiefly for the variety of colourful uniforms worn by the allied troops, most of which had not been seen on parade since 1939. Great cheers greeted the flypast of fifteen Spitfires led by Douglas Bader. I knew well and had flown with most of those pilots. The controller that day was another friend, Flying Officer Claire Legge of the WAAF. Her easily recognisable and calm voice, combined with their faith in her known controlling ability, had in the heat of battle given our pilots that added boost of confidence. Later as a wing commander she became the first woman to command an RAF station – the fighter control station at Neatishead in Norfolk. She married another friend of ours, Jeffrey Quill, who had been the Spitfire production test pilot. Upon retirement they lived near us in North Wales. I was not short of subject matter when I was asked to make the speech at Jeffrey's eightieth birthday party in London.

Despite the fact that we were celebrating victory, sad thoughts could not be dispelled. There were fears for the future too, as diplomacy seemed to be playing too strong a part. The Polish forces, who since 1939 had contributed so much to the allied victory, were not allowed to march that day. Presumably, this was to appease the Russians. I think political correctness was born that day. It was also a day tinged with sadness. Our special thoughts were of Peggie's only brother, a lieutenant in the Royal Welch Fusiliers, killed in February 1945 in the Reichswald Forest when the allied troops were making their final push towards the Rhine. I had known him as an exceptionally mischievous young boy with whom I had had many altercations when attempting to lord it over him as a school prefect. As a poacher turned gamekeeper, I was well aware of his calculated irritations. We did not forget the sadness of all those years of struggle that gained us eventual victory.

That night, as what seemed a fitting close to the day, we heard the unbelievably sweet song of a nightingale in a nearby wood. That was the first and only time that I heard a nightingale's song in England.

At Bracknell there were lots of social activities. Official cocktail parties, parties amongst ourselves, and even a garden party at which Field Marshal Montgomery was the chief guest. Some of the wives, mine included, thought they would challenge authority by questioning the wearing of hats as commanded on the invitation. During the war the Archbishop of Canterbury had announced that women need no longer wear hats for church. Their argument was that if hatlessness was good enough for God it should certainly be good enough for Montgomery!

They also asserted that they were not subject to military orders. We were rather pleased that they had entered into what we thought was the right spirit. Very few hats had been made during the war and there were still very few new ones obtainable. The wearing of headscarves, particularly made by Jacqmar, was the universal war-time fashion. Those rebellious wives, one by one, lost their nerve. Het was the last to give in. Consequently, there was little left to choose from in the one hat shop in Camberley. She vowed that the one she bought was the only one left in the shop. I had no reason to believe otherwise as she wore it only once!

Het and I at last had six happy months together in peacetime England. Our seventh anniversary in 1946 was the first we had spent together, and our best man was there too! There were not many accompanying wives. Quite a few had been lost on the way. As there were no married quarters at Bracknell married couples had to find their own accommodation. The fact that we were scattered over a wide area of Berkshire and Surrey did not inhibit our social life but often made the return journey a little more hazardous.

Whilst I was still in Germany Het had twice journeyed to Bracknell from Wales in an attempt to find somewhere for us to live. Eventually, after much searching, we ended up renting part of Lightwater Court, a remote, dilapidated mansion near Bagshot about ten miles away from the staff college. There it was that for the first time we lived together as a family. I knew little of my daughter, who was then two-and-a-half. She had seen me only during the few times that I had been on leave since she had been born in 1943. I was told that she was a beautifully behaved baby; this was hard to believe as whenever I saw her she cried and screamed at the nasty man who disrupted her life with her mother.

Many of my fellow students were also learning to be fathers. It was a long, hard struggle and staff college lectures certainly gave us no guidance!

During the mid-term break in July we spent ten days holidaying with two new friends. Group Captain Charlie Bale's wife was a Channel Islander. He had met her in May 1940 whilst leading a flight of his squadron at their forward base in Jersey. This move had been necessitated by the rapid advance made by the German army. In June when France fell and it became evident that the Channel Islands could no longer be defended, this RAF contingent was withdrawn after only a five-week stay. Flying out from Guernsey in his aircraft with Charlie was his newly-found girlfriend. Later he married her, and later still divorced her.

In 1946 we felt lucky to have her as our guide in Guernsey. The ins and outs of the place were known to her. Perhaps more of the inns, than the outs.

Although the war had been over for a year, we found Guernsey to be very run down. We were told that there had been a rapid decline after D-Day. As the allies advanced on the continent they blocked all supplies to the German garrison on the Channel Islands. As a result they had none of the materials required for regular maintenance and for keeping up the standards of sanitation and cleanliness. At our hotel, which had been a German headquarters, they were still struggling to improve the neglected bathrooms and lavatories. The many glasshouses in which tomatoes had been produced chiefly for export to the mainland were also derelict.

Coming from Britain, where there was still food rationing and a shortage of many other foods, we enjoyed all that Guernsey had to offer. Especially plentiful were the eggs and rich Guernsey butter. Most nights we ate at a fish and chip café in St. Peter Port where for half-a-crown we had a rare treat – eggs with our chips. This was always followed by an invitation to visit the proprietress in her parlour. There we were freely entertained with coffee and liqueurs, both of which were still in short supply. She was very blatantly anti-German as her husband had died whilst doing forced labour in Germany. Foremost in her mind was the belief that any member of the RAF deserved VIP treatment.

Despite the peace that everyone should have been enjoying, we were soon aware of much underlying animosity within the local community. There was evidence everywhere of bitter resentment towards those who had undoubtedly co-operated with the German garrison.

During this trip I revelled in wearing civilian clothes once again as we had not been allowed to previously even when on leave. Rather remarkably, all my clothes had survived wartime attacks by moths. I was told that this was because they had been regularly hung out in the sun. My 'tidy' appearance was our downfall. We were identified as 'collaborators' by a Royal Marine commando on demob leave in his native Guernsey. He decided to follow us round and as the week, and particularly the evenings, wore on he became more and more abusive. He seemed to be always there. I am ashamed to admit that after five days of this persistent nuisance I got so aggravated that I lashed out, knocking him through a glass door. Never had I done such a thing before, and never have since. I got into great trouble – not for throwing the punch but from Het, as the glass splinters had made numerous cuts in my new tweed jacket. Clothes were rationed and good tweed jackets in short supply. As we had used all our clothing coupons in acquiring it (with some influence), I had to go on wearing it for many years in its far from pristine condition.

It was at about this time that Het had the idea that we should emigrate. Having had what she regarded as her fill of war, she wanted nothing more to do with anything that had any war-like connection. This, of course, would have meant me leaving the RAF. She was strongly in favour of Southern Rhodesia. There, far away from conflict, we could live in peace happily ever after. After some months she dropped all thoughts of this. She was finally convinced by my constant assurance that I was not in the RAF to make war but to see that we were so efficient that we would prevent war starting. Throughout my service career I always worked with this belief in the forefront of my mind. We all did. After all, we had seen and experienced the ghastliness of war.

In October, at the end of six very pleasant months, the course came to an end. There was only one failure. Regrettably, this was Cedric Masterman. The rest of us, realising at the last moment that our future could depend upon it, treated the final exercise with great seriousness. Cedric alone chose not to do so. He wrote two lines explaining why he wished to play no part in what could only result in total disaster. The rest of us managed two pages of serious thought.

Our postings came through in September. Mine was as wing commander (night-fighter ops) at Fighter Command HQ, Bentley Priory, Stanmore. The majority of us felt that we had had our fun and were now ready to get down to serious work again. A few, albeit with outstanding wartime records, resigned their commissions. They decided that the peacetime RAF was not for them. They departed to seek adventure and their fortunes in Rhodesia, South Africa, Australia and Hong Kong. I was sad to bid farewell to some good friends. All flourished in their new jobs and countries. We met later from time to time when my RAF travels took me overseas. They were always anxious for news of the RAF. Despite all that they had later achieved, they often expressed regret that they had left the Royal Air Force.

HQ FIGHTER COMMAND
BENTLEY PRIORY OCTOBER 1946-MARCH 1947

With the rapid disbandment of squadrons my job at Bentley Priory soon became almost redundant. As there were no married quarters available, Het and Elisabeth moved into quarters at a former fighter station, Hawkinge, near Folkestone in Kent. It had been decided that Hawkinge was no longer viable as an operational station but that the much-needed housing would be retained. Only four quarters were occupied. These were sparsely furnished and in an attempt to make Elisabeth happy there I bought her a black cocker spaniel which she decided to call Bingo.

With me at Bentley Priory during the week, Het was lonely and unhappy in this unheated flight lieutenant's quarter. I was not able to get back there until Saturday afternoon as in 1947 we worked on Saturday morning. Late on Sunday afternoon, I had to return to Bentley Priory.

After two unsatisfactory months there we moved two days before Christmas to The Old Workhouse at Ruislip Common. We drove there through a snowstorm which heralded the start of the very hard winter of 1947. We lived in a self-contained annexe in a lovely old stone country house. We were made most welcome by the owners who straightaway invited us to have Christmas lunch with their family. They were a very sociable, and humorous couple with whom we remained friendly until their deaths forty years later. We still keep in touch with their three children, at whose weddings we were front-row guests. We, despite shortages of almost everything and despite the intense cold, had returned to happier times. They were very good friends to us.

We were at the Old Workhouse for that long-remembered winter. The bitterly cold weather, compounded by a rapidly growing fuel shortage, affected every part of the country. Factories were shut. Gas pressure was so low that it took hours to cook a meal. Elisabeth felt the cold so much that when her fingers were blue with cold I would literally 'put her head in the gas oven'. "Bad Mr Shinwell" (the minister deemed responsible for our sad state) was a frequent utterance whenever this happened. She and Het spent much of their time attempting to keep warm in the tea shops of Ruislip. Our nights were spent under a tier of blankets. We had borrowed ten blankets from the RAF. This is no exaggeration. They were wartime issue manufactured with the minimum of wool. However, we survived.

In March 1947 I was asked if I would like to go to the USA for ten months on an unaccompanied tour. I refused on the grounds that, after such long separations during the war, I was not prepared to once again leave my wife and daughter. This was not held against me as within a week I was posted to Horsham St. Faith near Norwich as station commander.

HORSHAM ST. FAITH
APRIL 1947-JANUARY 1948

This was just the posting I wanted. I was delighted with it as I knew it gave me a chance to have a hand in shaping the peacetime Royal Air Force. We had learned much during our years at war. Now we were about to put some of those lessons to the test in peacetime conditions. I was also delighted to be back at a 'flying' station as I was again able to fly regularly in both the Meteors and Spitfires that we had situated on the base there.

I went to Horsham charged with putting into effect a new way of aircraft servicing, known as the 'Three-Pronged System'. I was allowed to choose my senior officers for the trial, all of whom I knew to be highly competent and keen. This combination worked so well together that the trial was an overwhelming success. The success meant that this new way of working was adopted generally throughout the RAF and was still used fifty years later.

At Horsham there were four Meteor cadre squadrons 74, 245, 257 and 263 (i.e. half-strength) and 695 Squadron (an anti-aircraft co-operation unit) equipped with Spitfires and an Oxford.

I had also been charged with 'cleaning up' the station. The RAF had just taken over the station from the Poles who had also occupied the neighbouring fighter station of Coltishall and it had been brought to the Air Ministry's notice that much of the 'black market dealing' that was still rife in East Anglia in the continuing days of rationing, could be traced back to Horsham St. Faith.

There was much to be done. Minor rackets flourished. I immediately discovered that the nearby Norwich Speedway not only had its motorbikes serviced in our hangars by RAF technicians but were also supplied with all the petrol necessary to keep the Speedway going.

The station warrant officer informed Het at their very first meeting that he could get as much chocolate as she wished (I never found out how he knew that she was a chocoholic). A very junior officer, who obviously had an eye on promotion, indicated that through him we could be ensured a constant supply of red meat. Those were but a few.

After a little amateur sleuthing, followed by a spot-check on all financial ledgers, I decided to call in the police. The much-liked civilian adjutant, after a trial found himself in Norwich jail. The middle-aged, over-confident RAF accounts officer was sentenced to three years detention. Consequent to these enquiries we got to know the chief constable of Norfolk and the town clerk of Norwich very well, and made them honorary members of the mess. We were invited by them to many official and non-official functions in Norwich. I remember vividly the visit in July 1947 of the King and Queen. In 1946 and 1947 they visited many places throughout the British Isles to thank their subjects for their contribution to victory.

Another event was the unveiling of the City of Norwich War Memorial by Air Chief Marshal Sir Arthur Tedder. I had great respect for him. He recalled some amusing incidents from the times I had served under him in the Western Desert and northern Europe.

Norwich, only two miles away, was a lovely old city. A joy to the eye were the newly refurbished stalls of the open-air market in the centre of the city. There, under the brightly striped awnings, was a huge variety and quantity of local produce such as we had not seen for years. We frequently visited the market, both to buy and admire. At that time Norwich had several shoe factories. These had made nothing but military footwear for years but were producing women's shoes once again. Shoes were still rationed but seconds (only just!) could be queued for on Friday afternoons. Many of our wives could be found in these queues.

They told us that they were happy to be able to queue and were delighted to be in a place where such lucky breaks occurred. These must seem such small things but they all contributed to a feeling of peace-time well-being which was reflected in the high morale of the station. This was helped by the lovely summer weather of 1947.

The Castle Hotel, Norwich was our favourite meeting place. There we would rendezvous with a few friends for lunch on a Saturday. The wives would arrive from their morning shopping rather earlier than we working men.

We got to know and love Norfolk on this our first posting there. We loved its wide skies and the countryside which was so different from any other known to us at that time. Although our petrol ration was only five gallons per month (at a cost of 12½p per gallon), by pooling this with our friends we were able to take the children to the seaside at Cromer, Sheringham and Great Yarmouth. There we were once again able to walk on the shore and to play in the sand. Anti-invasion obstacles, mines and barbed wire had by then been removed from almost all the beaches.

Many Sundays of that long, warm summer were spent on the Broads. The mess had bought three dinghies and a small motor cruiser. On duller autumn Sundays we drove to Cromer where at the Queens Hotel we played mixed doubles on their indoor courts. Before the war the Annual Cromer Tournament held there was one of the foremost events in the sporting calendar. Following wartime occupancy by the army, the hotel had been refurbished and the tennis courts opened to the public. In 1947 there were very few such courts. I became a regular member of the Fighter Command tennis and squash teams. I used to travel to matches with my tennis partner, a young officer from nearby Coltishall, Christopher Blount, the son of an AVM killed in 1940. Chris, later as a squadron leader, became the Queen's equerry.

I was keen to encourage an interest in sport and as was customary in the pre-war RAF, declared Wednesday afternoon to be a sports afternoon. I played in the station rugger team. At thirty-two with an eight-year gap since last playing, I must admit that I did not really enjoy it, but did it to encourage others. We all worked together towards re-launching those pleasant social events which had been part and parcel of life on RAF stations in the thirties.

We had a summer ball, the like of which had not been seen for years. A young officer, later to become a well-known theatre impresario, was put in charge. He was so enthusiastic that, disregarding his demob date, he elected to serve an extra month in order to complete the job. He and his team, principally of young men awaiting their return to civilian life, exceeded all expectations. They were determined to leave the service trailing clouds of glory.

The mess was transformed – Parisian brothels, Bavarian wine cellars, Spanish bodegas, American honky-tonks. The British contribution was an oyster bar organised by another young man recently demobbed and back with the family firm in Whitstable. Although oysters were not rationed, they were still in short supply but not that night.

We reintroduced an annual station cocktail party, to which we invited 'official' guests from the local community and friendly local civilians. We also had a station sports day with a special section for the children.

The RAF was beginning to realise that looking after the families in this post-war era was not only a necessity but that it was to our advantage to have men supported by contented families. Accordingly, Het started a club for the airmen's wives. This was a new venture and probably the first of its kind. As time went by 'Wives' Clubs' grew in number, diversity and size and eventually flourished on every station.

Today, the Wives Clubs run thrift shops, toddler groups, libraries, car pools and such like, and have even been officially recognised by the Ministry of Defence. A committee with members elected from station Wives' Clubs has been able to influence decisions by putting forward the women's point of view.

Het's club, though, was strictly for entertainment, but definitely not for hers. Crown & Anchor and Housey-Housey (now known as Bingo) were long-time popular service games that worked well but were difficult to organise. And her attempts to raise the standard by giving lessons on smocking after three-year-old Elisabeth's smocked dresses were much admired were to no avail. Privately she used to describe the whole thing as a 'dead loss' and thought of closing the club but reluctantly succumbed to the wives' entreaties to continue with it. They assured her of its value as it meant a night out for them whilst their husbands were compelled to stay in and look after the children. Apparently this was the only night that the men did not go out to their various messes, or so she was told! They showed their appreciation by giving her a farewell party at which she was presented with a new style electric clock inscribed:

Mrs Rosier
From
Married Families
RAF Horsham St Faith

1947

That summer, we had two squadron visits. The County of Surrey Squadron of the Auxiliary Air Force came from their station at Kenley for their summer camp; and a squadron of the recently re-formed French air force came for a week's exchange duty. The auxiliaries, with their usual generosity, laid on a party to thank us. But the French, for whom we thought it polite to arrange a number of social activities on the station, spurned our efforts. Before 9.00 p.m. on the first evening every Frenchman had left our welcoming party announcing that he

was off to bed. They were later seen in Norwich! We therefore decided to cancel the rather tame social plans that we had made for them
and the next evening arranged a visit to the Samson and Hercules
dance hall, known as The Sodom and Gomorrah. The only snag was
that it was out of bounds to RAF personnel. This obviously delighted
those selected to accompany them.

The next morning the French CO asked for an interview with me
and with no preamble announced that his officers were going to London by train and would be back on Friday evening. He then produced
a scrap of paper on which were the names of three RAF officers whom
they thought would be the best to accompany them as their guides to
London. I recognised the handwriting and deduced from it the object
of the exercise and agreed with the names. But to call their bluff I
added the name of a pilot whose notorious exploits I conjectured made
him even better qualified. I had thought of naming the padre but upon
reflection, I thought it unlikely that Westminster Abbey was part of
the tour. On their return I did no delving as to what they had all been
up to but by means of the grapevine we gathered that a good time was
had by all.

At the end of October I was told that the station was to be upgraded.
Although the three squadrons commanded by squadron leaders had
done exceptionally well, it was decided that their jobs warranted the
rank of wing commander. This meant that automatically the job of
station commander would be upgraded to group captain. I was offered
the post as an acting unpaid group captain. This I refused. I had no
objection at all to acting the part, after all, I had been an acting group
captain for three years during the war, and thought I was pretty good
at it. But I did object strongly to the unpaid part of the deal. I have always thought that a man considered capable of doing a job should be
paid the going rate.

I was again offered a posting to the United States, which this time I
accepted as I would not have to go alone. It had been decided that all
overseas tours of two years or longer would be accompanied. This
condition would be met by my attending the five-month course at The
Armed Forces Staff College at Norfolk, Virginia, followed by two years
in an exchange posting with the USAF.

Although regretting that we had only two months left in Norfolk, we were excited to be going to the States. The next weeks were spent ensuring that the station would be handed over in as highly an efficient state as was possible. However, I had one unexpected setback. Almost the last visitors to my office were my friends the police.

After congratulating me on the Christmas spirit so evident throughout the station, they told me that they suspected that the beautiful and much-admired trees adorning the station in abundance were stolen. I did know that the 'window' which decorated the said trees (and which gently swayed and tinkled in the December breeze) had been 'borrowed' for operational purposes. But I did not know the trees were stolen. ('Window' was the name given to the strips of aluminium foil that had been dropped during the war to confuse enemy radar.)

In no time we ascertained that this accusation was true. A few airmen, who assured us that with no other thought than for the common good, had borrowed RAF transport and completely exhausted themselves chopping down and loading the trees. They were loyal to the flight sergeant whose orders they had carried out with such alacrity and enthusiasm. This revealed to me what a happy co-operative spirit there was on the station! So much for my fond belief that I had won the battle against crime.

In 1947, as many families were together at Christmas for the first time for many years, there was a general determination to make it 'the best Christmas ever'. Not wanting to miss these festivities, which were organised with the most meticulous detail, we did not leave the station until 1st January 1948. Rather weak after the New Year's Eve Ball we left by car for a few days leave in Wrexham.

That day we got only as far as Nottingham where we stayed with an old Desert Air Force friend Hugh O'Neil and his wife Billie. She was the widow of one of my pilots in 229 Squadron, Flight Lieutenant du Vivier, who in March 1941 had failed to return from a patrol over the Irish Sea. Het had had the awful task of giving her the sad news – a job undertaken with a heavy heart and with the knowledge that their roles could easily have been reversed. Our wives helped us a lot in dealing with such onerous duties which arose from time to time. Whilst I was away overseas Het and Billie had remained good friends and kept in touch. She stayed with us at Horsham in May 1947 whilst on demob leave from the WRNS. There she met Squadron Leader

Hugh O'Neil. Six months later we attended their wedding in London.

We drove to Wrexham the next day. I was now fully convinced that the air force life was for me. I had had no hesitation in refusing the offer of my great friend Denys Gillam that I should join him in Halifax running the family carpet business, Homfreys. Het wavered a bit when we visited them when she was told how difficult it had been for the chemist to get the right pink for dyeing the 800 yards of carpet in their house. This was at a time when we had only one rug in our brown lino-covered bedroom and at a time when the general public could only obtain what was called 'utility carpet' with a permit that was difficult to procure. However, she readily agreed with me when I told her it would never work. I simply could not have Denys as my boss. We remained very great friends, visiting each other from time to time and place to place. He was at our Golden Wedding party in 1989. In 1947 he joined the Yorkshire squadron of the reconstituted Auxiliary Air Force at Finningley as a flight lieutenant. Many distinguished wartime flyers willingly dropped two or three ranks in order to continue flying.

Chapter 9

A NEW CHAPTER
IN THE US

USA ARMED FORCES STAFF COLLEGE
JANUARY 1948-JULY 1948

I can remember little of those few days in Wrexham, but still dominant in my mind are my efforts to sell my car, a large pre-war Vauxhall, and to get rid of everything that seemed unnecessary and cumbersome as I needed some available cash in order to take advantage of what the United States had to offer. I had virtually nothing in my bank account. The miserly war bonus of £190 had disappeared at Horsham where, as station commander in 1947, the entertainment allowance I received was still the pre-war rate of half a crown per day (2/6d – now 12½ pence) and I had had to entertain a lot of visitors. January 1948 proved to be one of the earliest examples of my long line of financial mistakes. I sold my Purdy 12-bore shotgun for £12 and the Vauxhall at a give-away price to a vet who convinced me that it was suitable only for the transportation of sick animals.

I left Het and Elisabeth in Wrexham for a few days whilst I reported to the Air Ministry for briefings from the various departments. I then met them at Paddington on Friday 9th January. Taxis were still not plentiful but I had managed through the RAF Club to get one to take us to Victoria. In the late afternoon we boarded the boat-train to Southampton. At Victoria the hustle and bustle made for an exciting start to our trip.

Ours was one of the earliest post-war Atlantic crossings by *The Queen Elizabeth* and there was a feeling in the air that once again luxury ocean travel was heralding the revival of British prestige. The ship had been refurbished to the highest standard. It had been reported to be sumptuously elegant and glamorous – with ballrooms and night clubs. Geraldo, the famous band leader, was in overall charge of four or five bands – known as Geraldo's Army. To travel first class on *The Queen Elizabeth* was a status symbol highly regarded by Hollywood stars and the rich and famous from both sides of the Atlantic. We in cabin class, who had embarked on the Friday evening, watched with interest as the first class passengers arrived on Saturday morning in a special boat-train made up entirely of first class coaches.

However we did not feel like second-class citizens. Our four-bunk cabin was quite small but well-equipped. We could not believe that when it was a troop ship the same cabin had fifteen bunks. Our steward, who had joined the ship in 1938, had served on her throughout the war. He had been with the first contingent of troops that had been brought from Sydney to the Middle East and Britain. After 1942 she made a number of quick dashes across the Atlantic filled to the gunnels with up to 5,000 American troops. Her final contribution to victory was to transport the quite considerable number of GI brides and children acquired by Americans whilst serving in the UK, to their new homes in the US. (There had been rumours that the two Queens were having their engines removed as these would be supplanted by the 1,000 'oars' on board!)

Our dinner on the first evening exceeded all possible expectations but the most memorable thing was the whiteness of the bread, the like of which we had not seen for many years. Het's immediate reaction was that she must send a sample of this whiter than white bread to her mother. It would be like the snowdrops, a harbinger of spring, as it promised a future when bread could once again be made from unadulterated flour. In the event, this was not to be until 1954. Interestingly, although bread had not been rationed during the war, it had become so in the early post-war years.

We left Southampton on the Saturday afternoon, steaming slowly along the south coast. At dusk we went on deck to catch our last

The author and his wife Het taking (her first, and only!) tea on board *Queen Elizabeth* en route to the USA, January 1948.

glimpse of England. Finally, with the lights of the Eddystone Light-house disappearing in our wake, we made our way to the dining room where we again marvelled at the sumptuousness of the décor and the quality and variety of food. Het was not to know that this was to be her last meal there. Next morning she was so stricken with sea-sickness that she did not leave the cabin, and rarely her bunk, for the rest of the voyage.

Although only just four, Elisabeth made her own way to the nursery every day where she became friends with the six-year-old son of the popular British actor, David Niven. He had remarried just before the ship sailed and was on the *Queen Elizabeth* honeymooning with his new wife, a Swedish model. We had known his late wife, Primrose, quite well when she was a WAAF officer. She had died in 1946 after falling down the cellar steps at their home in Hollywood.

After enduring a very rough voyage, we at last arrived in New York on the Thursday afternoon. As the ship was not fitted with stabilisers, she was forced to slow down so much that we eventually docked twenty-eight hours late. Noon on that Thursday saw us on deck as the skyline of New York came into view. Seeing the Statue of Liberty I remember wondering about the welcome I would receive from the United States Air Force and how different life would be from that in a still bleak Britain.

We were met by an agent, an American employed by the British Government. His job was to expedite the passage through customs of those diplomats and servicemen taking up posts in the United States. Although he undoubtedly made use of his know-how, it seemed that we waited an inordinately long time in the bitter cold of the open customs sheds. When all business was completed we made our way through swirls of snow to a car in which he chauffeured us through Manhattan's rush hour traffic en-route to the Governor Clinton Hotel. There I gave him what I considered to be a huge tip. During my briefing in London I had been told how much to tip and had queried the amount, but was advised that this was what must be paid. I did as ordered. I began to understand how things worked in the US.

That evening we ventured out to do some sightseeing but the weather was so bitter that we managed no more than the Empire State Building. There, in the express lift, we were whisked at speed to the thirty-second floor, where we felt compelled to 'acclimatise' by having a hamburger and Coca Cola. It was my first and last.

Next morning we realised how many differences, albeit minor, that we were about to encounter. Upon arriving in the dining room for breakfast, we were directed to the coffee shop where our breakfast order consisted of fried eggs, 'sunny side up' accompanied by wafer-thin, crispy bacon and buckwheat pancakes with, to our amazement, maple syrup. The next day, sitting on high stools at the counter of the same coffee shop, we learned that if we wanted what we had always known as sausages, we must ask for 'links'. We also learned that to get what we called bacon we should ask for Canadian bacon. There was a whole new vocabulary to be learned.

For our trip to Washington the next morning we had only to cross the road to the Penn Station terminus of the Pennsylvania railroad. Here again it was an adventure in itself finding our way around this vast, bustling and noisy station as there was intense activity everywhere. Huge engines were belching out steam ready for the off. Red-hatted porters (Red Caps) seemed to be milling around everywhere.

Elisabeth, presuming that their skin colour was caused by the smoky atmosphere, asked her mother whether her face was also black. That, at the age of four in 1948, she had never seen a black person, illustrates graphically how great has been the change in the last fifty years from what we used to call 'Merrie England' to today's multi-cultural Britain.

On boarding the train we settled into a superbly furnished Pullman coach, red-curtained and tastefully upholstered with tables and red table lamps. We felt that this was a little ahead of the Great Western Railway on which we had journeyed to Paddington a few days previously.

Our four nights in Washington were spent at the Graylyn Hotel, just off Connecticut Circle. That first night, undeterred by the snow, we walked down an almost deserted Pennsylvania Avenue as far as the floodlit White House. This was an impressive sight, tempered somewhat by, what seemed to us, a profligate use of electricity. The brightly lit shop windows had been a pleasant surprise. Understandably we were chiefly fascinated by the fully stocked liquor shops and the huge car lots filled to capacity. At home drinks and cars were at the top of our list of shortages.

We then spent Sunday with Zulu Morris, who had been SASO of 84 Group during the campaign in northern Europe, and who was now a student at the US National Defense College. I was to succeed him eighteen years later as commander-in-chief of Fighter Command. On the Monday morning I reported to British Joint Services Mission (BJSM) for further briefings and on the Wednesday evening we set out on the last leg of our journey by taking the overnight ferry to Norfolk, Virginia. When we arrived to embark at Washington's Fisherman's Wharf we were somewhat surprised to find that we were to board a rather ancient-looking paddle steamer. It was no doubt adequately equipped for the job but the crunching noises made when we failed to avoid the floating ice blocks did cause us some alarm. However, after clearing the Potomac for the open sea, all was well.

We arrived at the Norfolk naval base at 7.00 a.m. There, awaiting our arrival, was the car we had bought from a British colonel on the previous course who was now safely back in Camberley. What a sad sight; we soon discovered that it was well known in those parts as the Purple Peril. We were very quickly to discover that its mechanical deficiencies did indeed make it perilous.

We set out in the Purple Peril along the coast road to Virginia Beach, about twenty miles away. There we took over a house from my RAF predecessor on No.2 Course. This grey clapboard house was within a few yards of the ocean, overlooking a deserted beach washed by a dull, angry sea. The house itself, usually a summer-only letting, was sparsely furnished and lacking those comforts we had been expecting. This did nothing to lift our spirits. However, our landlords the Halls, who lived close by, were very welcoming. Throughout the whole of our time there they were most helpful and hospitable. They were Southerners through and through with their oft-declared dislike of Yankees and 'white trash'. During our first week there we had the first fall of snow for forty years; which caused great excitement. The naval base was closed for the first time ever. Much impromptu partying ensued.

With the coming of an early spring only a few weeks later, we knew we were going to love living there. We very much enjoyed the rest of the five months that we lived in that house. Our newly-found American friends loved it too. Living in rather cramped apartments on the naval base, they frequently made a point of getting out to the beach at weekends where they treated our house as their headquarters. With duty-free gin at eight shillings a bottle and a four-bushel sack of oysters costing five shillings, we could afford to entertain lavishly. However, they never could understand how or why we drank hot tea even when the temperature was in the 80s.

Virginia Beach was a fashionable resort dominated by the Cavalier Hotel built at the turn of the century by a railway millionaire. This, and the town itself, were 'restricted'. It was some time before I learned that this meant that no Jews were allowed there. Garden City on Long Island, where we lived later, was similarly restricted. This was in 1948 in the 'Land of the Free'.

Elisabeth went to Mrs Everett's, a private school. There she quickly learned much that no doubt helped later when she became an American citizen. Returning home on her second day, she asked her mother if she knew that George Washington was our first president. She was far from popular when Pearl Harbor was mentioned and she told her teacher that her daddy said: "Pearl Harbor was where the Americans were caught with their pants down!"

My day started early as, in order to get to the Armed Forces Staff College by 8.00 a.m., I had to leave at 6.15 as Virginia Beach was in a different time zone. Our work, consisting of lectures, exercises and visits, was taken fairly light-heartedly by the four British officers there. In addition to the 100 US students, there were also three Canadians. We seven made up some sort of opposition, united in argument. The Americans treated the course far more seriously than we did. They had more to lose! They diligently read all the set books. We did not. At the end of June however we all graduated and received our 'sheep-skins'.

For us the social activities were the highlight of the course. We never missed the weekly Friday night dances. There we heard for the first time many of the 'state songs', such as The Eyes of Texas are Upon You, Way Back in Indiana and The Blue Ridge Mountains of Virginia. The last dance was always Bongo, Bongo, Bongo, I Don't Want to Leave the Congo. We certainly had fun.

In celebration of the silver wedding of King George VI and Queen Elizabeth, the British and Canadian contingent, with the help of our duty-free allowances, gave a party for about 100 people. This was re-garded as the social highlight of the course. Invitations were eagerly sought after. Most of the American women bought new dresses for what they insisted on calling 'The Silvo Wedding'.

We made several lifelong friends at the staff college with whom we got together whenever we went to the States and whenever they were assigned to Europe. Amongst these was Davy Jones who arrived in Norfolk in 1951 to command the newly-opened USAF bomber base at Sculthorpe on the very same day that I arrived to be group captain flying at the Central Fighter Establishment at West Raynham five miles away. In 1968 when I was C-in-C Fighter Command, Het and I and a team from the headquarters visited him in Florida where he was the general in charge of the rocket base there. Throughout his career he was known as 'Tokyo Jones' as he had been on the Dolittle Raid in 1942, made famous by the order: "Fly there, find your own way home."

Another was Frank Murdoch who had married Denny in 1944 in Hampshire, where he was stationed prior to D-Day. She was the widow of a pilot killed in action in August 1940, a few weeks before their daughter was born. Her brother, Peter Powell, whom I knew well, had also flown in the Battle of Britain. She was a great-niece of Baden-Powell, founder of the Boy Scout Movement. Denny made herself known to us at the 'welcome reception' where we had the new experience of being greeted and passed down the line of thirteen generals and their wives.

We stayed with the Murdochs in Paris in 1956 and Verona in 1965 and also, following his retirement as a brigadier general, on their farm near Roanoke, Virginia where he was rearing and training horses, helped by two horse-mad daughters. All of his family of one son and four daughters had inherited his skill and interest in horses. He had been in the US riding team in the 1948 Olympics and a member of the 7th Cavalry before the war and before mechanisation. In 1950 we had accompanied the Murdochs to West Point for Frank's fifteenth class reunion. There I was made an honorary member of the 7th Cavalry. I was to work with a number of them later in NATO and in particular in CENTO where in Ankara in 1970 there were three generals who were all former 7th Cavalry officers.

When the course ended in early July we went our separate ways. I was posted to Continental Air Command (ConAC). ConAC, under General George Stratemeyer, and based at Mitchel Air Force Base 'Mitchell Field' on Long Island just outside New York, was tasked with establishing an Air Defense Command. At the time General Gordon Seville, who was shortly to be followed by General Bob Webster, was in charge of Eastern Air Defense Force. As a result of their efforts, Air Defense Command was finally established in 1951. Then, under General Ennis Whitehead ('Ennis the Menace'), it moved to Colorado Springs where, playing a vital part in the US security, it has remained to this day.

I had been given the choice of going to Mitchel or to the Tactical Air Force Headquarters at Langley Field. Having worked in the tactical world since 1941, I thought it time for a change. The Berlin Air Lift, which was taking place at this time, made me aware that in the further necessary developments of air defence, there would be much interesting work.

We left Virginia Beach, taking the ferry across to Cape Henry, and drove to New York overnight. Hampton Roads, which abounded with ferries in those days, is now criss-crossed with long, high bridges. However we were not in the Purple Peril which had lasted less than a month. There was general agreement that I had been conned; yet another financial mistake! With our meagre dollar allowance the necessary purchase of another car had been difficult. Finally, we had acquired a brand-new Austin A40. Unfortunately this was another financial disaster. I had paid for it at four dollars to the pound two days before Sir Stafford Cripps devalued the pound to two dollars-eighty cents, despite his constant assurances that he would never do so. This confirmed my opinion about politicians.

MITCHELL FIELD, LONG ISLAND
JULY 1948-JUNE 1950

On reporting for duty at ConAC HQ I found I was assigned to research evaluation which suited me well. However, although everyone in the office was welcoming and friendly, I quickly became aware that I was simply marking time. No work of any importance was passed to me. Papers marked 'secret' by-passed me completely. After six weeks of having virtually nothing to do, I asked to see the general. I explained to him that as I could see no point in wasting my time there, I was about to write to Tedder, then CAS, to ask for my recall. This would obviously reflect badly on the much-heralded exchange programme just introduced between the two air forces. The general apparently got on to the Pentagon straight away and I was told the very next afternoon that I was 'fully cleared'. From then on I was to take part in every aspect of the development of Air Defense Command.

We were an enthusiastic bunch. We travelled widely mostly flying ourselves. As a result, during my time at Mitchell Field I qualified to fly the F80, the F84 and F86, the B25 and B26 and the C47. We made frequent visits to Boston where, at the Massachusetts Institute of Technology (MIT), a department had been set up solely for the development of air defence. We regularly visited aircraft factories, most of which were situated on the West Coast; I must have made half a dozen trips to Lockheeds in California and we visited USAF bases all over the US. Little did I think on my visits to Coco Beach in Florida that it would develop into Cape Canaveral and the Kennedy Space Center.

Nor did I imagine that, when we attended the official opening of the small Idlewild Airport nearby on Long Island, it would eventually become New York's Kennedy Airport.

There were lighter sides to our 'business trips'. We would fly up to Maine with the sole object of bringing back lobsters for pre-arranged office lobster suppers. On one trip my co-pilot, Colonel Cary, and I found time to fly the length of the Grand Canyon. With some luck we managed to be in Indianapolis for their annual motor racing bonanza, the Indianapolis 500. The fact that the USAF worked on a system known as 'cutting your own orders' was a great help. I can remember that only once was a trip cancelled because there was nothing left in the budget that month.

During my tour I spent a few days flying F84s as a member of a fighter squadron at Otis Field, Cape Cod and at Selfridge Field near Detroit. I even gave a lecture on air defence at the Air University at Maxwell Field, Montgomery, Alabama.

At that time great changes were taking place as the USAF had become a separate service and was no longer the US Army Air Force. Although very keen on this development, the officers were reluctant to give up their old, fine quality, gabardine uniforms. They disliked the blue lightweight material of what they deemed a badly designed new uniform. They loved their 'olives' and their 'pinks' which they mixed and matched at will. It was inevitable that the wearing of the new uniform would become compulsory. When we left in June 1950 all were wearing blue.

The order for racial integration was put into effect at that time. This resulted in three very smartly dressed wives of three black officers turning up at the officers' club for the first time in February 1949 for a Valentine's Day lunch, which it so happened was being hosted by the wives of 'our' office. Consternation reigned. After a 'pow-wow' Het was allowed to talk to them, but on no account was she to introduce them to anyone else. That, unbelievably, was the state of things in the US in 1949.

On my many visits to the US Air Force since then I have observed the great progress that has been made in this area. I have always thought what brave pioneers those three wives were. Het never fails to remind me that at that time in the UK women were not allowed into the RAF Club through the main door in Piccadilly. They had to enter through a door in a side street which was especially reserved for women and for officers' baggage!

I was determined that we should see as much as possible of the US. Whenever I went on attachments to fighter squadrons Het and Elisabeth came too. We had ten days at Otis Field on Cape Cod when I was attached to a F84 squadron. There, we were able to explore and take part in the activities of this fashionable holiday playground. We visited the summer theatres which flourished there and saw a New York production of 'The Second Mrs Tanqueray'. Playing the lead was a very well known actress, Tallulah Bankhead.

Het and Lis also came on my attachment to an F84 squadron at Selfridge Field, near Detroit, from where we went on to Toronto and came home via Niagara Falls. We had previously been on two other Canadian trips to Montreal and Ottawa. Compared with the USA, Canada seemed terribly old-fashioned. Forgetting about Britain, we found it hard to believe that there were places where shops still closed at noon on Saturday! However, in Canada we felt at home again. Everywhere there were posters stating 'Buy British' and 'British is Best'.

In the summer of 1949 I returned to England for a few days to attend the annual 'fighter tactical convention' at the Central Fighter Establishment at West Raynham. There I met many old friends.

That autumn we drove to Boston along the Maple Leaf Trail. In winter we skied in the Adirondacks in upstate New York and we made frequent trips to nearby Coney Island in the summer. We also got to know New York City very well. We went to Carnegie Hall a number of times and at the Metropolitan Opera House saw Margot Fontaine appearing with the Royal Ballet on its first overseas tour.

We were lucky to attend a New York 'society wedding'. A poverty-stricken friend of mine, Wing Commander Hedley Cliff, was marrying Tucky Astor. In 1949 she held the record for having received a one million dollar alimony settlement. The champagne flowed very freely at the reception during which Het was admonished by Tucky's cousin Gloria, then in her eighties, because the new British Ambassador, Sir Oliver Franks, had been in the US for a month but had not yet called on her. Het made the excuse that he was only forty-two, thus inferring that he had a lot to learn and no doubt wisdom would come with age.

This excuse was dismissed by Gloria Astor. And Het felt that the only way to hold her own was to refuse Gloria's invitation to have tea with the Duke and Duchess of Windsor on the following Sunday afternoon, as 'she had a previous luncheon engagement'. I knew nothing of this until the next morning when she shot up in bed and told me that we had refused to have tea with the Windsors. She warned me that I was not to tell anyone, especially our lunch guests the Ashkins! Of course I did. Nearly fifty years later, whilst staying with them in Santa Barbara, California, they still remembered this incident and told us that they had wondered if we were quite sane. No doubt this is the reason that we got on so well. Jane Ashkins became David's godmother.

In April 1950 I took three weeks leave with the sole purpose of seeing more of the States. I was conscious of the fact that Het had not seen as much of the country as I had. Unfortunately, we had neither the time nor money to go further west than New Orleans. We started by driving through the Carolinas to the Deep South where, in the acres and acres of cotton fields, the cotton was still being picked by hand.

In New Orleans we did all that tourists were expected to do. We had dinner at Antoines, where we ate Oysters Rockefeller. We then made our way from one end to the other of Basin Street listening to a variety of bands playing jazz and the blues.

From New Orleans we made our way along the Gulf coast of Florida where we stayed for a few days at Sarasota. It was then a village comprised almost entirely of the winter quarters of the Ringling Brothers and Barnum and Bailey Circus. At the Ringling Hotel, where we were staying, we met a number of the performers. When Het arrived from putting Elisabeth to bed she was surprised to find me chatting at the bar with Bette Davis. She managed to whisper to me, but the name meant nothing.

We were welcomed heartily by a brother and sister acrobatic team from the circus. Despite the broadest of Yorkshire accents, having been born near Sheffield, they were known as the 'Great Alanzas'. They kept their promise to invite us to Madison Square Garden when the circus opened in New York. We were most impressed by their very daring performance and appreciated their kindness in inviting us backstage

After Sarasota we decided to return to Long Island by driving up the Atlantic coast. This entailed crossing the Everglades to Miami. In those days this was regarded as quite an adventurous trip as it was not until some time later that the Everglades were opened up as a tourist attraction. As Miami did not appeal to us, we stayed at a small village a few miles to the north. Returning there forty years on we marvelled how it had grown into Fort Lauderdale, the starting point or port of call for most Caribbean cruises.

The next morning we drove further north to Daytona Beach where we spent a week. We were attracted by the long stretch of silver sands where the British driver, Sir Henry Segrave, had broken the world land-speed record in 1927. Thirty years later, whenever we stayed with Elisabeth and her husband who was working at the Space Center in Florida, we always paid Daytona a nostalgic visit. Driving on the beach is still permitted to the general public.

Within ten days of returning to Mitchell Field I was told that my tour had been curtailed. I had been posted to the directing staff of the Joint Services Staff College at Latimer in Buckinghamshire. My superiors thought that I should get to know the ropes by reporting there for the last few weeks of the current course, which ended in late July. After that I could have my disembarkation leave until the next course began in early September.

On 31st May I was told that we would be leaving on Saturday 10th June on the Cunard liner, the *Caronia*. Panic ensued. There was much to be done as we had not yet purchased many of the goods that we wanted which were not obtainable back in Britain. Our American friends panicked too. Every single night we attended farewell parties. At one, neither Het nor I could recollect ever having previously met the hosts. Obviously any excuse for a party!

After ten hectic days of shopping, which also involved some 'weight guessing', came the fateful day. The weight guessing was necessary because of the constant reminder from BJSM (British Joint Services Mission), Washington that if we had goods in excess of a wing commander's weight allowance we would have to pay for them. I recognise now how foolish we must have seemed to the salesman who was selling us a washing machine. We insisted on lifting the various machines and bought the one we judged to be the lightest, not the one that we thought was probably the best.

At about 10.00 a.m. on the day we were due to leave, a motorcade of five cars turned up to take us to Pier 9D on Manhattan Island. On boarding the *Caronia* about twenty people, including my commanding general, General Webster, and his wife, squeezed into our cabin for a cheerful farewell party. Het missed more of the party than she had bargained for. She had deemed it her motherly duty to take Elisabeth to the Empire State Building for a final viewing of New York. Our cabin jollifications had gone on for some time before I realised that my wife and daughter were missing. I left immediately in search of them. It transpired that the flight sergeant with whom I had entrusted their boarding passes had failed to recognise Het in the smart new hat that she had not been able to resist buying on her way to the ship. As a result she had been waiting on the dock for an hour and was so angry that she threatened not to return to the UK with me. I thought it most unfair as she was the one who had bought the hat!

At 2.30 p.m. we weighed anchor. The owners of the tugs operating in New York harbour were the Gillans, friends who lived near us at Rockville Center, Long Island. They had warned us that the tug masters had been told that when casting the *Caronia* free they were to give three farewell toots rather than the usual two. Apparently three toots were given only when VIPs were on board. Meanwhile our friends had rushed to the Staten Island ferry. As we sailed past the Statue of Liberty we glimpsed them waving until we disappeared from sight.

After our hectic final few days we were ready to relax on what was virtually to be a seven-day summer cruise. I was delighted to find an old friend, Tubby Butler, on board who was returning from a two-year posting at the Pentagon. He was later to command the Parachute Brigade at Suez and later still became a four-star general. He was excellent company although his behaviour was somewhat unorthodox! His notoriety stemmed from the fact that before the war, whilst serving as an ADC, he had eloped with his general's wife. He had been forced to leave the army but at the start of war had rejoined as a private soldier. All was forgiven by the authorities but not, I believe, by the general himself. He was re-commissioned and, when the general agreed to a divorce in 1941, married the general's former wife. She and her eighteen-year-old daughter were with him. With his usual charm and Irish blarney he soon made his mark with the head barman.

As a result he volunteered to introduce us to the customs officer when he came aboard from his launch before we docked at Southampton on the Saturday morning.

We were duly introduced and after a drink or two he got down to business. We answered all questions in line with his promptings. He returned with us to our cabins, put some chalk squiggles on our luggage and finally gave us instructions concerning the number of the customs desk that we were to use. There we were charged £3 for all the goods we had accumulated during our two-year stay in the United States which included a smart fur jacket, a washing machine, a waffle iron, some long-playing records that were not available in the UK, and about a dozen pairs of nylon stockings which were available but not easily obtainable.

It had been our intention to drive away in my Austin A40 which had accompanied us on the *Caronia*. However, we took a rather jaundiced view of our motherland when we were told by customs that, as it was nearing noon, it was too late to contact my bank to find out whether my cheque to the car licensing authorities could be met. Despite my protestations, we were told to return on Monday at 11.00 a.m. We therefore spent the weekend at our friends the McEvoys at Kenley, where Mac was the AOC of a flying training group. On the Monday morning, having collected our car, we left for North Wales where Het and Lis stayed for the next two months. Since leaving in January 1948 we had lived in five houses and Elisabeth had attended three schools.

Chapter 10

RETURN TO
DUTY IN THE UK

JOINT SERVICES STAFF COLLEGE, LATIMER
JULY 1950-APRIL 1952

After less than a week at home in Wrexham, I reported to Air Ministry for an intensive debriefing, lasting three days. From there I left for the Joint Services Staff College (JSSC) at Latimer for the final three weeks of Course 6, at the end of which I was able to take five weeks disembarkation leave. After these first weeks I had the feeling that we were going to enjoy this posting. Much as we had appreciated our stay in the United States, I felt we were ready for what promised to be a pleasant interlude back in rural England.

Latimer House, near Chesham, was situated above the River Chess in delightful Buckinghamshire countryside. The house in which I was to work reminded me of Hampton Court. The beautiful stacks of tall octagonal chimney shafts were particularly pleasing to the eye. The interior of the house which could best be described as Victorian Gothic was disappointing. After a fire in 1830, it was recreated in what was then a popular style. In addition, in 1950 there was still evidence of the adaptations that had been made to enable it to fulfil its wartime role as a prisoner of war reception centre.

Early in 1942, Latimer had become the permanent home of a so-called distribution centre. Which was in fact the Combined Services

Detailed Interrogation Centre. Where all high-ranking German prisoners of war were held for a few months before being assigned to a
prisoner of war camp in South Wales. In 1950 some students were oc-
cupying the still unmodernised cells of the wartime prisoners. As a bit
of memorabilia, the central watch tower was still there. The students
professed to believe that the directing staff used it for spying on them.
How else could we have such detailed knowledge of the students' 'go-
ings on'? Actually, one or two of us had infiltrated the 'enemy' as lots
of fun was always to be had.

The JSSC had been established in 1947 'to nourish among the
higher command of all services that mutual understanding and com-
radeship which had been so successful in war'. When I arrived in September 1950, these aims had been further clarified. By then the stated
purpose was 'the training of officers to fill appointments on joint staffs
by widening their knowledge of subjects with which as staff officers
they might have to deal'. Most important was the development of a
mutual understanding between the services.

There were seventy-two students consisting of British officers from
all three services, Commonwealth and United States service representatives, and five first class civilians. I was one of the four RAF officers
who were members of the fifteen-strong directing staff.

On reporting to the commandant, Major-General Bill Stratton, he
made it clear to me that as the students were of much the same rank
and age as the directing staff co-operation was the name of the game.
This was so different from the way we war-battered students had been
treated at the RAF Staff College. Most of the students had recent active
service experience in ranks often higher than those they then held.
DSO and DSC was as frequent a collection of letters after the name of
naval students as DSO and MC was of the army students and DSO
and DFC was of the RAF men.

We DS found we had much to learn from our students who were
eager to share their experiences. I was constantly impressed by the
way, often reluctantly and modestly, we were told of the nature and
reasons behind the decisions they had made in highly dangerous sit-
uations. These usually had resulted in acts of great gallantry. Amongst
the worthy warriors in my first syndicate was Willie Tate, the most
highly decorated bomber pilot who, amongst other achievements, was

credited with sinking the *Scharnhorst*. Rather shyly, he explained to us the tactics he had employed in finding and sinking this most elusive of German battle cruisers.

Another syndicate member was Lieutenant Colonel Mike Carver whom I had known in the Western Desert. As a brigadier at the age of twenty-seven, he served in the 7th Armoured Division (The Desert Rats) at the Battle of El Alamein in 1942. As directors of army and RAF planning respectively, we were to work together in 1960 as joint planners under Lord Mountbatten. We made great efforts to understand each other's viewpoints (some in our respective services thought too much!). Many years later Field Marshal Lord Carver, a former CDS, took it in good humour when I pointed out that much of his success in life should be attributed to my guidance.

During my time at Latimer the way that world politics was evolving, and the development of new weapons, resulted in less time being spent discussing the past and more focus given to the future. We arranged visits to Portsmouth, Salisbury Plain and Germany, where we saw some of the new ideas in navy, army and air force thinking in the process of being tested. In addition, exchange visits began with the French École Supèrior, and my old alma mater, the American Armed Forces Staff College.

In early August 1950, we journeyed from Wrexham to Amersham with the intention of finding a furnished house somewhere in that area. We stayed at The Crown where on our first evening we met a Mr Aston who was on leave from Penang where he was the British Resident. We were invited to have a drink at his home in Old Amersham, which he was looking to rent out. We so liked Wych Cottage that we thought it was worth waiting the ten weeks until he returned to Penang in November, despite the fact that we would have to find somewhere to stay for the interim.

Luckily, we were able to find accommodation in a wing of a large Victorian house at The Lee, a village in the Chilterns above Great Missenden. Our landlady, Mrs Stainer, was the widow of a former organist at Westminster Abbey, composer of Stainer's Crucifixion. She was exceedingly kind and helpful to us. Over fifty years later, Elisabeth told us of a different recollection. She remembers her as a very bad-tempered old woman. No doubt she was on the Sunday morning when she was woken by Elisabeth playing in her drawing room with her antique spinning wheel.

It was on Mrs Stainer's recommendation that Elisabeth had her first taste of English schooling at Hyde House, Hyde Heath. Usually I dropped her off by taking a roundabout route to Latimer; but when I was away on exercise, she had to cycle the four miles accompanied by Het on a borrowed ramshackle bicycle. How Het hated those early morning sorties negotiating the steep ups and downs of the Chiltern country lanes. When we moved to Amersham, Elisabeth was able to continue at Hyde House, catching public transport from almost outside our front door to where she was able to board the school bus at Amersham on the Hill. Later, from our Latimer quarter, she arrived at school 'in state' in a service car driven by a WRAF corporal. Elisabeth felt she was unjustly treated when on one occasion the headmistress upbraided her – not the driver whom she had spied gathering daffodils which were growing in profusion on either side of the drive.

When we left The Lee in late November 1950, we took it for granted that we would be spending the rest of the tour at Wych Cottage in Amersham. However, ten months later, we moved again to some newly built quarters within the grounds of Latimer House.

With the JSSC now firmly established, the Treasury was persuaded that the time had come for domestic development. The cricket ground (formerly used by Latimer village) was made playable once again, squash courts were built and two blocks of semi-detached married quarters were built overlooking the picturesque cricket field. These four quarters were occupied by DS with an RAF preponderance of three to one. I should mention here that there was so little house building after the war that to get four houses built at Latimer was truly an achievement. Moving in in September 1951 amidst an indescribable amount of mud and builders' rubble, we suffered from a number of teething troubles, which we attributed to post-war shortages. Luckily we had very little of that same teething trouble from our son, David, who was by then five months old. He had arrived on the first day of Course 8. This was not really the most convenient time for me as I had to leave the 'Assembly Party' early just in time for a fast drive at midnight with Het to RAF Hospital Halton. An excellent start to the course!

When we moved to 'Cathedral Precincts', a name laughingly conjured up by the student body, we became involved in the action at Latimer House and got better acquainted with the students, the majority of whom chose to be weekly boarders. My old friend, 'Splinters' Smallwood, and fellow DS, and I had realised at our first official cocktail party that there was a serious lack of 'spiritual knowledge' in the entertainment committee. We inveigled ourselves into the job of joint bar officers and straight away upgraded the bitterly criticised 'Squirrels Widdle' to a stronger and tastier potion. Everyone was most grateful. Not so Het. She wasn't too pleased to have to cope with my 'exuberance' caused by the prolonged mixing and tasting needed to produce such an excellent brew.

I remember that for a payment of two shillings (ten pence) every Friday, I collected from the kitchen garden as much produce as we could possibly need. The head gardener, who had been there for at least forty years, told me that at one time in 1944 he had had twenty-three German and Italian generals working for him!

During my time at Latimer, I kept up my flying – mostly Tiger Moths – at Booker, a civilian grass airfield on the Chilterns overlooking High Wycombe. Being only about twenty miles away, student friends were always happy to accept a lift to their distant homes. I always hoped that, as a result, the military would appreciate the value of the air arm!

In early January 1952, half way through my third course as a DS, I was told that my next posting was to be as group captain flying at the Central Fighter Establishment at West Raynham in Norfolk. I was overjoyed, not only was I going back to flying but I was also to be promoted.

I spent the whole of that February in the RAF Hospital Halton. During the war, I had developed a stomach ulcer which, for some years, had been giving me lots of pain. Despite various 'cures', I was in constant pain. The doctors recommended surgery but ultimately agreed to try medication consisting of four weeks of rest and sedation. It worked; but regrettably only for a few months.

Six weeks later in early April, we left for West Raynham in the wilds of Norfolk.

CENTRAL FIGHTER ESTABLISH-MENT, WEST RAYNHAM APRIL 1952-FEBRUARY 1954

In early April 1952 I arrived at West Raynham in Norfolk, the place where every keen fighter pilot had dreams of being posted. The Central Fighter Establishment (CFE) was the academy of air fighting, the testing ground for all new ideas about fighter operations. It had been founded in 1944 at Tangmere by expanding a unit whose mission was 'to promote leadership, efficiency and skill in both the interception and ground-attack roles'. In 1945 this unit was moved to West Raynham, where its functions were further expanded to take in all test functions of fighter operations. Here, these most fortunate pilots were controlled by newly-developed radar systems, whilst flying the newest fighter aircraft equipped with the latest instruments and weapons.

On the operational side there were three main units: **The Air Fighting Development Squadron (AFDS)**. This unit was concerned with day fighting tactics and techniques. Much of the work was secret, e.g. research into high altitude interception techniques. At first, the Meteor was used until the eagerly awaited Hunter arrived in 1954 for general handling trials. Many improvements in air-frame and engine design came from close relations with the aircraft industry and with test pilots.

The second was: **The All-Weather Wing.** This unit was responsible for the development of night and all-weather operational procedures, i.e. where the target cannot be seen. Here there was even closer secrecy than in AFDS as the wing was concerned with developing an all-weather fighter.

Finally there was: **The Interception Analysis Unit.** This unit specialised in controlling aircraft interception and the investigation of air control problems. It was felt essential that facilities on the ground should keep up with those in the air.

These three units liaised closely with the aircraft industry, the RAF research establishments at Farnborough and Boscombe Down, and the radar research unit at Malvern. There were frequent visits to and from Eglin Field in Florida where there was a unit similar to CFE. This liaison was felt to be of so much importance that for a number of years an RAF group captain was on exchange duty there. In my time the post was held by Teddy Morris, my long-time friend from Desert Air Force days. Later, he became our son John's godfather. At CFE we had an exchange USAF captain flying with the air fighting development boys.

In addition, there were two training units: firstly, **The Day Fighter Leader's School**. This was the original unit from which CFE had evolved. It had continued in its aim of promoting leadership, efficiency and skill in interception and ground-attack roles. The six-week course, comprising forty-six sorties, was attended by RAF officers from all over the world joined by members of the Fleet Air Arm and Commonwealth air forces. All aspects of fighter operations were undertaken. They learned from each other's experiences as the briefing and leading was done by the students themselves whist the staff flew in subordinate positions. Debriefings between staff and students often resulted in the modification of operational procedures and techniques.

The second training unit was the **Instrument Training Squadron**. This unit undertook the training of selected pilots to become instrument rating examiners. The aim was that they should go back to their squadrons and take responsibility for instructing and testing their colleagues on 'instrument flying'.

I loved the CFE as I was back on a flying station and flew almost every day, initially mainly in the different marks of Meteor at the station. On 21st July 1952 I note from my log book that I took a trip down memory lane by flying a Tiger Moth to RAF Hospital Halton for an X-ray on what turned out to be a stomach ulcer, returning the next day.

During my time at the CFE I also flew Venoms and Vampires, F84s and Swifts.

Situated in sparsely populated north-west Norfolk, West Raynham was designated a 'remote station'. As such every month we were entitled to a long weekend off from Friday mid-day until Monday night.

This special leave was granted 'subject to the exigencies of the service'. We saw to it that there were no 'exigencies' on these weekends.

On the Monday nights coaches filled with mostly reluctant airmen left Marble Arch at midnight bound for West Raynham. These were the days of National Service! We 'regulars' looked forward to this break and usually spent a day in Norwich. Though little more than thirty miles away, it took one-and-a-half hours along the winding country roads of Norfolk. Sometimes we would visit King's Lynn which was nineteen miles away. Before going we always compiled lists of those things we were not able to get in the small market town of Fakenham seven miles away. With no bus service, West Raynham was rightly dubbed 'remote'.

It was four-and-a-half years since we had last lived amongst RAF folk. Although I was excited at the prospect, Het thought that returning to life on a remote airfield was for her a somewhat retrograde step. She felt that life in America and amongst the army and navy at Latimer had broadened her outlook. We moved into a large married quarter on the patch and for a few weeks Het was depressed. However, things soon looked up. We quickly made friends and it is no exaggeration to say that we made more lasting friendships at West Raynham than at any other time in our service life. The Rosiers, the Bird-Wilsons, the Ricky Wrights, the Freers, the Boxers, the Oxprings, the Waltons, the Frank Davisons in Adelaide and the Hugh Tudors have always kept closely in touch.

Ricky Wright and Birdie, both Battle of Britain pilots, became god-fathers of Nicholas when he was christened in the station church on Battle of Britain Sunday 1953. The closeness that developed between us was undoubtedly the result of West Raynham's remote situation. As a result we relied upon each other for so much. Very few Saturday nights went by without a party in the mess. Most of these were hosted and organised by one or other of the various sections. We flying chaps were normally able to find some 'business' reason for flying to Germany earlier in the week and we returned with duty-free drink for the party.

I note from my log book that from 10th to 16th August 1952 the Commandant Air Commodore Paddy Crisham and I spent some time in Germany initially flying in an Anson to Gütersloh. On that trip I flew a Vampire from Wunstorf. For the same reason it was only with much prompting that the earth-bound engineering officers gave a party. Poor chaps, their supplies had to be obtained locally from the much-maligned station NAAFI which was not noted for its variety of stock or its all-round efficiency. Once it ran out of sugar for four days and this was when it was still rationed. Luckily for our sugarless neighbours we were able to save the day as I had recently returned from Australia with a sack of sugar. This, I had promised an Australian to send to his relatives in the Midlands. Believing that charity began at home I wrote to him with an explanation, but had no acknowledgement!

In the heart of the country with time on our hands, a number of us showed an interest in gardening. We grew our own vegetables, specialising in developing those new species which were first being introduced into post-war Britain. Service men and women posted all over the world had developed a taste for what were in 1952 regarded as the more exotic vegetables such as sweetcorn, spinach and squash.

We became so keen that we formed the West Raynham Gardening Club. The competition became so intense that one member was expelled. He had colluded with a winning exhibitor at the annual show at East Rudham, our nearest village. Shortly after the show his leeks and onions doubled in size overnight. I was also given a warning for using an abandoned Spitfire canopy as a cucumber frame!

There was no Wives' Club as such, but there was friendly co-operation amongst the wives. Thursday mornings saw two or three cars heading for Fakenham. They returned with fresh market produce to supplement our NAAFI fare and garden produce. Cromer crabs were always a must and when in season samphire, a plant with small, fleshy leaves and a taste vaguely resembling asparagus, which grew freely on the dunes during July and August. We used to have a weekly visit by a horse-drawn contraption loaded with samphire freshly picked that morning. We bought it at give-away prices. Forty years later that we saw it again at a top London restaurant at what we thought was a truly outrageous price.

Once a month the wives would change their venue to King's Lynn's

Tuesday market. This trip, which always culminated in a cheerful lunch at the Dukes Head was known to the husbands as 'The Gallivant'.

In 1952 we ran what must have been the first free launderette for our special friends. We were the only ones who possessed a washing machine and an electric iron, both of which we had bought in the United States. In attempting to buy a steam iron in 1954 when Morphy Richards were introducing the iron into the UK, Het, who wanted one for her mother's Christmas present, tried shop after shop in Norfolk. In more than one she was told that they would not be stocking it as 'water and electricity did not mix'.

The highlight of each year was the Tactical Convention held in June, when the CFE presented its most up to date ideas on fighter operations. The experts in the audience were given full opportunity to comment freely on the views expressed and practical conclusions were hammered out. There were also flying and static displays in which the latest fighter aircraft and equipment were put on view. These conventions grew in size and scope. In my time we had more than 300 delegates from all corners of the globe – squadron commanders, wing leaders, sector commanders and fighter station commanders. They were joined by representatives of the Royal Navy, the British army, the air forces of the Dominions and US Air Force and navy representatives. In 1949 I had attended as a representative of the US Air Force Air Defense Command. There was, of course, also a galaxy of distinguished senior officers. Subsequently, a report on the proceedings was circulated throughout the RAF and sent to all the overseas representatives.

During the convention, as well as work there was play in the form of endless official parties. It was a great gathering of friends – what a week it was!

In 1952 we also held a Test Pilot's Convention which the following year was expanded into a Designer's Convention. This audience was composed of designers of fighter aircraft and their test pilots, and the designers of engines and weapons. In addition, there were a few service officers; staff from the Ministry of Supply and staff from the experimental units. The designers of each component of the defence system had the opportunity of seeing how their particular part was keyed into the system by the users of their product.

Another annual event eagerly looked forward to was the long week-end visit of the Auxiliary Air Force. There was some flying, but it was the partying that was enjoyed by all. The wives found them a charming lot! I think they fell for their red socks and the red silk linings of their immaculately cut tunics. Little did I know then that in a very short time as group captain plans at Fighter Command I would recommend the disbandment of the Auxiliary Air Force. Put simply, they were not value for money considering what was being expended on them. Being a fighter pilot had become a full-time job.

The West Raynham balls were the envy of other RAF stations. In those days we had both summer and winter balls. Their theme and organisation was left to the outstanding group of young flight lieutenants whose only interest at that time seemed to be flying and having fun. There were few likely girl-friends in remote Norfolk but their time was well occupied!

There was much social contact between West Raynham and the recently reactivated US Air Force base at Sculthorpe, seven miles away. Two days after our arrival at West Raynham, Davy 'Tokyo' Jones arrived to command the base. He had been a friend since our first days at the Armed Forces Staff College. He it was who invited us to our very first party on our arrival in the United States by asking bluntly: "Hi, you folk. Do you go to parties?" On replying, "Yes, if anyone asks us" we were told the number of his quarters at the naval base where he'd be expecting us at 5.00 p.m. the next day. We left at 6.00 a.m. the following morning! That was the first of many parties we had with Davy. He had been in Stalagluft III with Douglas Bader, Bob Tuck and many other of our friends.

Het likes to think that she helped with the settling in of the American wives. To help them acclimatise, all families were issued with a booklet entitled *Over Here*, which was meant to help them understand our peculiar ways but this lacked explanations of many things that they came across in rural England. She was invited by Davy's wife, Anita, to the Wives' Club meetings where she held a question and answer session. So great was the diversity of the questions that providing answers often tested her ingenuity. The very first question was: "What is a foot?" After further questioning by Het she discovered that the questioner had had an invitation to a village 'fête'. She found it hard to explain what sort of clothes they should wear and what would be going on there.

There were many questions about etiquette and table manners; they particularly found eating lamb chops a problem. The majority had never come across lamb in the USA. The problem was that they were forced to leave so much meat attached to the bone. They were much relieved when she told them that they could pick the bone up as long as they used both hands.

They had been told in *Over Here* that *The Times* was the best paper. They had bought it and were not convinced. Het tentatively suggested *The Daily Telegraph* but advocated a visit to the local newsagent whom she was sure would allow them to peruse his selection before they decided which was the one for them. Throughout she was fortified appropriately by the ladies with Bristol Cream.

1953 was an auspicious year. It started with a bang. We had a new young Queen and General Eisenhower had been sworn in as United States President in January.

That January I was away on a trip to the Far East (during which I saw my brother Bill who, with his family, had recently emigrated to Australia) Het remembers snow storms, driving rain and the continual howling of the wind off the North Sea. When the dykes broke nearer the coast causing extensive damage and loss of life, Queen Elizabeth visited the flooded area to give her support.

On 26th January 1953, I set off in a Hastings on a CFE tour to Singapore, Hong Kong, Australia and New Zealand accompanied by Wing Commanders Oxspring and Bird-Wilson and Squadron Leaders Tudor, Cumming and Wilson and Flight Lieutenant Jenkins. The joy of this trip was that the Hastings was fitted with beds which were much needed as at every stop we had the most 'VIPist' of welcomes. I can recall that when we returned to West Raynham eight weeks later on 24th March we were all exhausted.

June was the Coronation month, looked forward to with much anticipation by everyone. There was a holiday on Coronation Day on 2nd June. The nation celebrated with street parties, with beacons and fireworks. The station also celebrated in style – there was a sports day and parties in the various messes.

In those early days of television Het, David and I watched the

ceremony on a small black and white television in the mess. To everyone's amusement he recognised and shouted out the Duke of Embry's
name.

Elizabeth (aged nine) was lucky enough to be in London with Het's
brother Stewart where she remembers watching the parade in pouring
rain in a seat in front of the new Air Ministry building in Whitehall.
This was also located opposite Downing Street and a great cheer went
up when Sir Winston and Lady Churchill left No.10 for the abbey.
The rain stopped for a short time several hours later as the Gold Coach
came into view glimmering in the sun. The Queen of Tonga was not
so lucky but insisted on waving cheerfully to the crowds in pouring
rain in an open carriage.

Nicholas our second son was born on 15th June – quite a momen-
tous month all round.

Prior to the Queen's Coronation Review at Odiham on 19th July,
much time was spent perfecting the part we were to play. A Swift of
AFDS took part in the fly-past but the *pièce de résistance* was to be the
performance of five Venoms of AFDS led by Wing Commander Bird-
Wilson who were to write 'EIIR' and 'VIVAT' in the sky over Odiham.
We had devised a way of 'painting' in the sky. 'E' was easy, but the 'R'
needed much practising. I think that this was the first time that Venoms were used in that way. Het vividly remembers their return to
Raynham the next morning, when they gave their wives a repeat performance, finishing by swooping perilously low, it seemed, over the
quarters trailing red, white and blue smoke.

The whole station rejoiced in the achievement. Unbelievably, one
miserable wife complained that her washing was soiled by the smoke!
Nowadays, nearly fifty years later, in the grand finale of the Red Arrows
flying displays we see them flying off into the far blue yonder trailing
the same red, white and blue smoke.

I was unable to go to Odiham. This I greatly regretted but my future
in the RAF was my first concern. A few weeks earlier I had been instructed to attend the Central Medical Establishment (CME) in London
for a medical prior to promotion. I was fearful of this as my ulcer was
again troublesome. The station medical officer (MO) hatched a plan
that, with a fortnight in bed under sedation and with his medication
and care, which included a diet of endless rice puddings, he hoped

we would hoodwink the medical fraternity at CME. It did not and I was declared unfit for flying duties. They suggested that I should transfer from the general duties (GD) branch to the administrative or equipment branch. Such a prospect was appalling. I demanded an interview with the head of the medical branch, Air Marshal Sir Aubrey Rumbold, whom I had known well during the war and hoped that he would have some sympathy for me. I told him firmly that I was not leaving until he and I had spoken to Sir Basil Embry, C-in-C of Fighter Command. There I remained until 6.00 p.m. when at last Sir Basil was contacted. The outcome of the conversation was a compromise. I was passed fit for flying as long as I did not fly for more that forty-five minutes at a time. This limitation was soon forgotten!

In 1953 HRH the Duke of Edinburgh resumed his flying training at Raynham, carrying out ground approaches in a De Havilland Chipmunk of The Queen's Flight. Some time before this he had told me that Winston Churchill was very much opposed to his flying. I feel that it was as a result of this that we were invited by the Queen for drinks at Sandringham later in the year.

In January 1954 I went on another trip down memory lane to North Africa. From 2nd to 26th January I flew in my Meteor 8 to North Africa – calling in at many of the airfields I had been at during my time in the Desert Air Force: Tunis, El Adem, Kabrit, Abu Sueir and Habbaniya. During the trip, after a brief visit to Cyprus, I flew to Aden via Wadi Halfa and Khartoum, before returning to West Raynham via Luqa in Malta and Istres in the South of France. During this trip the chief magistrate in Aden found his credulity being questioned when he announced at a party that I attended the same Sunday School as him. This was welcomed with great cheers.

One of the joys of CFE was that I was able to fly so many of the new aircraft types. I note from my log book that on 26th June 1954, having flown to Boscombe Down, I made my first flight in a Hawker Hunter Mark 1 and that there was 'complete hydraulic failure'. Later in the year on 6th October 1954 I flew a B45 from Sculthorpe with Colonel Jones to Heidelberg in Germany, returning the same day.

On 19th October I left on a CFE visit to the USA. We flew in a Constellation from London to New York via Prestwick, Keflavik and Goose Bay. The party was led by Commandant Air Commodore Geoffrey

Stephenson and in addition to myself included Wing Commanders David Mawhood, Ricky Wright and Edward Crew and Squadron Leader Dennis Walton. The purpose of the visit was for us to update ourselves on the latest developments in the air defence of the US.

After the initial briefing at the Pentagon which I see from my notes I described as 'poor as it was superficial and most of the material was well known to us beforehand', the team split into two parties, Air Commodore Stephenson, Mawhood and I leaving for New England to go to MIT, the Cambridge Research Centre, Rome Air Development Centre and the GE factory plant at Syracuse, whilst Wright, Crew and Walton went to the Wright Paterson Air Development Center and Edwards Air Force Base. A week later we joined up in Los Angeles and in three days we visited the factories of the North American, Lockheed, Convair and Hughes, and then went on to the Air Defense Command at Colorado Springs before moving on to Eglin Air Force Base via Kansas City, New Orleans and Pensacola.

Very sadly, during this trip, on 8th November Geoffrey Stephenson was killed, crashing soon after take-off in an F100 at Eglin. A dejected CFE party returned to London from New York on the 12th in a Stratocruiser. Many years later when visiting Elisabeth we went to his grave there among the thirty RAF flying cadets who were killed whilst training at nearby Maxwell Field.

Towards the end of 1954 my next posting came through. I was to be group captain operations at Fighter Command headquarters at Bentley Priory. This was a post that qualified me for immediate occupancy of a married quarter. Two days before we were due to leave for Stanmore, I was telephoned by the Commander-in-Chief Air Marshal Sir Dermot Boyle to be told that my posting had been changed to that of group captain plans which did not automatically entitle me to a quarter! Therefore, we would have to go on the waiting list. Panic ensued in the Rosier household. Two days later just before Christmas I left for Fighter Command. The family remained at West Raynham until March.

Over ten years later, when I was C-in-C Fighter Command I found a letter in a file which explained this last minute change of plan. Unbeknownst to me, my original posting had been changed to Royal Aircraft Establishment (RAE) Farnborough. This was not to the liking of Sir Dermot Boyle who evidently wished to retain me in Fighter Command. Though he fought vigorously it was not until the last moment that 'postings' compromised with him. I could go to Fighter Command HQ but not as group captain operations. I feel sure that this was career planning. I had had much experience of operations, in the Western Desert; of the operations of 84 Group before D-Day and in Europe, but had had no experience of planning.

Very sadly, I missed my farewell party at West Raynham. Every Saturday afternoon I journeyed from London to King's Lynn on 'The Fenman'. On the Saturday afternoon of my party in early February the snow fell so thick and fast that the car that was to collect me from King's Lynn station became snowbound. Thankfully I was rescued by an old school friend's brother who was the town clerk. Whilst I was enjoying quite a good party at the King's Lynn Yacht Club my so-called friends had persuaded Het that she should have the farewell party at West Raynham without me. At about 10.00 p.m. the station MO announced that he had recently been issued with a four-wheel drive ambulance and now was the time to try it out. With four volunteers from the party as medical attendants they battled their way through the snow for the next three hours. Having picked me up in King's Lynn we arrived back at the mess at 3.30 a.m. where most of my guests were awaiting my arrival and continuing the party. They had not left my house until after midnight. I was subsequently particularly sad at the size of my mess bill. Apparently, when my cellar had been drunk dry there were constant phonecalls to the mess for further supplies. Het assures me that at 11.00 p.m. despite encouragement to continue, she vetoed further calls to the mess and moreover, did her best to persuade the guests to go home. They had insisted that it would be extremely impolite not to wait until I arrived at my own party! That night was remembered for many years, not least by me for the size of my mess bill.

Thus our time at West Raynham came to an end. We had both been very happy there, we had gained a third child, Nicholas, and life had been even more interesting than we had anticipated but it was time to move on.

Chapter 11

CLIMBING TO
THE TOP

FIGHTER COMMAND – AGAIN!
1955-1956

I was not exactly filled with joy when, on a cold dreary winter's day in late December 1954, I arrived at Bentley Priory to take up my new post. As I was unable to move into a tied quarter straight away, I was depressed at the prospect of living a bachelor's life in the mess for at least six months. Despite this gloomy outlook, I quickly settled down in 'plans' and soon realised that I had the best group captain's job in the headquarters.

There was a very friendly atmosphere as most of the staff officers were friends who had fought together, had experienced the differing fighter rolls; and had served in most theatres of war. Together there was a vast amount of expertise to be called upon in the planning of a much smaller air force, which had to be adapted to changing world politics. Work was a challenge and a joy as effective plans were vital to contain the expected enemy attacks from the east. There were no signs that the Cold War was getting warmer and plans had to be made that would allow us to deter what we understood to be the threat from the Soviet bloc.

In this role I worked closely with Paddy Dunn who, as air commodore plans, was my immediate boss. Our job was to produce both short and long-term plans to counter the perceived Soviet threat. It was an awesome task. Our long-term plan was to improve our defences everywhere. The short-term plans involved our own Fighter Command stations where we had to make sure that our fighter airfields would be able to operate in the event of an attack on them.

In order to develop these plans, we had meetings with and briefings from all branches of the RAF, the army and the Royal Navy. We also visited the US Air Force bases, SHAPE, NATO HQ in Brussels, MI5, GCHQ in Cheltenham, and the communications station near Malvern. The result of these briefings and visits was the decision that, in times of tension, dispersal would be the solution for the fighter stations. It was further agreed that, to counter any attack by Russia, there would always be aircraft on stand-by for immediate take-off. Reinforced concrete-sided pens were set up on the perimeters of fighter airfields. Aircrew were at readiness day and night. Such was the nature of their job. Thankfully these measures were never put to the test.

The long-term plan demanded much thought and even speculation. Our knowledge of the threat, supplied by the intelligence agencies, was limited. This plan was naturally not published but remained top secret. Over thirty years later in 1989, after the break-up of the Soviet bloc, when much was revealed about the Soviet military machine, it became clear that in its last years we had over-estimated the Russian capabilities. They had problems of their own too.

Whilst living in the mess I decided to reduce the boredom by practising my night-flying. For some reason I targeted West Raynham midweek. Imagine my surprise when I was called in by the AOA to be told that I was doing too much! In those days 'desk wallas' were encouraged by the Air Ministry to keep up their flying skills by getting in as many hours as we could. Consequently, during my time at Bentley Priory I made every effort to keep up my flying, mainly taking a Meteor from Bovingdon. On one occasion in October 1956 I 'borrowed' an Anson for a weekend trip to Scotland. The length of the runway at Leuchars was the sole reason I survived to tell the tale of this trip. Half way down the runway just after taking off, the engines of the Anson made a terrible clanking noise and cut out. I put the Anson down on the remaining runway just coming to a halt seconds before hitting the sea. The subsequent investigation revealed that the

Anson had been refuelled with paraffin rather than aviation fuel. A po-
tentially deadly mistake.

At the beginning of March I took up the offer of a 'hiring' in Dev-
ereux Drive, Watford. After two months separation the family were
again together. Het's struggle with a large, difficult to heat, quarter
had been lightened by our civilian batman – Steward (an apt name)
– who had been allowed to 'stay on' after I left. We stayed in Watford
for a couple of months before moving into quarters at the Highway
in Stanmore. Elisabeth, whom we had left with friends at West Raynham, joined us there at Easter.

At just about the same time two of our greatest friends also moved
into quarters at The Highway, a small 'patch' of ten houses. Pete and
Annette Brothers, James and Di Leathart and the Rosiers constantly
provided any help needed by the others. We were all ardent party-
goers and an excuse for a party came when, in the Queen's Birthday
Honours List on 9th June 1955, I was awarded the CBE. Subsequently
we all kept in touch visiting each other frequently. Our children became close friends too. Fighter Command in 1955 and '56 was the
place to be with its many official functions attended by all mess members. Non-attendance was unthinkable. Now I am told things are
very different. Mess functions are very few and far between.

Bentley Priory was a happy place to work. During my time I was
involved in disbanding the Auxiliary Air Force, but the work was not
all destruction as planning for the future air force was my primary job.
To keep in touch with the current thoughts in the workplace, I frequently visited our stations in the United Kingdom, and RAF airfields
in Germany.

My two years at Bentley Priory stand out as a time of broadening
my education. The constant visits and briefings expanded my knowledge of the desperate problems that were facing the UK at that time.
Thankfully, our plans were never tested by the Russian hordes.

In June 1956, whilst at Bentley Priory, I was included in a delegation
headed by the Air Minister Duncan Sandys, to visit Russia. This visit
was undoubtedly the highlight of the posting. Earlier that year a delegation from Russia led by ministers Bulganin and Krushchev had been
invited to the United Kingdom. One of the places that they and their
experts visited was RAF Marham, a bomber station in Norfolk. Whilst

they were there a suggestion was made that the RAF pay a return visit. To most at the time this idea was almost unimaginable.

However as a result, on 23rd June eight of us including the C-in-C of Fighter Command, Sir Thomas Pike, set out, accompanied by a large press contingent, into the virtual unknown as guests of Marshal Zhukov. We left Heathrow on a Saturday morning in a Comet 2. It was the first flight of the Comet since it was grounded eighteen months previously following the loss of one in the Mediterranean. I am told by my wife that there was a cloud of doom and gloom among the wives seeing us off that morning. However, my three children seemed very cheerful.

The Russians had arranged a most interesting 'business' trip including visits to the air academy and a nuclear power station, and very much 'guided' trips around Moscow and Leningrad (previously and now again St. Petersburg) where we visited the Winter Palace. We were much impressed by what we were allowed to see of these cities and even more by the ambassador's wife, Lady Hayter, when, at a dinner in our honour at the British Embassy, she appeared not to notice that the contents of a bowl of hot soup had landed in her lap. We were most unimpressed with everything to do with their civil aviation. It seemed a completely ramshackle organisation. I had never been so terrified as when flying back in an Ilyushin 14 airliner from Leningrad, where we had been shown around an aircraft factory, we ran into an electric storm – quite the most violent I had ever experienced.

At this aircraft factory, a few miles outside Leningrad, we had been invited to question Mr Tupolev, the aircraft designer. In reply he said he had no intention of revealing any details of his new Tupolev bomber, as, during the whole of his recent visit to Britain, we had not shown or told him anything of any importance. He would therefore do exactly the same. The Russians would not equivocate as he was well aware we had done. We knew after this exactly where we stood.

The highlight of the visit, as reported widely in British newspapers, was an open-air reception given by B & K (Bulganin & Krushchev) in the Kremlin grounds. Being rather hot and tired, Air Marshal Broadhurst and I wandered over and sat at some empty tables set up under the trees. Soon B & K and their senior commissars arrived and sat down at the tables accompanied by Duncan Sandys,

USAF General Twining and the head of our delegation, Air Chief Marshal Ivelaw-Chapman (DCAS). We were invited to stay. The eating and drinking, which started at 5.00 p.m., did not finish until after midnight. There were many toasts, drunk in Russian vodka every time. As B & K got drunker and drunker their accompanying speeches revealed how great was their dislike of each other. When the US Air Attaché, (who had been a fellow classmate at the US Armed Forces College in 1948) was caught pouring away a drink, he was publicly reprimanded being told, "We Russians would never do such a thing". He immediately drank his refilled glass but honour was not yet satisfied. He was presented with another full glass which he had to down in one before a cheering bunch of drunken Russians. The press reported at length about such carousing – the likes of which they had never before seen.

In a letter to Het from Hotel Sovetskaya in Moscow on 29th June I wrote:

Darlingest,

The programme arranged by the Russians goes on until 3rd July (after we had planned to return to the UK). As the secretary of state felt that it would be wrong for the whole of the British team to leave before that date the DCAS and I have to stay.

It's been an incredible week; an excellent air display on Sunday was followed by a reception at which I met B and K, Zhukov, and several others of the top rank. For the first hour or so things were reasonably orderly, in fact it was similar to a garden party – with Bulganin rowing the secretary of state on a lake. But then the fun started with B and K as central figures. Apart from a few speeches by the heads of delegations, these two held the floor almost continuously for three hours. At least fifteen toasts were proposed which meant for those sitting close fifteen glasses (full ones) of brandy. Broady, Bing and I had ringside seats and could hardly believe our eyes. Even the ambassador said he had never known anything like it.

*On Monday, Tuesday and Wednesday we visited
an operational station where we saw some of the latest
types, an air force academy where engineers are trained
in great numbers and an engine and airframe factory.
In the evenings we had dinner with the air attaché,
the ambassador and on Wednesday went to the Bol-
shoi Theatre to see the opera Aida. This theatre is
quite magnificent, contrasting vividly with the dowdi-
ness of the people and the streets.*

*Yesterday we flew to Stalingrad in a VIP aircraft
after getting up at 5.00 a.m. They reconstructed the
battle for us and took us on a tour of the city. It was
a remarkable day. The people are much more cheerful
here than in Moscow. After another large dinner and
several toasts we flew back to arrive at the central airport here in the dark and rather relieved to be safely
on the ground again. Their technique of flying in bad
weather is more hair-raising than ours.*

After the main party returned to the UK, Air Marshal Pike and I
stayed on for a few days. The press rang up my wife to tell her that
I had not returned with the main party. As she has not yet received
my letter she feared that I had said or done something wrong and
was on my way to Siberia. She was even more upset when my so-
called pals suggested that she was going to be the accompanying wife
of the first RAF exchange officer in Russia.

On 3rd July we returned in a Comet to Hatfield and, as a consequence of having had to surrender all my allowance of roubles to the
Russians, I had to buy the children's presents from 'Russia' at White-
leys in London. My wife showed little appreciation of the heavy Russian perfume which had been presented to us in Moscow. She indicated
that she too would have preferred something bought in London.

On my return I was delighted to be told that I had been selected
for the 1957 course at the Imperial Defence College in Belgrave
Square. I left my post as group captain plans at Bentley Priory a few
days before Christmas 1956.

IMPERIAL DEFENCE COLLEGE (IDC)
1957

The IDC was the foremost military college in the country. In 1922 a cabinet committee presided over by Winston Churchill, then secretary of state for the colonies, had advocated that representatives of the armed forces should work together and get to know each other. But it was not until 1927 that the IDC was opened at 9 Buckingham Gate where it remained until its closure at the outbreak of war in 1939.

During the Second World War many past students in key appointments all over the world had shown the effectiveness of their training at this highest level. Consequently, at the end of hostilities the government thought that this proven success of ex-IDC students warranted its re-instatement. It was re-opened at Seaford House, Belgrave Square in 1946.

There we chosen few assembled in early January 1957. There were about seventy of us. Predominantly service officers we were leavened by high-flying civilians. There were twelve army officers at brigadier/colonel rank and an equivalent number from the Royal Navy and Royal Air Force, most of whom had known each other whilst working together during the war. Others had met at Latimer, the Joint Services Staff College, as students or directing staff. There were similarly qualified service officers from the military forces of Australia, New Zealand, Canada, India, Pakistan and the United States.

We rather over-confident 'service types' were joined by a mixed bag of civilians. There were civil servants from those departments that had dealings with the services: the Treasury, Ministry of Transport, and the three separate armed services departments. Members of our Foreign Office and those of Australia, New Zealand and Canada were joined by a member of the US State Department, Coburn Kidd, who had been serving in the embassy in Berkeley Square. Among those we termed 'odd jobs' was a Hong Kong civil servant who professed he was delighted to be away from its hustle and bustle. Very odd we thought! Another 'odd job' was the chief constable of Lancashire, Eric St. Johnston.

In later years many of these like-minded people either worked together or were always willing to give advice or extend a helping hand. For example Eric St. Johnston certainly did over ten years later when he was commissioner of the Metropolitan Police. From Ankara, where I was the UK representative at the Central Treaty Organisation (CENTO), I asked him to issue an invitation to the army general commanding the Turkish police force to visit the Metropolitan Police. Within days the general with three henchmen and wives were off. On the eleventh day of what was supposed to be a meticulously planned four-day visit, I received a somewhat humorous but extremely rude signal from Scotland Yard. It stated that never again would he entertain any of my so-called friends. Although I never found out what happened I was sorry at the loss of Eric's regard; however my popularity with the Turks knew no bounds. It was almost impossible to convince them that I was unable 'to fix' any more trips to London.

Our friend Coburn Kidd co-opted us into a number of his attempts to make friends with senior members of the Labour Party. I did not feel that we were any good in helping him; but I suppose I acted as a catalyst. We thoroughly enjoyed the dinner parties at his home in Pont Street. These had added interest when George Brown, the shadow foreign minister was there. He never failed to entertain and shock with his unorthodox behaviour.

A few years later whilst in Aden we greatly appreciated the periodic delivery of a Foreign Office bag which came on an aircraft passing through Mogadishu. This contained the freshest of grapefruit picked a few hours earlier in the garden of a fellow student, by then the ambassador there. In addition there was always a hearty welcome in Hong Kong for those of us who contrived visits there.

Apart from these frivolities, most of our future dealings with members of the course were of a serious nature. There was always a friendly ear in a key senior post with whom we could have 'a quiet word'. We valued their opinions and their willingness to give any possible help.

The year at the IDC was meant to be a respite from responsibility: a time when we would broaden our knowledge of world politics and recharge our batteries in preparation for those greater responsibilities which we confidently hoped would be thrust upon us. The lecturers were of the highest calibre. We especially enjoyed challenging and occasionally rubbishing the theories which they expounded. We felt that this was what we were tasked to do. For my part I greatly enjoyed hectoring my former C-in-C at Fighter Command! During the year we went on two trips. One was an industrial tour taken just before the Easter break. I was in the West Midlands group based in Birmingham. We visited Dunlops, the *Birmingham Evening Post* and the small workshops of the jewellery quarter. We also visited a newly sunk coal mine in Staffordshire which had been widely acclaimed as the most modern and most productive coal mine in Britain. There we spent a couple of hours underground and were greatly impressed and filled with hope for the future of British coal-mining. Less than twenty years later that mine was closed, practically marking the end of coal mining in Britain.

The much longer overseas tour of six weeks took place during the summer break. I was detailed to join the group of ten destined for Pakistan and India which was a most interesting and educational visit. All was new to me as it was the first time that I had visited the Indian sub-continent. I never again visited India but returned to Pakistan for a seven-day visit in March 1970 when I was the British permanent military deputy to CENTO in Ankara.

Before the trip began Het and I and the family had an enjoyable week besides the sea at Dinas Head in Pembrokeshire. There I was presented with a tie embossed with daffodils and saucepans whilst being elected a member of Llanelli Rugby Club. That honour had been earned by the fervent rendering of rugby songs at the local pub The Ship Aground.

In late July we set off from RAF Northolt in a Hastings tasked to deliver us wherever this fact-finding-come-sight-seeing trip was programmed. In each country we visited the most important bases of the three services; the capital cities of New Delhi and Islamabad, where it was hoped we would gain some understanding of the prevailing diplomatic situation; and in tourist mode the Taj Mahal, Amritsar and the Khyber Pass. In Kashmir we found it hard to reconcile the contradictory reports about the diplomatic situation of which we had a plentiful supply on our journeying round the sub-continent.

During this six-week trip I was buoyed up by letters from home with news of the family and in turn I wrote regularly. On 4th September I wrote to Het from Deans Hotel in Peshawar:

Sweetheart, and now for the diary.

After lunch at Flashman's Hotel in Rawalpindi where for the first time I had a fool of a 'room boy' we drove out to the old city of Taxila which was in a fine state of preservation. This was followed by a cocktail party at the Rawalpindi Club.

The following day, Saturday, we were up early for a briefing by the army COS. My impression here is that the army is the dominant service. It takes eighty per cent of the budget revenues and certainly rules the roost.

That same morning we left in Jeeps for Murree which is about 7,000 feet up in glorious wooded country and the transformation from the heat of the plain is most marked. We went to the local services club where we were royally entertained by Haq Nawaz commanding a division there. I felt somewhat embarrassed when he held my hand for some three or four minutes. He asked after you and the family. After the dinner we were entertained by displays of tribal dancing. There were three teams, one Punjabi and two from frontier tribal territories. It was quite fierce stuff.

Next morning we set off for Muzaffarabad in Azad (free) Kashmir. Again, tremendous scenery with the Himalayas in the distance. For a great part of the way the road followed a wide, swift-flowing river but for the rest it was a succession of hair pin bends with sheer drops of thousands of feet on one side. On arrival we were given cold drinks and tea by the army before meeting the Kashmir president. He spoke at long length about the Kashmir problem whilst bearers kept bringing more and more tea (tea is a sign of hospitality). After a question period we were each presented with a carved walnut cigarette box.

The following day, on the way to Peshawar, we stopped at an ordnance factory for an inspection and tea. The next stop was an old fort at the junction of the Kabul and Indus rivers where we again had tea, and some twenty miles further the whole thing was repeated at a Cavalry mess.

Went shopping and bathing the first evening in Peshawar before being entertained by the air force at dinner. It was the first time our party was actually conscious that an air force even existed. Instead of a military band there was a jazz band, and women guests were present. This is almost unheard of in the army.

Yesterday, Tuesday, we had one of the most enjoyable days. After a briefing by the head of the Civil Armed Forces – a brigadier who was born a tribesman, we went with him up the Khyber Pass to the Afghanistan border. The Pass is better than I expected, picture book forts, tribesmen all carrying rifles and forbidding mountains. On the way back we stopped in the Pass at the headquarters of the Khyber Rifles. It was an oasis in the middle of nothing, beautiful lawns and flower borders and again an excellent band, but the same monotonous food.

Oh, I forgot to tell you, I was given a knife by the Khyber Rifles.

And now must finish darlingest, missing you and the children, but won't be long now.

By early September I had had enough of travelling and was happy to be returning home. I know Het, who had coped with the children, albeit then only three of them, through the long summer holiday, was delighted to have me back.

At Seaford House frequent cocktail parties, film shows, and seminar parties were well attended events. Ascending the beautiful sweeping marble staircase seemed to add glamour to the occasions. Theatre visits were arranged and, chiefly for the overseas families, we took trips to such places as Kew, Greenwich and the British Museum.

The IDC course was a marvellous break from the usual routine of service life. For the first two months I travelled by tube from Stanmore to St. James's Park at the gentlemanly hour of 9.30 a.m. Usually I was able to leave for home in mid-afternoon. Housing was the only problem. As the course lasted more than six months, Queens Regulations required that we vacate our quarter within sixty days. Having searched unsuccessfully for affordable accommodation in London we left our quarter at The Highway for yet another hiring at Coulsdon in Surrey. From there I had a train journey of an hour. I became a commuter, complete with bowler hat and umbrella.

To make life easier at Coulsdon we had a Hungarian au-pair recommended by Het's brother who was on the staff of the International Interpreters School in Zurich. She proved to be an unmitigated failure – it quickly became obvious that she had made her way to England to take advantage of our National Health Service. She came to breakfast on the first morning with a large x-ray of her back. She requested the name and address of the nearest doctor and hoped that I would be able to fix some boards on her bed before nightfall! We knew immediately that we had been conned. Neighbours reported that the boys were playing in their pyjamas in the garden at 10.30 p.m., and we could not understand why a call at 7.30 p.m. was not answered. When questioned about this she explained that she had eased the burden of baby-sitting by retiring to her room with her ears tightly stuffed with cotton wool. She left shortly after to live with a Swiss friend. This episode I think added to our dislike of the whole 'Coulsdon Experience'.

New schools had to be found for Elisabeth and David. Elisabeth, by now thirteen, had already attended six schools. We decided that the time had come to find a school where she could remain wherever I was posted. After visiting and rejecting Howell's School, Denbigh, we visited Cheltenham Ladies College. The headmistress suggested that she should be coached in Latin prior to the entrance examination at the end of March and recommended a former Cheltenham classics mistress, a brigadier's widow living in Kensington. There Elisabeth had two hours daily coaching for six weeks. On passing the examination she

214 BE BOLD

became a 'Cheltenham Lady' for the next four years.

In 1957 special school trains were the order of the day. Paddington at about mid-day on the first day of term was a seething mass of uniformed pupils seeking out their 'special' which was already belching out smoke ready for the journey westwards to the nearest station to their school. David had a much shorter journey to a newly built elementary school. This entailed a five-minute walk. There he remained for just under six months until with great rejoicing on his part he returned to his former school on Stanmore Hill in October 1957.

On returning from the India and Pakistan trip, I decided to visit P staff in quest of my next posting. This was the first and last time that I ever did this. I was a believer in leaving such things to fate. I had assembled a number of reasons in favour of my being posted overseas. These I quite forgot when greeted by the AVM in charge who congratulated me on being about to get what he called, "the best job in the RAF". It sounded pretty good to me although it was in London. I was to be director of plans in the Air Ministry reporting to the CAS Sir Dermot Boyle. In addition, I was entitled to an Air Ministry quarter.

As a result, in October we moved into 16 Finucane Rise, on a 'patch' which had not yet been completed, at Bushey Heath between Stanmore and Watford. An ocean of mud is my memory of those early days there. David was able to go by bus to his former school in Stanmore while I once again took the tube to the IDC until starting at the Air Ministry in January. We were all glad to return to RAF quarters and to be leaving Coulsdon where we had made no friends. In fact we had the feeling that itinerant service families were not welcome to dwell amongst those folk in their leafy suburb. They had seemingly forgotten how thankful they had been less than twenty years earlier when they saw patrolling fighter aircraft from nearby Kenley and Biggin Hill. At Bushey, surrounded by like-minded friendly families, we felt we had returned home.

AIR MINISTRY AND MINISTRY OF DEFENCE
1958-1960

1958 started well with my promotion to air commodore and my new job in Whitehall as director of plans at the Air Ministry. At that time I also became an ADC to the Queen.

My first task in my new job was to mastermind 'Exercise Prospect'. Two months of extremely hard work culminated in a three-day conference at Cranwell attended by the members of the Air Council and over 100 senior RAF officers and civil servants. The objective was to look ten years forward at what might be the global defence requirements of the United Kingdom and its overseas interests and thereby establish the RAF's strategic priorities. The purpose was to ensure that the RAF's structure, equipment and manning accorded with the intelligence picture and the government's policy of maintaining a deterrent strategy against the Russian threat.

My team made an extensive presentation and concluded that strategically, both for deterrent and global war purposes, the main nuclear deterrent was probably best mounted in ballistic missiles dispersed among underground sites. I also suggested that on a limited scale, for political reasons, active defence of cities against Russian missile and winged attacks might be desirable. The team I led thought that limited wars, i.e. non-nuclear, were no longer likely. We thought that the most likely threat to the UK's interests would come from comparatively small local disturbances particularly in the Middle East.

We argued that as missiles were inflexible the RAF would continue to require manned aircraft: a low-level bomber force, a fighter force for air defence and defence of the deterrent force, and an air-to-ground guided weapons system. We concluded that by 1970 the RAF would need a deterrent force of a minimum of 100 to 150 ballistic missiles, thirty-two V bombers, ten sites for anti-ballistic missile defence and thirty-two fighters for air defence of the UK.

In order to cope with local disturbances, we felt there would be an overseas requirement of thirty-two strike\recce aircraft in Aden and eight medium-range transport. The same would be needed in Cyprus to support the Baghdad Pact with the same again in the Far East.

Having made the presentation to the Air Council it was decided by the CAS Sir Dermot Boyle that we should make a similar presentation on 6th May at the Royal Empire Society's Hall. In addition to the Duke of Edinburgh and service chiefs, the conference was attended by a selected civilian audience of over 300, consisting of 'eminent civilians associated either directly or indirectly with the well-being of this country' – the great and the good – 'with the aim of outlining how the RAF was playing its part in the defence of the United Kingdom and its interests overseas'.

In his introduction to the conference, Sir Dermot Boyle told those at the conference that they had been included because there was great confusion in many minds about the present and future role of the RAF. "We feel that this is bad for the country and bad for the service."

The conference caused a huge furore both in the press and in parliament as it was suggested that in 'going public' the RAF was 'lobbying' against the secretary of state for defence. Duncan Sandys' final decision was to end the development of manned fighter planes and high-level bombers in favour of a nuclear deterrent carried by guided missiles. The press and the Labour opposition made much of this, questioning the constitutional propriety of 'Prospect'.

This did not seem to worry the CAS who wrote to me on 7th May:

My Dear Fred

This is to congratulate you and your Exercise staff on the excellence of everything to do with Prospect 1 and Prospect 2.

I know the enormous amount of work that you have put into these projects but I assure you that in the event nothing could have been more worthwhile.

I congratulate you personally on the excellence of your individual performance and indeed the standard of acting by all the performers was first class.

You can now relax and get down to the simple task for which you have been appointed to the Air Ministry!

Again, very many thanks.

Dermot Boyle

The coup in Iraq and the assassination of King Faisal in the summer of 1958 resulted in the cancellation of our planned camping holiday in Europe as I was fully occupied with planning for different possible scenarios. As a result Het took the children to a caravan at Calshot on Southampton Water and I joined them in the mud at weekends.

Meanwhile in Whitehall, Secretary of State for Defence Duncan Sandys, as well as ending National Service was determined to cut down the power of the individual services and to centralise power within the Ministry of Defence. As part of this process Lord Mountbatten, who had become CDS in 1959, formed a new post – chairman of the joint planning staffs – and I was selected for the job, which started in July 1959. Previously the three service directors of plans had held the post of chairman by rotation for one month. As part of my new job as permanent chairman of the joint planning staff I attended all the meetings of the chiefs of staff and was responsible to Mountbatten for all operational joint planning.

I enjoyed working for Mountbatten. He was also most entertaining. At the end of our working day it was usually the practice for us to have a whisky and soda, over which we would chat. He told me many interesting stories, often enhanced by his great skill at mimicry. He explained to me that the reason he had returned to the Royal Navy as a captain, after having reached the supreme heights as viceroy of India, was that he realised he was becoming a megalomaniac and was beginning to think that everything he did was right. His standing and power in India had been such that no one had ever dared to contradict him. He realised that back in the navy he would be amongst people who would not hesitate to criticise his actions when they thought it necessary.

There was a widespread belief at that time that Mountbatten rejoined the navy as he was determined to be First Sea Lord to avenge his father's memory. His father, Prince Henry of Battenburg, had been dismissed from that post at the outbreak of war in 1914. Popular clamour had demanded this because of his German name and ancestry. When I joined Mountbatten in 1959 as his director of plans, he had already achieved that ambition and more by also becoming CDS.

However, he had not forgotten how to make use of his position. This I heard being employed most amusingly in February 1960, a few days before Prince Andrew's birth. The Queen and Duke of Edinburgh were to dine with the Mountbattens at their home at 2 Wilton Crescent. He had the idea that after dinner the Queen would enjoy being entertained by a team of performing dogs. (When I told my wife she said in an exasperated manner: "Poor Queen – men?!" She informed me that a woman in such an advanced state of pregnancy, and in the

late evening, needs no entertaining – least of all by dogs.) These dogs
and their American trainer were appearing at the London Palladium.
However, after each performance the Ministry of Agriculture & Fish-
eries insisted that they returned under escort direct to their quarantine
kennels.

Not to be thwarted, Mountbatten rang up insisting that he spoke
to the permanent under secretary (PUS), whose name he well knew.
He was told by the PUS that it was quite impossible for the dogs to be
dropped off at Wilton Street. Upon hearing this, he asked for the PUS's
name as he wanted to be able to tell the Queen the name of the man
who had refused her request (not his!) to see those wonderful dogs.
Of course, she saw them.

Towards the end of August 1960, I was told that early in 1961 I
would be posted to Supreme Headquarters Allied Powers in Europe
(SHAPE) which was situated at Fontainebleau, just outside Paris, for
a job there as an AVM. Het and I were delighted with this news.

We were joined two weeks later at our bi-weekly chiefs of staff
meeting by a senior general from SHAPE. On leaving he turned to
me and said that he was looking forward to my arrival at his headquarters. Greatly to everyone's surprise and my consternation, Tom
Pike, by then CAS quietly informed him that the RAF now had different plans for Rosier. To me this was a complete bombshell. I followed him back to his office and asked that I be told there and then
what exactly was this change of plans. I learned that I was to be
posted to Aden as AOC Air Forces Middle East (AFME). I was delighted. To my mind a command job in the heat and sand of the
'Barren Rocks' of Aden, was far preferable to a staff officer's job in
Paris. Quite understandably my wife, who had been looking forward
to living in Paris, was not of the same mind. Aden hitherto had been
known as a 'punishment posting'. Her instant reaction on hearing
the news was that she was not going to accompany me. However,
by morning she had decided that come what may she was not going
to miss out on what was likely to be a great adventure.

I was told that although I would still be leaving the Ministry of Defence at the end of the year, I would not be taking over in Aden until
the latter part of July. Meanwhile, I was to re-charge my batteries
whilst preparing for my tour. I duly left the MOD after Christmas,

handing over to Brigadier Powell-Jones, and was delighted to receive
the CB – Companion of the Order of the Bath – in the New Year's Honours list. The CDS wrote to congratulate me:

My Dear Fred
No-one has more richly earned the CB than you for
so successfully establishing the hotly opposed and yet
vitally necessary job of chairman of the joint planners.
*   I am sure this recognition will give equal pleasure*
to your many friends in all three services.
*   Mountbatten of Burma*

Over the next six months I completed a three-week jet refresher course
on Meteors at RAF Manby in Lincolnshire where I did not enjoy being
known by the other pupils as 'Fred the Retread'. I then spent a week
flying Hunters at Chivenor. As my personal aircraft in Aden was to be
a Canberra, I completed the Canberra conversion course at RAF Bass-
ingbourn in Cambridgeshire. I also did a survival course at
Portsmouth. In between all this I found time to redecorate the entire
quarter at Finucane Rise, and had plenty of time to be a dutiful husband to a pregnant Het. Our third son, John, was born on 25th June
1961 and in mid-July I left my wife and family for what was to be one
of the most enjoyable postings of my entire career.

On 18th July, after flying out to Aden, I took over from Air Vice-
Marshal David Lee. After nearly five years in London I was very excited by the prospect of becoming AOC Air Forces Middle East which
was probably the best AVM's job in the Royal Air Force.

ADEN
JULY 1961-OCTOBER 1963

Middle East (Aden) Command with its headquarters at Steamer Point
had, in 1959, become the first 'unified command', shortly followed
by the Far East and Near East in Singapore and Cyprus respectively.
Combining the three services under one joint commander had long
been the aim of Duncan Sandys and the CDS Admiral of the Fleet
Lord Louis Mountbatten.

At that time the C-in-C of Middle East Command was Air Marshal Sir Charles 'Sam' Elworthy, a New Zealander, later to become CAS and then CDS. (He was succeeded in 1963 by General Sir Charles Harington.) He was loyally served by 'two star' officers of the three services, Major General Jim Robertson, Rear Admiral Fitzroy Talbot and myself. The majority of the admiral's staff were with us in Aden but he remained at his subordinate headquarters in Bahrain for the few months until his residence in Aden was ready for occupation. Having been built on a former gun emplacement, this became known as the 'Round House'. The cost of constructing and furnishing this house became the subject of much criticism in the press at home in the UK.

Aden with its searing, unrelenting heat was of enormous strategic importance. It was home to the largest oil bunkering port in the world, handling over 5,000 ships per year. All the ships sailing from Asia to Europe via the Red Sea and the Suez Canal refuelled there. It was no longer regarded as a somewhat forgotten 'punishment station'. Accommodating the men and the families of the fast growing Aden garrison had necessitated much building and construction work. Flats were built for the rapidly growing population of all three services. Roads were upgraded, one of these – wide and flanked on either side by tall blocks of flats occupied by the families of servicemen – was known as the Maala Straight. In 1962 a visiting ambassador from the Lebanon declared it was the finest road in the Middle East.

I spent the first three months in Aden 'unaccompanied' as Het had stayed behind in England for the summer holidays with our new baby and the boys. In September she sent our second son Nicholas off to join his elder brother David at King's College School, Cambridge. Having 'handed over' 16 Finucane Rise, Het, Elisabeth, who had left Cheltenham Ladies College that summer, and baby John then travelled out to Aden on the troopship SS *Nevasa*, arriving in Aden in early October.

They joined me in our temporary residence No.11 Tarshyne where we were staying while Air House was being refurbished. This house was a colonial-style bungalow built in the thirties on a promontory above the sea, close to Government House. We spent Christmas there where we were joined by David and Nicholas for the holidays. Living close by in Tarshyne was the air officer administration Air Commodore 'Bob' Hodges and his wife Elisabeth and their two sons David and Nigel who became great friends, and the SASO Air Commodore Peter Cribb. (Air Chief Marshal Sir Lewis Hodges was in 1973 to take over from me in Holland as DCINCENT.)

In March 1962 we moved into Air House, high above Telegraph Bay. Flagstaff House, the residence of the GOC Jim Robertson – a former Gurkha – was next door. Further down the hill was Command House, the residence of the commander-in-chief, 'Sam' Elworthy.

My first ADC was Flight Lieutenant David Downey, a navigator, who hailed from Kenya where his family ran the well known Kerr and Downey Safari company. He was succeeded a year later by Flight Lieutenant Hugh Cracroft, a Hunter pilot from one of the RAF Khormaksar squadrons.

My driver was Corporal Nettle who drove me round Aden in great state in a Humber Pullman with the number plate RAF 1. The house staff was headed by Corporal Smith and included Ali our skilled and volatile Yemeni cook, Ahmed and Abdullah, the 'bearers', and the sweeper Mohammed. The statuesque Somali ayah (or nanny) Fatima was succeeded by the equally statuesque Medinah.

As AOC Air Forces Middle East my responsibilities extended from the Persian Gulf down through East Africa to Rhodesia and to the British protectorates of Bechuanaland and Swaziland and the crown colony of Basutoland in southern Africa. In addition, I had certain responsibilities for British Somaliland and Mogadishu. As a result I had two sub-headquarters in Bahrain and Nairobi commanded by air commodores.

I recall that we gave Somalia assistance in coping with the floods in 1962 by dropping food packages. Imagine my surprise when visiting there I discovered that the head of state, like myself, had been educated at a Welsh county school. His Welsh mother had married a Somali seaman. We also had regular contact with Ethiopia where the air attaché was attached to our HQ.

For transport I had my personal gleaming white Canberra which I christened 'Queen of the Arabian skies', and a Valetta, the RAF version of the Viking. I used the Canberra with my ADC as navigator on my monthly visits to the RAF stations in Nairobi and Bahrain. I also made frequent visits to the chain of RAF airfields along the Arabian coast and the Persian Gulf: Riyan, Salalah, Masirah and Sharjah.

My daily routine was to get to my office at the headquarters at Steamer Point by 7.00 a.m. Work for the day finished at 1.00 p.m., by which time I had often been home for a change of uniform. The climate in the summer months from May to September was oppressively hot due as much to the high humidity of eighty per cent or more as to the temperature which rarely rose above 100°F. After lunch we rested and then in the relative cool of the late afternoon there was much to do in either the sea or sun. There were two beach clubs for officers, one at Ras Tarshyne in the bay below Air House and a privately run one for senior servicemen and civilians at Gold Mohur, a little further along the rocky coast. Both had shark-nets. No one swam in the open sea. There were cinemas at the two service clubs, and an open-air cinema in the town close to the much patronised Charlie's Fish & Chips.

RAF Khormaksar was one of the RAF's largest stations. In 1961 it was home to 8 and 208 Squadrons equipped with Hawker Hunter FGA mark 9s. My old squadron, 43, also equipped with Hunters arrived from Cyprus in March 1963. In addition, there was 37 Squadron flying Shackletons, 78 Squadron flying Twin Pioneers, 84 Squadron flying Beverleys and 233 Squadron equipped with Valettas and Dakotas. To increase the helicopter flight which consisted of only three Sycamores, 26 Squadron, equipped with Belvedere helicopters, arrived in 1963.

In addition there was the RAF Marine Craft Unit, which included extremely powerful air sea rescue launches. These came in useful for weekend boat trips to swim and picnic at a group of rocks known as the Blue Grotto off Little Aden.

Most of the army were stationed in barracks in Little Aden which, until shortly before we arrived, had been a tented camp. Their role was ostensibly to provide protection for the BP refinery situated there. During our time the cavalry regiment was 11th Hussars, known as the 'cherrypickers' as a result of their red trousers. They were followed by the Queens Royal Irish Hussars and then in early 1963 by 17th/21st Lancers. 45 Commando were also stationed here, as was 1 RHA. In addition the King's Own Scottish Borderers (KOSB) and the Queen's

Royal Surreys were based at Waterloo barracks close to Khormaksar.

Although Aden itself stayed reasonably quiet all the time we were there, there were continuous operations in the Aden Protectorate and the Oman. In 1962 a civil war in the Yemen started with the Egyptian-backed republican coup. This prompted the beginning of civil unrest from nationalist and tribal elements, aided and abetted by President Nasser. For decades the RAF had been the instrument of British policy in the region and during my time the RAF was used to support the army whose convoys up-country to Dhala in the north of the protectorate were regularly subject to ambushes.

In September 1962, the crown colony of Aden merged with the Aden Protectorate states to become the Federation of South Arabia with its government headquarters at Al Ittihad on the road from Khormaksar to Little Aden. Things were moving too in Africa and during our time in Aden Het and I attended the independence ceremonies in Uganda and Tanganyika. The governor of Aden was Sir Charles Johnston with whom I frequently played tennis at Government House.

My job regularly took me to Kenya where I had a subsidiary HQ at RAF Eastleigh commanded by Air Commodore Macdonald. I would return from these trips with the bomb compartment of the Canberra filled with fresh fruit including pawpaw, avocado pears and artichokes – virtually unknown in the UK at that time – and fresh flowers. Once, when we returned to Air House with some brussels sprouts, Ali could not understand why the memsahib had allowed herself to be palmed off with such small cabbages!

In order to get away from the searing heat of Aden we occasionally flew up for the weekend to Air Cottage which was a small house several thousand feet up in the hills close to the up-country airstrip of Mukeiras near the Yemen border. The house had been given to the RAF in the thirties by the local ruler in memory of an RAF pilot who had been killed while providing air support for the ruler. The lush green fields and the need to wear a jersey in the evenings made us feel we were back at home.

From Aden as a family we also flew to visit the island of Perim, a former coaling station 100 miles west of Aden and the island of Socotra where there was a former RAF airfield. There we swam in crystal blue sea.

Frequent visitors in the form of defence reporters became a great nuisance. Chapman Pincher, the doyen of them all, stayed for a week with us at Air House. We looked after him meticulously and on his return to London the *Daily Express* reported that all was well with the services in Aden. We became great friends.

In August 1962, after David and Nicholas had arrived from school for the summer holidays, we all flew down to Kenya in my Valetta. Having spent the first night in Nairobi we drove north to Naro Moru near Nanyuki and the foothills of Mount Kenya where we spent a week or so staying in a farmhouse fishing for trout and visiting the local game reserves.

We then flew in a Pembroke to the Queen Elizabeth game park in Uganda where we took a boat trip up the Nile to the Victoria Falls and saw crocodile, hippopotamus and water buffalo. Next stop was the Ngorongoro Crater game reserve in Tanganyika – not yet Tanzania – where Charlie Chaplin was staying in the same hotel. Here we were guided by Masai tribesmen who showed us gazelle, zebra, wildebeest and lion. We then flew back to Nairobi where we saw cheetah and monkeys in the local game park and played a round of golf at the Royal Nairobi golf club before returning to Aden.

In May 1963 Minister of War John Profumo, and his wife arrived in Aden on their way home from Hong Kong and Singapore where he had been visiting the British forces stationed there. I do not remember why we put the Profumos up, rather than the army, but I do remember how great was the excitement of the Air House staff at the prospect of their visit. The only British member of staff, Corporal Smith, had undoubtedly overdone his description of the beauty of Profumo's wife, Valerie Hobson, the well-known British actress. They could not hide their excitement at the prospect of meeting this young, world-renowned beauty. On meeting her, their faces fell. My wife immediately detected their disappointment. Valerie Hobson was charming and, I was later to discover, well versed in military matters. But she was no longer the twenty-year-old beauty anticipated by the Arabs.

The Profumos stayed at Air House for ten days whilst he visited the army in Aden and the Aden Protectorate. After John Profumo had delivered a well-received message to the troops over BBC Aden we saw them off from RAF Khormaksar on an RAF Britannia just after noon on a Wednesday in late May. I make a point of detailing this timing as two issues were involved. On that Wednesday the British press and the service authorities had been alerted that a scurrilous article entitled 'The Love Life of the Forces in Aden' was to appear in the Thursday issue of *The Dhow*, the local forces weekly newspaper published in Aden. A certain section of the British press immediately leapt into action. They were certainly in luck as the only weekly direct flight to Aden left on a Wednesday evening. Arriving early on Thursday morning they learned that the Profumo scandal had 'broken' in the British papers that morning. Against this, the Aden sex scandal stood no chance. It was very small fry compared with the sex life of Profumo and his friends – British and Russian. They waited impatiently and with increasing frustration in the intense heat of a May day until 10.30 that night when they were able to return on the same aircraft to Heathrow, and busy themselves with the long, drawn-out Profumo scandal.

The service chiefs were very grateful to Profumo. On leaving Aden he had promised to give them what help he could. He kept his promise! The Aden story – sensational as it was – would no doubt have provided material for various parliamentary questions, gravely reflecting on the morale (and morals) of the British troops and their wives and questioning the competence of their service commanders.

Some weeks later, when the Profumo name was worldwide news, the Sheriff of Beihan, the ruler of an up-country Arab state, questioned me as to whether Profumo was the same man whom he had met at dinner in my house. When I assured him that it was the same man he asked whether it was true that he would never again be a minister. When I assured him that it was true indeed, he vehemently asserted, "That's wrong, wrong, wrong. It could happen to me, it could happen to you." I had no doubt that it could have happened to this handsome, bearded Arab, generally reputed to have fifty-seven wives.

In March 1963, after spending eighteen months with us in Aden, where she was much in demand by the young RAF and army officers and by then a nineteen-year-old, Lis returned to the UK to start her nursing course at St Thomas's Hospital in London.

In 1963 Het and I visited the three territories in southern Africa for which I had responsibility. We flew on to South Africa where we stayed with Admiral Sir Fitzoy Talbot who had been with me in Aden. On our journey north we landed at Ladysmith where we visited Sailor Malan, a well-known fighter ace of the Second World War, who was in hospital there, suffering from the last phase of Parkinson's disease. Sadly we could not understand what he said but his pleasure at seeing us was obvious.

The last stop was in Southern Rhodesia where we were welcomed by the AOC of the Rhodesian air force AVM Ralph Bentley who had served with me in 43 Squadron before the war.

During the summer holidays of 1963 we spent two weeks in Ethiopia where we camped next to the lakes south of Addis Ababa. It was here that David, then aged twelve, shot his first guinea fowl. We ended the holiday staying at the British Embassy in Addis Ababa where we heard the news of 'The Great Train Robbery'.

Two months later in October 1963 we left Aden where I was succeeded as AOC by the wartime fighter ace Air Vice-Marshal Johnnie Johnson just as the insurgency began to hot up. We travelled back to England on the SS *Canberra* via the Suez Canal, Marseilles and Gibraltar arriving back in London in late October.

Chapter 12

FIGHTER COMMAND FINALE

TRANSPORT COMMAND
MARCH 1964-MARCH 1966

I left Aden in mid-October 1963 knowing that I would not be taking up my next post as SASO at Transport Command until March 1964. This extra leave, for recharging my batteries, was based on my having served three months over the allotted time in Aden. The Air Ministry had decided that two years was the limit that a man could endure in that hostile climate. The all-year-round humidity and high temperatures took their toll.

On arriving back in England, we spent four months in the former station commander's married quarter at, the moth-balled, RAF Bircham Newton in north-west Norfolk, before moving in early March to RAF Upavon in Wiltshire, the headquarters of Transport Command. This posting was a 'one off' for me. My superiors thought it essential for the furthering of my career that I should widen my understanding of other aspects of the RAF. I looked forward to this.

My first few days at Transport Command were the final few days as C-in-C of Teddy Huddleston who had been appointed vice chief of the air staff (VCAS). I had been his group captain operations in north-west Europe twenty years previously when he commanded 84 Group in the 2nd Tactical Air Force. The few days I had with him were in-valuable. He put me in the picture of the workings, difficulties and plans for the long-term development of Transport Command.

On his departure I was confident that I was equipped with the knowledge that would enable me to tackle the job successfully. The new C-in-C was Bing Cross, my old friend and colleague from the Western Desert days.

We lived a few miles away from RAF Upavon, one of the original RAF stations, in a house called The Beeches in the village of Upavon. The Beeches had been bought by the RAF in 1915 and the founder of the RAF Lord Trenchard had lived there at one stage. The house which had originally been two cottages, had a grass tennis court and was a few yards from the river Avon where David and Nicholas canoed and fished for trout courtesy of the local landowner Barry Wookey, whose family we got to know well.

My personal staff included my excellent ADC Pilot Officer Patricia 'Pat' Davis. Pat later married a young RAF officer, later to become Air Chief Marshal Sir Michael Knight, and became Lady Knight. Her many duties in 1964 included babysitting our three-year-old son John. I also had my driver from Aden, Corporal Nettle, who drove my official car, a Humber Super Snipe.

Being new to the transport world I had a very interesting two years. The principal 'trooping' aircraft were Comet 4s and Britannias based at RAF Lyneham. During my time the VC 10 was introduced to the transport fleet, replacing the Comet, and these were based at RAF Brize Norton. In addition, during my tour the Hercules replaced the Argosy at RAF Colerne. 38 Group, with its helicopters and Hawker Hunters and its HQ at RAF Odiham, was especially fun to visit as the AOC was my old friend Air Commodore 'Mickey' Martin of Dambusters fame.

All 'trooping' was by then done by air rather than sea and Transport Command was responsible for carrying army, navy and air force per-sonnel and their families to, amongst other places, Aden, Singapore and Hong Kong. In addition we worked closely with the Parachute Regiment and regularly exercised with them. I went on some of their jumps. Often on very short notice we flew VIPs to their destinations.

In l963, Rhodesia under Ian Smith, had declared Unilateral Decla-
ration of Independence (UDI). We were much involved in the Rhodesian crisis and flew a constant stream of VIPs to Salisbury trying to solve
the problem. We also flew in the Parachute Regiment when our political
masters decided the military should intervene. On this occasion I was
awakened during the night to be told that the government wanted the
paras to 'go in' as soon as possible. From my bedroom I discussed with
my staff the problems posed by countries we were not allowed to over-
fly. After some hours, we eventually devised a route. My wife, who listened to my side of the conversation, was most puzzled as to what was
going on. Her several inspired guesses were completely wrong.

It did not strike me at the time that I was being disloyal when the
ex-chief of the Royal Rhodesian Air Force and his wife stayed with us
at Upavon for the weekend. He was on his way to Washington as Ian
Smith's ambassador to the USA. I had known Ralph Bentley since 1937
when we were great friends in our days in 43 Squadron at Tangmere.
We had renewed this friendship and that of our two air forces when I
was in Aden.

Early in June l965 I was summoned by Chief of the Air Staff Sam
Elworthy, to the Air Ministry to be told that I would take over the next
command to become vacant. This was to be RAF Germany. Naturally
I was delighted at the prospect of being promoted to air marshal and
looked forward to serving in Germany. The next vacancy after Germany was likely to be Fighter Command to which Air Vice-Marshal
Denis Spotswood would be appointed as C-in-C.

About ten days later Sam Elworthy summoned me again to the sixth
floor of the new MOD building. There, in his room, which looked
down on Dowding's memorial on the Embankment, he told me that
the Air Council had agreed to the C-in-C Germany's request for early
retirement. Meanwhile Zulu Morris the C-in-C Fighter Command, for
reasons involved with his pension, had been allowed to stay on until
April 1966. This would mean that Denis Spotswood, and the newly
promoted AVM who was about to take over his job at 3 Group, would
have a nine-month wait before taking over. As this was deemed to be
too long a 'gardening leave' it had been decided that Denis would go to
Germany and I would go to Fighter. As it was some time off until I was
to take over, the announcement that I was going to Fighter Command

The author leading the escort of Battle of Britain pilots at the unveiling of the memorial to Sir Winston Churchill in Westminster Abbey.

would not be made for some months. I could not believe my luck.

My pals, whom I suspect had an inkling of what was going on, were lurking in the 'corridors of power' with the sole purpose of assessing my demeanour as I left CAS' office. Noting my rather sheepish grin they decided on the spot that Fighter was my destination. Of course I denied it, as did Het when rung up by Air Vice-Marshal 'Splinters' Smallwood. He and she both had quite a penchant for forecasting postings. This time she was not co-operating. No doubt there was something in our voices that gave us away.

The rumours spread so fast that about ten days later Teddy Donaldson, an old friend from Tangmere days, who as Air Commander E.M. Donaldson was then the highly regarded air correspondent of the *Daily Telegraph*, wrote a glowing account of how delighted the young pilots of Fighter Command were with the prospect of having me as their commander-in-chief.

One of the highlights of my time at Transport Command was to be asked to lead the escort party of Battle of Britain pilots at the unveiling of Winston Churchill's memorial at Westminster Abbey by Her Majesty the Queen on 19th September 1965.

In early January 1966 I was relieved as SASO at Transport Command by an old friend of mine Air Vice-Marshal David McKinley. Het and I spent the next six weeks visiting Malta, Cyprus, Singapore, Hong Kong and Malaya. We then spent some weeks at Het's home in Wrexham, North Wales where I played golf every day in an attempt to get fit and lose a few pounds.

By the end of March with my batteries recharged I was raring to go again.

FIGHTER COMMAND
APRIL 1966-APRIL 1968

On 1st April 1966 I was promoted to air marshal and became AOC in C Fighter Command. Having joined my first fighter squadron in 1936, the year Fighter Command was formed, thirty years later I felt immensely proud to become the C-in-C of that famous command. Little did I know, on taking over, that I was to be the last in that position. My office was the same office in Bentley Priory from which Dowding had directed his fighter forces in the Battle of Britain. It was on this appointment that I was knighted, receiving the KCB – Knight Commander of the Order of the Bath – from Her Majesty the Queen at Buckingham Palace in June 1966.

I had a tremendous two years at Fighter Command. We lived in fine style in the C-in-C's residence Montrose, a large Edwardian house in Gordon Avenue in nearby Stanmore. My PSO was Squadron Leader John Pugh and my ADC was Flight Lieutenant John Graham. We had an excellent chef Sergeant Vallance and I was lucky to retain my driver from Aden and Transport Command Sergeant Nettle, who proudly drove me around on official duty in an Austin Princess. It was in 1966 that Nicholas started at Haileybury while David took his 'O' Levels at Winchester.

The primary objective of the command was the air defence of the

UK. At the time the main task was to protect UK air space from the Russian threat. The main aircraft in the command was the English Electric Lightning, with the McDonnell Phantom F4 coming into service, firstly at RAF Leuchars, during my time. In addition we had Hunters for advanced training purposes at Chivenor. Although this might sound an impressive array of firepower, in reality our air defences were at a low ebb for, in addition to the surface-to-air missiles, at one stage I had only five front-line Lightning squadrons to defend the UK. This meant that 100 per cent effort by all personnel was required.

The command stretched from Chivenor in Devon to Saxa Vord in the Shetland Islands. As well as the front-line air defence stations of Wattisham, Coltishall, Binbrook and Leuchars, there was a chain of early warning radar stations stretching along the east coast of the UK and one in Northern Ireland. There were also several training stations: Chivenor, Brawdy and Coningsby in Lincolnshire, the latter was eventually to become the base for the next RAF fighter, the Tornado. In addition, in a remote spot on the coast of Cardigan Bay was Aberporth, a ground-to-air missile station.

In an even more remote spot on the Yorkshire moors was Fylingdales, the site of the latest, state of the art early warning and eavesdropping systems which were used to monitor the Russian air force's activities. An assortment of RAF and USAF boffins manned the station. An American colonel was the local commander of the base. With the help of Fylingdales' radar we were able to intercept enemy aircraft far out into the North Sea. In order to keep the peace in the so-called 'Cold War', our aircraft would intercept the Russian 'Bears' and fly side by side with them as if in formation. When this occurred they would return with photographs. On one occasion when taking Merlyn Rees, the air minister, to visit Saxa Vord, we called in at RAF Leuchars to refuel. There the minister saw two RAF Phantoms setting out to intercept a Russian aircraft. A few hours later, when the air minister arrived at Saxa Vord, awaiting him was a photograph of the interception. Nothing could be done about these Russian patrols, but we made sure that the Russians were aware that we knew they were there!

The early warning radar station at RAF Bawdsey on the Suffolk coast was probably the most well known to the public. It was here that Sir Robert Watson-Watt had carried out his early experiments with radar.

Happily radar was in operation at the beginning of the Battle of Britain allowing us to take off and intercept the enemy raiders in the air rather than them catching us still on the ground.

I was determined to make my mark by visiting every station in the command within four months of taking over. These visits, mainly in my personal aircraft, a Devon, were limited to the times when my hectic programme at Bentley Priory allowed me to get away. I was lucky in that I was allowed to use the commercial airfield at Leavesden which was only a few miles away on the outskirts of London. Accordingly three days after taking over, on 4th April, I visited Binbrook to take the salute as the station was being accorded the Freedom of Grimsby. That day it poured with rain for so long that my service dress hat shrunk so much that I was unable to wear it again. My ever-supportive wife suggested that my elevated position had gone to my head!

Throughout my two years as C-in-C I made frequent visits to the flying stations of Wattisham, Coltishall and Binbrook and particularly relished the success achieved by Leuchars with the introduction of the Phantom.

A major part of my job was liaising with the commanders of the NATO air forces. Each year the 'Tiger' squadrons from all the NATO air forces competed for a trophy. In 1966 this trophy had been won by 74 Squadron based at RAF Leuchars and consequently in 1967 the RAF hosted the 'Tiger Meet' at the station.

I remember arriving for this event to see one of the competitors crashing and bursting into flames. However, 'the show went on'. Another highlight of 1967 was the Battle of Britain 'Open Day' also at Leuchars. On my way there I called in on the other stations in the command that were holding open days. Het and I arrived just before lunch in the mess and afterwards were treated, along with almost 20,000 others, to a superbly organised flying display. I was very proud of the hard work that had obviously been put in by all ranks.

Early in 1967 I was approached by the Home Office to become the chief inspector of prisons. This would obviously have meant retiring early from the service. I decided to seek the advice of Sam Elworthy, who was by then CDS, as to my future prospects in the RAF. He told me confidentially that my name had been pencilled in as the successor to John Grandy as CAS but cautioned me that long-term plans

often changed. He suggested, however, that out of politeness, I should go and see Roy Jenkins, the then Home Secretary, to discuss the matter. This I duly did and following the meeting wrote to him declining the job.

Some months later Air Secretary Donald Evans informed me that there had been a change of plan and Denis Spotswood was to succeed John Grandy as CAS. I never really knew the reason for this change of heart but suspect it was because I was not a particularly good 'politician' and always spoke my mind, not least in defending Fighter Command and the future structure of Strike Command. I know that some 'senior airmen' also thought that my views on joint operations were too close to those of Mountbatten and that I was in danger of 'selling the RAF down the river'. It did occur to me at the time that, had the original plan of my becoming C-in-C RAF Germany come to fruition, I would not have been put in the position of having to take the flak for defending Fighter Command.

As a result, towards the end of 1967 I began to think seriously about leaving the service as the post of DCAS for which I had been earmarked was disestablished and the only other post available was the UK member of the Permanent Military Deputies Group at the Central Treaty Organisation (CENTO) whose headquarters was in Ankara, Turkey. However, my links with the service proved too strong and so out to Ankara I decided to go, taking over from Air Marshal Sir Tim Piper and joining the other members of the group from Pakistan, Iran, Turkey and the United States.

Despite my protestations, during 1967 the decision was made to merge Fighter Command with Bomber Command to form Strike Command. Fighter Command became '11 Group' of Strike Command. As a result, my farewell visits to the different stations of the command were even more poignant. Most memorable was the last time I went to RAF Coltishall on 10th April. As my eldest son David was the cadet warrant officer in charge of the RAF section of the Winchester College CCF and the date happened to be his seventeenth birthday, I decided that he should get some additional 'air experience'. Having flown up

Opposite: The author being interviewed at the disbandment parade of Fighter Command, held at the HQ at Bentley Priory, 25th April 1968. He and other veterans reflected on the events of the day and the development of the RAF during his years in the service, and also mourned the end of an era for Fighter Command.

to Coltishall with me in my Devon, he flew 1,000 mph in an English
Electric Lightning piloted by Squadron Leader Nick Galpin who pre-
sented him, while airborne at 50,000 ft over the North Sea, with his
'Ten-Ton Club' tie.

Our flight back to London that afternoon was unforgettably emotional as we were escorted by a Hurricane and Spitfire of the Battle of
Britain Memorial Flight.

I left Fighter satisfied with what we had achieved. I had magnificent
support from several young men who were later to reach high rank in
the RAF. Keith Williamson, a wing commander at Leuchars, became
CAS. John Nicholls, the station commander at Leuchars, became
VCAS, whilst Mike Graydon, later to be my PSO at AFCENT, and even
later to become CAS as Air Chief Marshal Sir Michael Graydon, was a
flight commander at Wattisham. George Black, wing commander flying at Wattisham was later to become an AVM.

My last duty at Fighter Command was to preside over its disbandment parade on 30th April 1968. The parade and flypast, which was
attended by many dignitaries and Battle of Britain veterans, was a sad
and moving occasion. There were few dry eyes when a Hurricane and
Spitfire did an aerobatic display as the finale to the parade.

ANKARA
AUGUST 1968-MARCH 1970

After this fitting and fond farewell to Fighter we moved out of Montrose and into a quarter, Cherry Tree Cottage in Gordon Avenue, Stanmore, for a couple of months leave before setting out to drive to Turkey
once the school summer holidays began in July. Notable during this
leave was my inspection of the Winchester College CCF of which
David was the head of the RAF section.

In mid-July Het, David, Nicholas, John and I left for Turkey in our
Fiat estate car towing a trailer. As we were not allowed to visit Yu-
goslavia, we drove and camped through France, Switzerland and Italy
before taking the ferry from Brindisi to Greece where we stayed for
three days in Corfu. We then drove through the mountains of northern
Greece before crossing the Turkish border. After a night outside Istanbul and taking the ferry across the Bosphorus, we were met a few miles
short of Ankara by my new ADC Flight Lieutenant Bruce Moore and

Family photo taken in Ankara, 1969.

my new military assistant Lieutenant Colonel Mike McNab of the Black Watch. They led us to our apartment close to the British Embassy in Çankaya, the 'diplomatic area', which sits above the bowl, and in those days the smog of Ankara.

The apartment we moved into was unsatisfactory in that it was far too small for our family and for the 'official' entertaining which we were expected to do. It was therefore agreed that we could look for another larger apartment. This was not easy as space was at a premium in Ankara. However, we eventually found a nearly completed apartment block where we were able to make the two flats on one floor into one large apartment. In December 1968 we moved in with the help

BE BOLD

238   BE BOLD

of our very resourceful ADC Bruce Moore, our head steward Sergeant
Phillips, who had previously been with us at Upavon, and our loyal
driver Baha.

My office was in the British Embassy. The ambassador at the time
was Sir Roderick Sarell with whom Het and I got on well and with
whom I frequently enjoyed a game of tennis. His wife Pam, having
two boys of similar age to David and Nicholas, was especially kind to
them.

In addition to Bruce Moore and Mike McNab, Flight Lieutenant
David Golby, who was on the administrative staff at CENTO, was also
a great support.

As my job was not over taxing we decided to see as much of Turkey
as possible and made frequent camping trips to the east coast: Troy,
Izmir, Kusadasi (for Ephesus) and Bodrum, and to the south coast:
Side, Marmaris and Alanya. On the way we visited the Troglodyte
caves of Göreme and the hot springs of Pamukkale. We also made frequent visits to Istanbul where we stayed in the faded splendour of the
consulate general. This building in the heart of old Istanbul had been
built as the embassy in the mid nineteenth century when Stratford
Canning was the ambassador. The embassy moved to Ankara in the
mid 1930s when Atatürk moved the capital of Turkey from Istanbul
to the more central, Ankara.

My job took me on official visits to Iran and Pakistan and we also
visited Cyprus frequently where Air Marshal 'Tap' Jones was the C-in-
C. The main reason for the Cyprus visits was that our eight-year-old
son John contracted a tubercular gland in his neck from drinking the
milk (non-tuberculin tested) in Turkey. As a result in 1969 he spent
several months in the RAF hospital at Akrotiri. On one of these visits
I was looked after by Mike Graydon who at that time was a flight commander of 56 Squadron flying Lightnings and who has written the
foreword to this book..

I had thought that Ankara might be my last posting and was therefore delighted to be told in November 1969 that in the following April
I would be taking over from Air Chief Marshal Sir Augustus 'Gus'
Walker as the deputy commander-in-chief of Allied Forces Central Europe (AFCENT), whose headquarters was at Brunssum in Holland. As
a result I was promoted to ACM in January 1970.

I was pleased to be going to a job back in the mainstream where I would again be working with senior planners of the three services and not to the MOD.

Although we only spent twenty months in Ankara we very much enjoyed our time there and made many friends. It was in Ankara, when visiting us, that our daughter Elisabeth met her future husband, Captain Charles 'Chuck' Carver who was the aide to the CENTO chief of staff, a US two star general – Major General Anthis.

In early March 1970, having been relieved by Air Marshal Sir 'Jimmy' Stack, we left Ankara. We few by Argosy into RAF Lyneham for a two-week spell of leave in the UK. Our baggage was sent direct to Holland accompanied by Bruce Moore who was to continue as my ADC at AFCENT.

It was during this period of leave that, wearing the Moneypenny sword, I led the escort of Battle of Britain pilots at the memorial service for Lord Dowding in Westminster Abbey.

AFCENT
APRIL 1970-JUNE 1973

Following the withdrawal of France from NATO, in the mid 1960s, the Supreme Headquarters Allied Powers Europe (SHAPE) had moved from Fontainebleau to Mons in Belgium and the headquarters of Allied Forces Central Europe (AFCENT) to a former coalmine at Brunssum in the south of Holland.

The commander-in-chief of AFCENT was a four-star general from the German army Jürgen Bennecke. Under his responsibility came northern and central army groups and the allied air forces in Central Europe which were divided into the 2nd Allied Tactical Air Force (2 ATAF) in the north of the central region and 4 ATAF in the south. As the deputy commander-in-chief my main responsibility was for the central region air forces.

2 ATAF, whose headquarters was at Rheindahlen, was commanded by an RAF air marshal – happily for most of my time by my great friend Air Marshal Sir Harold 'Mickey' Martin. 4 ATAF based at Ramstein was commanded by an American four star general who again happily was my old friend General Davy Jones.

During my time at AFCENT I spent considerable energy arguing strongly against what I thought was the politically motivated American proposal to re-organise the central region air forces by establishing a separate Central Region Air Forces Headquarters (AIRCENT) commanded by a US general which would control 2 and 4 ATAFs. While recognising the need for greater centralisation of our air forces, I felt that the proposal flew in the face of all that had been learnt about tactical air support since my days in the desert when, in order to provide close air support, the need for the air HQ to be co-located with the army HQ was first established.

I felt that the sub-plot behind this move by the Americans was their desire to control the tactics of the air forces in the region. They wanted to use the same tactics that they had developed in Vietnam, of operating under radar control at medium to high level in order to avoid low level flak. I argued that these tactics were not appropriate in northern Europe with its poor weather and with the lack of aircraft available. The tactics of the UK and German air forces were to operate at low level below the radar system and to work closely with the army on the ground. For example, our Harrier force was co-located with the army; unfortunately the US air force did not have such a close relationship with their army. As it was impossible to come to an agreement over this, the compromise was made that 2 ATAF and 4 ATAF would use different tactics.

With a very busy schedule it was imperative that my personal office ran like clockwork and during my time at AFCENT I was lucky to have the support of an excellent PSO, the afore-mentioned Squadron Leader Michael Graydon who had just finished staff college. He and his delightful wife Elizabeth became great friends and often entertained our nine-year-old son John. After an illustrious career which included commanding Strike Command, the successor to Fighter Command, Mike Graydon eventually became CAS in the early 1990s. *[He subsequently gave the address at my father's funeral in September 1998 and at his memorial service at St Clement Dane's in December of the same year.]*

I was also lucky to have Colonel John West, late Royal Signals, as my MA. John had been a young signals officer in the desert and remembered meeting me on my return from my 'Desert Walk' in November 1941.

On my frequent visits to the many different air force units and airfields, normally in my personal Pembroke aircraft, John usually managed the office while Mike Graydon accompanied me. John and his wife Joy lived near us in Valkenburg and remained close friends over the years. Bruce Moore, my long suffering and highly amusing ADC, by then promoted to squadron leader, completed my personal staff.

The month of September 1970 was memorable as our daughter Elisabeth was married to Captain Charles F Carver III in the RAF church, St. Clement Dane's in London. The reception afterwards was held at the RAF Club.

On the domestic front our official residence was a pretty Dutch stone farm house in the village of Houthem St. Gerlach which was on the road between Meerssen and Valkenburg, and was about ten miles drive from Brunssum. Our house staff, led by the able and charming Sergeant McNiffe, coped admirably with the endless official and unofficial entertaining that we did. In the kitchen we again had Chef Sergeant Vallance who as Corporal Vallance had been with us at Fighter Command. Another member of the house staff was the ever cheerful Corporal Morris who as an SAC had been one of our house stewards at Fighter Command, and who had in the meantime married Susan, another of our stewards. My driver during my time at AFCENT was the excellent and ever resourceful Sergeant Jarrett. In a triumph of organisation in May 1972 my personal staff organised David's twenty-first birthday drinks party in the garden of his Oxford college, Keble, flying in the staff, food and drink to nearby RAF Brize Norton. This certainly could not have happened today in these cost-conscious times!

With all the official entertainment that we were obliged to give it was imperative that I kept myself fit. I did this by playing a lot of tennis, where my partner was normally Mike Graydon. The final nail in the coffin for my career came when Mike and I beat the CDS, Field Marshal Lord Carver and one of his staff officers, when they were visiting AFCENT.

Shortly after my promotion to ACM I was appointed as a principal Air ADC to Her Majesty the Queen and in the Birthday Honours List of 1972 was advanced from KCB to GCB – Knight Grand Cross of the Order of the Bath. I was very proud of both of these appointments as a culmination to my RAF career. The icing on the cake was being asked to represent Her Majesty at the Battle of Britain Thanksgiving Service that year.

In preparation for my return to 'civvy street' after thirty-eight years in the service I wrote to Lord Mountbatten, my erstwhile boss when I was his chairman of the joint planning staff at the MOD, asking if he would be prepared to give me a reference. His reply was simply, 'Dear Rosie, any time, anywhere'.

My farewell trip to AFSOUTH took Het and I to Greece, Malta and Naples where we were royally entertained. This was a marvellous trip capped by the party that General Davy Jones (later chief of staff of the US Air Force) gave for us at the US Air Force HQ in Germany.

Although sad to be leaving AFCENT, I was delighted that my successor as DCINCENT was to be my old friend from Aden days and before, Bob Hodges or, as he was by then, Air Chief Marshal Sir Lewis Hodges.

On my departure from AFCENT in June 1973 I was given the honour of a farewell parade to which David and Nicholas, unbeknownst to me, were flown over from England. This was an emotional occasion as it marked the end of my service life. The next day, moving from the sublime to the ridiculous, Het and I left for the UK towing our caravan behind us.

Epilogue

LIFE AFTER THE RAF

I was sad to leave the service in September 1973 but I was nearly fifty-eight and had had a good innings. On leaving I was given a dinner by the Air Council and received a note from Secretary of State for Defence Lord Carrington which read as follows:

> *'I have it in command from Her Majesty the Queen to convey to you on leaving the active list of the Royal Air Force her thanks for your long and valuable services.*
>
> *May I take this opportunity of wishing you all good fortune in the future.'*

However, the most memorable of my farewells was the thirty-minute audience I had with Her Majesty the Queen.

I was not prepared to sit back, not least because my retired pay was just £7,032 per annum and I still had John's school fees to pay at Haileybury. Within a month or so I became military adviser to the British Aircraft Corporation (BAC), later to become the privatised British Aerospace, and a director of the board of their Preston division.

On the domestic front, on returning to the UK we moved into a quarter at RAF Bicester for my final few months in the service. My first job was to find us a home, for we had never owned one. In October we bought a flat in Latymer Court, Hammersmith which was convenient for both Weybridge, where I had my office, and Heathrow from where I frequently flew.

Apart from making aeroplanes, BAC had a big contract in Saudi Arabia where, in addition to local labour, we had over 2,000 British pilots, technicians, civil engineers, teachers, doctors and nursing staff. As well as providing the technical support for their three Lightning squadrons and the Strikemaster trainers, we were responsible for the training of the pilots and the technicians for the Royal Saudi Air Force. In 1977 I became the director of this operation and Het and I, joined by John during his holidays, moved to Riyadh.

Het and I enjoyed our time in Saudi where we lived in some style in Riyadh but managed to get away into the desert most weekends. The main reason for being onsite rather than directing long-distance was to ensure that the British retained their influence with the Saudis against stiff opposition from the USA and France. In September 1977 I was therefore delighted to represent British Aerospace at the signing of Great Britain's largest ever single export order, worth in excess of £500 million between Saudi Arabia and the British Government. Three years later in 1980 at the age of sixty-five, I retired again.

While on leave from Saudi we bought a cottage, Ty Haul, overlooking the Dee valley close to Llangollen in North Wales and also close to Wrexham and Corwen where Het and I had spent the first twenty years of our lives. Following my retirement we divided our time between London and North Wales but spent as much time in North Wales as possible.

One of the things that brought me to London was that, having been chairman of the Victory Services Club from 1974 to 1977 before moving to Riyadh, I became president from 1989 to 1993.

In May 1990 I was 'installed' by Her Majesty the Queen as a Knight Grand Cross of the Order of the Bath in the Henry VII Chapel in Westminster Abbey. In order to do so I had to have a coat of arms drawn up by the heralds at the College of Arms. My son David helped me do this and we eventually agreed that the 'supporters' should be a Welsh dragon and a Polish eagle. In the centre of the shield was the portcullis and sword of Fighter Command. This was surrounded by red roses. The crest, which sat on an astral crown, was an arm holding the Arabian 'Jambiya' or curved knife from the crest of the Middle East Air Force. I chose as my motto 'Be Bold' – which was also the motto that Mac Macguire and I had chosen for 229 Squadron early in the Second World War. This crest can be seen in the introduction to the book.

A memorable moment in the early 1990s was the occasion when I was a guest on the 'This is Your Life' programme when the subject was Mike Graydon, by then CAS.

Having for some years been chairman of the Polish Air Force Benevolent Fund, I was very pleased that in 1990 the Polish Government awarded me the honour of a knighthood in the Order of Polonia Restituta. I subsequently led the appeal to restore the Polish air force war memorial at Northolt which was unveiled in the presence of HRH The Duke of Gloucester in September 1996. I was even more delighted when in 1998 I was given the Commander's Cross with Star of the Order of Merit of the Republic of Poland.

Of our children, Lis lived the life of an American air force wife until Chuck retired as a lieutenant colonel and they eventually settled in Montgomery, Alabama. David, after Oxford, spent five years in the army before becoming an investment manager in the City. Nicholas trained at the Middlesex Hospital and became an army doctor for seven years before becoming a GP in Wisbech. Finally, John our youngest also went to Oxford where he won a rugby blue and then, like David, became an investment manager in the City. From their marriages we were very lucky to have had the joy of eleven grandchildren.

POSTSCRIPT

My father died in Wrexham Hospital on 10th September 1998 at the age of eighty-two. After a funeral in St. Collen's Parish Church in Llangollen, he was buried in the burial ground overlooking the River Dee, in which he had swum and fished as a boy, and the Llangollen to Corwen railway line, on which he had travelled every day in his youth.

Following his memorial service at St. Clement Dane's on 14th December, the CAS, Air Chief Marshal Sir Michael Graydon arranged for a flypast of four Tornados from 43 (F) Squadron from Leuchars, my father's first squadron.

To commemorate my father's life my mother gave a silver salver – the Rosier trophy – to 43 Squadron, which is presented annually to 'the officer, NCO or airman who has done the best to foster the fighting spirit of 43 (Fighter) Squadron'. The trophy was presented to the squadron in 2000 and the first winner was Flight Lieutenant Mark Chappell.

In addition, my mother endowed a consulting room at King Edward VII's Hospital in London which bears my father's name.

David Rosier

ENDNOTES

1 My brother, William Henry, was apprenticed in early 1939 to a mining surveyor at Gresford colliery near Wrexham, the scene of the great disaster in 1934 resulting in the tragic loss of more than 300 lives. When war came his job was designated a 'reserved occupation'. However, in 1943, at the age of twenty-one he joined the RAF; volunteering for flying duties was the only way he could get away from his 'reserved' job. In South Africa he failed his pilot's course but re-trained as a navigator, qualifying just as the war was ending. In 1945/46 he was based at Scampton (Lincs) in a squadron then chiefly engaged in repatriating prisoners of war. There he met Sybil Jones, a WAAF. They married in Northampton, her home town, in 1946.

On leaving the RAF in 1947 he worked for British Thomson Houston at Stafford and later for ICI in Northwich, Cheshire. Having qualified as a member of the Institution of Structural Engineers and of the Institution of Civil Engineers he left for Australia in 1952 to work on the Snowy Mountain Project. Five years later he started his own business in Paramatta near Sydney. On retirement he lived between Sydney and Paramatta, the original capital of NSW. His son George and daughter Penny live nearby. Both George and Penny were born in England, in 1948 and 1950 respectively. Bill died in 2007.

My sister Rose, who after mother's death took every advantage of the 'laissez faire' attitude of father, in 1939 married a man twenty years older. He was an unprepossessing trade union leader at the big steel works at Shotton, to me a most boring man. She died soon after father died in 1942, leaving two sons, Kerry and Howard.

Marion married an ex-professional footballer – a forward, I think. I never met him. Again, some twenty years older. They lived in Wellington (Salop) where they ran a pub. Their only child, Robert, became a school master. After her husband's death in 1971 Marion went out to Australia to stay with Bill and his wife Sybil. Whilst there she heard the tragic news that her son had been killed in a car accident whilst changing a tyre. The Robert Prouse Hall at Kimbolton School was named as a memorial to him. Marion returned to Wellington but could not settle and twelve months later emigrated to Australia. On a bus trip to Ayres' Rock she met and eventually married a retired electrical engineer – Michael Barrett, an Ulsterman, who, having served as a submariner during the war, decided to be demobilised in Australia, rather than Britain. Surrounded by a profusion of plants, trees and exotic bird life, they live in a house they built in Dorrigo in the north of New South Wales.

2 Thirty-three years later, whilst at a luncheon following my farewell ceremony at AFCENT, I just missed meeting this helpful Frenchman. The wife of a United States officer serving in AFCENT told my wife that she had been approached at the ceremony by an elderly Frenchman who had told her that he had put me on his motor cycle after seeing me floating down in flames. He said he would wait outside the mess. My wife and the American went in search of him, only to find that all civilian sightseers had been ordered away by the guard. I was very sorry that I was unable to thank him.

3 I had served with many Australians in the desert and some became lifelong friends. Many years later, in 1984, Het and I flew to Australia with the intention of seeing my brother Bill and his family, my sister Marion and some of those old friends. We stayed for a few days just outside Sydney with the above-mentioned Bobby Gibbes and his wife. As a surprise he had organised a get-together of RAF fighter pilots of desert days. We had met a few of

them since the war as they would always get in touch on their visits to the UK. When we arrived at the party we were not only delighted but amazed and touched that our friends had taken the trouble to come to Sydney from Adelaide, Melbourne, Brisbane and places further west and north.

4 It was in the Reichswald Forest that Peggie Henderson's brother Noel was killed whilst attacking with the 7th Battalion Royal Welch Fusiliers. Peggie and Het had been in the same form at Grove Park together and were still best friends some eighty years later.

APPENDIX A

Aircraft types flown by Frederick Rosier between 1935 and 1973:

Tiger Moth	Puss Moth
Gipsy Moth	Hart
Fury 1 & 2	Monospar
Audax	Magister
Gladiator	Wapiti
Monospar	Nimrod
Demon	Battle
Blenheim	Cygnet
Whitney Straight	Hurricane (various marks)
Tomahawk	Kittyhawk
Lysander	Spitfire (various marks)
Vega Gull	Mustang
Mosquito	Master
Hornet	Harvard
Proctor	Meteor
B25	A26
Dakota	F80
F84	Vampire
Venom	Desford Trainer (prone position)
Hunter	Anson
Oxford	Canberra
Twin Pioneer	Beverley
Valetta	Argosy
Dominie	Jet Provost
Jaguar	Lightning
Phantom	Pembroke
Devon	Dove
Harrier	F104

Helicopters:

Belvedere	Wessex
Whirlwind	Sycamore

BIBLIOGRAPHY

Beedel, J. *43 F Squadron - "The Fighting Cocks"* Beaumont Aviation Literature, 1966

Bishop, P. *Fighter Boys* Harper Collins, 2003

Brown, R. *Shark Squadron: History of 112 Squadron 1917-75* Crecy Publishing, 1994

Cross, Sir K. & Orange, V. *Straight and Level* Grub Street, 1995

Cull, B. & Lander, B. *Twelve Days in May* Grub Street, 1995

Drake, B. & Shores, C. *Billy Drake Fighter Leader* Grub Street, 2002

Gelb, N. *Scramble* M. Joseph, 1986

Houghton, G.W. *They Flew Through Sand*, 1942

McKinstry, L. *Hurricane Victor of the Battle of Britain* John Murray, 2010

Scott, D. *Typhoon Pilot* Arrow Books Ltd, 1991

Sutton, B. *The Way of a Pilot* Macmillan and co, 1942

Townsend, P. *Duel of Eagles* Weidenfeld & Nicolson, 2000

254   BE BOLD